UNRAVELING THE MYSTERIES OF ADDICTION
THROUGH CUTTING-EDGE BRAIN SCIENCE

THE
ADDICTION
SOLUTION

DAVID KIPPER, MD
and STEVEN WHITNEY

RODALE

© 2010 by David Kipper and Steven Whitney

Rodale books may be purchased for business or promotional use or for special sales. For information, please write to:

Special Markets Department, Rodale Inc., 733 Third Avenue, New York, NY 10017

Printed in the United States of America
Rodale Inc. makes every effort to use acid-free ♾, recycled paper ♻.

Illustrations by Karen Kuchar

Book design by Joanna Williams

Library of Congress Cataloging-in-Publication Data is on file with the publisher.

ISBN-10 1–60529–291–5
ISBN-13 978–1–60529–291–5

Distributed to the trade by Macmillan

2   4   6   8   10   9   7   5   3   1   hardcover

We inspire and enable people to improve their lives and the world around them.

To Sam, Chanel, and Jessi . . .
our reward pathways

Contents

PART 1:
ADDICTION 101

PART 2:
THE ADDICTION SOLUTION

PART 3:
CASE STUDIES

Preface

THE FUTURE OF ADDICTION TREATMENT

Two decades ago—about the time my son Sam was born—doctors were limited in what we understood and could do for many diseases, especially the disease of addiction. Back then, there wasn't even a valid medical approach to addiction. Campaigns like "Just Say No" and the government's costly but ineffective War on Drugs were all we had.

But during Sam's lifetime we have seen an explosion in medical research and technology that has led to new and successful treatments for chronic conditions like heart disease, cancer, and—yes—addiction.

An avalanche of information—much of it coming from cracking open the long-hidden code of human genetic makeup—has revealed the true origins of addiction. Previously mistaken as a behavioral problem, addiction has been proven to be a chronic disease. This knowledge has opened the floodgates to new, smart-targeted, and successful medical treatments that no longer depend on the failed behavioral approach.

Like Sam, the field of addiction medicine has grown up. His generation has the opportunity to understand the science behind addiction and to manage it, much in the same way that my generation learned to better manage diabetes, heart disease, and cancer.

Indeed, diagnostic and treatment breakthroughs are revolutionizing the entire world of addiction.

The Human Genome Project has identified specific genes and biomarkers that allow doctors to chart the origins of addiction and to predict those people most at risk for this disease. (Even Your Addiction Prediction on page 40 can readily and simplistically identify who is at risk and the specific substances they are most likely to abuse.)

We now have the ability to create an "addiction blood panel" much like the blood tests for cholesterol, arthritis, and liver disease that allow us to detect, evaluate, and monitor these problems.

Imaging techniques such as functional MRIs allow us to go beyond external behaviors and glimpse the areas of the brain responsible for addictive behaviors. With a new technology called brain mapping, we can actually *see* the brain as it "heals" from addiction. Having clear pictures that show the progressive stages of recovery encourages patients to maintain their commitment to therapy.

A close corollary to these advances were the heart scans developed in the 1980s that allowed patients who were vulnerable to coronary artery disease to see their own heart arteries—for the first time enabling them to know if they were truly at risk. These simple, noninvasive 10-minute tests became the gold standard for diagnosing heart disease and quickly rendered the less-sensitive electrocardiograms, treadmills, and blood tests obsolete. Those with a family history of heart attacks could take this scan, identify their impending risks with their own eyes, and intervene long before the disease progressed to an irreversible situation.

Indeed, the discovery that addiction originates in brain chemistry brings a new era of successful medical treatment of addiction. This is the new paradigm, the cornerstone of *The Addiction Solution*.

Under the new paradigm, addiction treatment succeeds only when it becomes more personalized, replacing cookie-cutter behavioral therapies that have not worked on their own with customized treatments that relate to individual chemical imbalances in our brains. The clues to solving the medical causes of addiction are found in family trees and in the contributing factors of genetic imprinting and environment.

Medicine is doing all that right now. And by continuing to address the real scientific and medical issues, it spells just the beginning of an amazingly successful turnabout in treating addiction.

Within the next few years, as the success of the new paradigm settles in, Sam's generation will witness a total makeover in the ways addiction is viewed and treated.

- The new paradigm will universally establish addiction as a medical disease, not a behavioral malfunction.
- With this new understanding, the negative connotations of addiction and of being an addict will largely vanish.
- Punitive attitudes toward addicts will be replaced by positive and healing support systems.
- Dual diagnosis will become the essential tool of addiction therapy, with medical treatment seen as primary and behavioral methods viewed as secondary and supportive.
- Medical treatment in the new paradigm will rely primarily on pharmacologic breakthroughs that target neurotransmitter imbalances.

- Vaccines are being developed to target cocaine and other abused substances.
- Every advance in the addiction solution will come from science and not from the exhausted behavioral model.
- Patients will be given new tools to better manage their stress and to address associated medical issues like sleep disorders and chronic pain syndromes.
- The revolution in awareness will inspire a greater number of professionals to dedicate themselves to the field of addiction medicine.
- Along with doctors, other professionals—including neuropharmacologists, psychologists, nutritionists, physical trainers, homeopaths, and pain management specialists—will collaborate as teams to integrate the medical and behavioral aspects of dual diagnosis.
- Exclusive 28-day inpatient treatment programs will be replaced by comprehensive and personalized outpatient programs with long-term agendas.
- By personalizing addiction therapies, medical treatment will reverse the 90-plus percent failure rate of the outmoded, stand-alone behavioral treatment to a 90 percent success rate nationwide.
- Addiction will be a manageable and preventable disease controlled with the smarter-targeted diagnostics and therapeutics that are even now in development.
- These advances will allow health care professionals to target adolescents—the greatest at-risk population—with insight, counseling, and (when necessary) medications, so that treat-

ment will finally become preventive and proactive rather than after the fact and reactive.

Addiction is not a disease limited to any one population or demographic. It doesn't attack by class, income, religion, IQ, race, or culture. Addiction is and always has been an equal opportunity epidemic.

To deny anyone the basic right to medical treatment is immoral and a type of malpractice. Victims of addiction need access to doctors, medications, counselors, a wide assortment of psychological and behavioral therapies, pain management courses, and sleep and eating disorder programs.

Health care reform must recognize and support this new paradigm. Insurance carriers and Big Pharma must not discriminate against any chronic disease that negatively impacts our national health, including addictive disorders. The very best care must be provided whenever and wherever it is needed; it must be accessible to all, not just the privileged few, now and in the future.

And what a future that could be—a bold new era of addiction vaccines, in vitro genetic engineering, and other miracles of medical science hardly imaginable today.

By the time Sam is my age, it is my belief—and a real possibility—that there will be no further need for *The Addiction Solution* . . . because the addiction puzzle will already be solved.

David Kipper, MD
Beverly Hills, California

INTRODUCTION

Change is always in the wind.

In medicine, new ideas and discoveries lead to more accurate diagnoses and more successful treatments. Most often, these changes are incremental—baby steps that follow logically, one step after another, and eventually lead to an expected solution.

But every once in a while, lightning strikes: A triumphant breakthrough or startlingly new notion shatters conventional wisdom and challenges what we thought we knew about an illness. Ultimately, the innovation creates a new paradigm—a new gold standard of diagnosis and treatment that renders the older methods obsolete.

Think of penicillin, the Salk vaccine, and robotic surgery. Each of these advances unlocked the solution to a medical quandary. Each saved millions of lives.

In the same way, medical breakthroughs lead to improved treatment approaches and offer hope and healing for people with chronic (long-term) mental and physical health problems.

Looking back just a century ago, a person suffering from twitching, confusion, slurred and disconnected speech, and blurred vision probably would have been diagnosed as insane and tucked away in an asylum. Today, X-rays, CT scans, MRIs, and a host of other visualizing tools—all of which were new paradigms of their day—allow us to *see* the tumor (a benign or malignant growth) in that person's brain and determine that it's the tumor that is causing radical changes in the patient's behavior, temperament, and personality. It isn't madness at all—it's a medical disease.

The same goes for schizophrenia, once diagnosed as a severe type of insanity. Patients were shuttled off to sanitariums, where they often remained for life. Today, we know that schizophrenia is a medical disorder that can be successfully managed with medications that target its biochemical origins.

New paradigms aren't simply novel or forward-reaching ideas—they are fresh answers to old questions. They arrive with credible evidence—with proof. They are substantive, not theoretical. And it is that substance that propels them forward.

Now, after a century of frustration and failure, an extraordinary breakthrough is revolutionizing the diagnosis and treatment of what has become one of America's most serious health problems: addiction.

More than 100 million Americans suffer from some form of addiction. The use (and abuse) of alcohol, cigarettes, prescription drugs like Vicodin or OxyContin, and illegal substances like cocaine and heroin; behavioral issues like overeating and gambling; and any one (or combination) of a number of self-destructive actions and/or behaviors fall under the umbrella of addiction.

Addiction impacts other diseases. Smoking, for instance, can lead to lung cancer; overeating can set the stage for diabetes and heart disease. Shared needles are a leading contributor to AIDS. Rampant alcoholism can result in cirrhosis of the liver and death.

Addiction costs government, big corporations, and small businesses more money—in lost time, lost wages, low productivity, increased insurance and HMO premiums and payouts, and countless other ways—than any other disease. The losses from addiction create a tax burden that we all share.

Aside from medical and economic concerns, the human tragedy of addiction is staggering: millions of lives wasted, tens of thousands of families destroyed, countless friendships lost, and careers ruined.

Over the past century, traditional addiction treatment has been an unparalleled failure. Close to 90 percent of addicts return to substance abuse within a year of receiving treatment—the same rate of recidivism that existed 20 years ago . . . 50 years ago . . . even 100 years ago. Despite all our treatment centers, progressive programs ("the War on Drugs"), campaigns ("Just Say No"), and stern legal enforcements, addiction has exploded into a pandemic. Today, it is our country's number one health problem. Every facet of American life is touched in some way by addiction. Indeed, the US Department of Health and Human Services recently predicted that for those Americans presently age 40 or older, substance abuse would double by the year 2020. Unless, that is, a new and successful paradigm replaces the traditional method that has failed for the last half century.

What went so wrong? Why has traditional addiction treatment been mired in a 90 percent failure rate?

First and foremost, addiction was misdiagnosed as a social or character malady affecting those who didn't possess the morality, upbringing, or willpower to resist. Addicts were perceived as bad or weak people—the worst of society—who lacked the proper guidance to set them on the right path.

Second, addiction was treated as a stand-alone problem, something unrelated to anything else happening in the addict's mind, body, or environment. Addiction was addiction was addiction.

When making diagnoses, doctors are often confronted with the age-old chicken-or-egg dilemma. In medicine, this *causality dilemma* translates into a search for the root cause of any given problem—in other words, a diagnosis. With addiction, the question is: Which comes first, addictive behaviors or addiction itself? Since there was no other explanation at the time, traditional caregivers long ago chose to treat behaviors as the primary cause of addiction.

But this early judgment (which is still the core of conventional treatment) was utterly wrong. And since diagnosis *always* determines treatment, whenever a diagnosis is fundamentally misguided, the treatment stemming from it will be ineffective.

Clearly, the conventional treatment of addiction—the one with the 90 percent failure rate—has needed fixing for a long time. At long last, a new paradigm has arrived that can successfully treat addiction.

From the perspective of 2010, we can look at the incredible breakthroughs in modern medical technology achieved in the past 2 decades and know with absolute certainty that *addiction is not primarily a behavioral issue but a medical disease* that eventually causes behavioral problems by sparking biochemical "wantings" or needs.

Just over a decade ago, geneticists began to decode human DNA. They saw that certain genes determined specific biochemical flaws in brain chemistry. Almost simultaneously, other research scientists discovered a close relationship between these flaws and both addiction and radical alterations in behavior, temperament, and personality. With these synchronous findings, science finally *proved* that individual genetics determines the specific biochemical flaws that can lead to addiction. In simple terms, they proved that addiction isn't a social malady or character flaw—it is a bona fide medical disease that is determined by genetics, resides in brain chemistry, and is triggered largely by stress. It is affected by and impacts many other issues, both medical and behavioral.

This insight into the biochemical nature of addiction calls for a new treatment protocol based on the *dual diagnosis* concept, which entails diagnosing and treating the primary disease *and* the behaviors or symptoms that arise from it. Since the disease and its behaviors are entwined, effective treatment must address both issues in order: the primary first, then the secondary. Neglecting either fails to address the whole problem, and the subsequent treatment plan will spiral into failure.

From this revolutionary insight came the new paradigm for the medical treatment of addiction, which is supported by the American Society of Addiction Medicine and thousands of medical specialists throughout the world.

Here, in a nutshell, is the groundbreaking paradigm.

1. An inherited genetic flaw causes . . .
2. Specific imbalances in brain chemistry that, when . . .
3. Impacted by stress, create . . .
4. Biochemical "wantings," or needs, that show themselves as . . .
5. Bad feelings, uncharacteristic behavior, and/or . . .
6. Addiction, which is medically treated by a new family of . . .

7. Pharmaceutical medications that first regain and then stabilize the biochemical balance.
8. During the rehabilitation of the brain chemistry, the patient enters a personalized recovery program featuring behavioral and other therapies.

Traditional addiction treatment did not have the first seven steps, and rarely did it personalize behavioral recovery in the last step.

The new paradigm comes with accompanying advances that make treatment more comfortable and accessible.

- New types of pharmaceutical medications minister to the biochemical source of addiction and its behaviors.
- Withdrawal (and detox) under the new medical paradigm is safe, painless, effective, and relatively quick, sometimes achieved in a few hours. The nightmare of days-long withdrawals under traditional treatment has been sent packing.
- Traditional 28-day inpatient programs at treatment centers are now largely unnecessary. This is good news, since that kind of treatment costs from $50,000 to $100,000 per month. In contrast, the new medical paradigm is grounded in outpatient treatment, making it more affordable, especially with insurance and government benefits that define addiction as a medical disease. Thanks to the Mental Health Parity and Addiction Equity Act of 2008, insurers that offer substance abuse coverage must provide the same lifetime limits on payment as they provide for other medical diseases like diabetes, heart disease, and cancer.

- More subtly, the new approach replaces the expectation of failure attached to the old, traditional treatment with a tangible opportunity for success, including raising an addict's self-esteem.

The new paradigm does not discard every element of conventional treatment; it incorporates many excellent behavioral therapies. In that sense, the new paradigm is a key *addition* to recovery therapies rather than a wholesale replacement of them. What it adds is the focus on medical treatment that not only fixes the biochemical source of the disease but also sets an agenda for healthy living.

Think of a jigsaw puzzle. You work diligently to interlock all the pieces together. Then you discover that the last and most important piece, right in the center, is missing. Without it, you can never complete the picture, no matter how hard you try.

For years, traditional addiction treatment has been a puzzle with the most vital piece missing. The conventional method implemented many helpful pieces: 12-step programs, counseling, support groups, exercise regimens, nutrition plans, and other therapies. But it didn't address the biochemical imbalance, and thus it was missing the critical interlocking piece. And without that piece, addiction treatment could never be complete.

The new paradigm for the medical treatment of addiction changes recovery statistics dramatically: It moves from the traditional method's 90 percent failure rate to a potential success rate of over 90 percent.

The Addiction Solution details, clarifies, and expands on each point of the new paradigm. This book explains in plain language what addiction really is, where it originates, how it works, and how the new paradigm addresses addiction's insidious forms.

Part 1 offers a course, Addiction 101—the scientific elements of addiction. Part 2 looks into case studies, and Part 3 reviews substances and the medications needed to successfully treat their respective conditions. Glossaries, questions and answers, resource and contact guides, and links to useful Web sites round out the book. Everything—from the smallest topic to the most complex and controversial issues—is engaged with straight talk.

The Addiction Solution is a ticket to recovery, not only medically, but in myriad ways that enhance people's lives.

For now, start with this mantra—it is the first baby step to understanding addiction and learning how to fix it.

ADDICTION
ORIGINATES IN BRAIN CHEMISTRY,
IS DETERMINED BY GENETICS,
AND IS TRIGGERED BY STRESS.

Finally, hope and success ride on the winds of change.

PART 1 ADDICTION 101

A new paradigm demands a new beginning. We must revisit every-thing we thought we knew about addiction.

Make no mistake: Addiction is a disease—a clearly defined health problem that must be treated medically to ensure long-term success. Although addiction is a chronic (long-term) disease with many compo-nents, it is treatable.

Part 1 of this book provides a brief and vital course on the core issues of addiction. But don't worry; this "course" doesn't require specialized knowledge of medical terminology. It explains the basic facts and con-cepts you absolutely need to know to understand addiction—either your own or that of a relative or friend. It explains the root causes of addiction and its triggers, touches on addiction's possible prevention and treatment, and demonstrates the undeniable fact that addiction is a medical disease with its origins in brain chemistry.

Once you become familiar with these concepts, you may well know more about addiction than 95 percent of the world population. More important, you will have taken the first step to conquering addiction.

Origins and Triggers

HOMEOSTASIS

The concept of homeostasis is at the core of any discussion, diagnosis, or treatment of addiction.

What is homeostasis? It is *the process of maintaining the body's natural balance to achieve stability* (or a norm), not just in critical moments, but throughout a lifetime . . . one day at a time, one minute at a time, and one second at a time. Homeostasis is the central regulating system for the entire body, and it plays a crucial role in good health and bad.

In the mid-19th century, French physiologist Claude Bernard conceptualized the need for a constant (a condition or process that does not change) that regulates the body's "internal milieu" (internal environment) to make life both possible and sustainable. If that constant was lost—if the internal milieu was destabilized or thrown out of balance—life itself was threatened.

Over the following decades, the idea of a self-regulating constant at the center of life was applied to all biological systems: plants, animals, humans, and microorganisms.

This constant was given a name in the early 1930s by Walter Bradford Cannon, an American who joined two Greek words—*homos*, meaning "equal," and *histemi*, meaning "to stand." *Homeostasis* literally means "to stand equally" or "to remain the same." As it specifically relates to addiction, it means "to maintain a balanced state."

The term *constant* does not imply something unyielding. In fact, homeostasis is remarkably fluid and flexible in adapting to internal and external threats.

Think of a surfer on a board, riding a long wave to shore, expertly adjusting her balance and posture to counter each dip and swell of the ocean's current. Riding the waves of life, homeostasis does essentially the same thing—bending, countering, and adapting to each change or danger while maintaining the body's tenuous balance.

Homeostasis is a dynamic concept in continual flux, maintaining stability by moving fluidly within a narrow field, a constant range of normalcy.

For example, 98.6° Fahrenheit (37° Celsius) is commonly accepted as normal body temperature. But individual body temperature may vary. For some people, "normal" might be 98.4°F; for others, 98.9°F. Your normal temperature actually lies in a fluid range of about plus or minus 1 degree—in this case, from about 98.1°F to around 99.1°F.

Homeostasis strives to maintain the body's internal temperature within each person's normal range. A signal (like extremely hot or cold temperature) is picked up by a sensor and sent to a control center (the brain), which immediately sends back a response appropriate to restoring homeostasis. Three fast steps: input, processing, response.

A response can be an involuntary (or automatic) reaction. For instance, if it's warm outside, your body sweats, helping to cool the skin. If it's cool, you shiver or get goose bumps, both of which help warm the skin. Those involuntary reactions to external conditions are called homeostatic compensations.

A response can also be voluntary. Let's say it's a real scorcher outside, and you're sweating like Niagara Falls but you can't cool down. This is when the survival instinct—part of homeostasis—prompts a voluntary response: You fan yourself, jump in a swimming pool, sit in the shade with a cold drink, or walk inside where the air-conditioning is set at a comfortable 72°F.

Now imagine you're outside in the dead of winter. It's bitterly cold, and snow cascades from the sky. Standing there shivering is not going to keep you warm . . . so you put on a parka and gloves, stand under an outdoor heat lamp, or walk back inside where the heating system maintains a cozy temperature.

In any extreme condition, voluntary action is needed to maintain homeostasis—otherwise heatstroke or hypothermia would result. Yet whatever physical action is taken, it is *automatically cued* by an imbalance in homeostasis. Think of it as a red flag alerting the systems to impending trouble.

Homeostasis is not limited to controlling body temperature. It also maintains blood glucose balance and regulates the body's water level (thirst causes you to drink water; the body absorbs what it needs and releases the excess through evaporation and urination). In fact, homeostasis regulates the entire body and all its systems—millions of internal equilibriums (or balances) affecting everything from the smallest brain cells to the largest bones. At the same time, it reacts to every change and threat by making alterations of equal size and in opposing directions to those that created the disturbance. For instance, when physical danger threatens, homeostasis releases adrenaline to help the body combat it. During vigorous exercise, homeostasis cues the heart and respiration to race faster to keep the body's internal balance.

Whenever stability is at risk, the process of homeostasis takes steps to ensure that balance is restored so life may continue.

Homeostasis and Disease

Sometimes the body cannot restore balance on its own, and medical intervention is needed.

For example, homeostasis efficiently helps the body resist some viruses, like the common cold: The virus attacks, the immune system receives the signal to respond, and you get better. More virulent strains, like hepatitis, overwhelm the homeostatic process, and medical assistance is thus needed. Toxins and drugs can also overwhelm the system: Homeostasis can fight small amounts of mercury or lead or cocaine, but larger or concentrated doses of these and other poisons require medical treatment.

Many illnesses and diseases result from homeostatic imbalance, including diabetes, hypoglycemia, dehydration, gout, any malady caused by a foreign chemical or substance in the bloodstream—and the disease of addiction. These problems usually occur when there's a flaw in the homeostatic mechanism or when an increased amount of a specific substance (a toxin, a drug, or a metabolite like uric acid that leads to gout) engulfs one or more of the body's operating systems. These situations require medical intervention.

In every case of medical intervention, the goal is to restore the body's chemical balance—its homeostasis.

Homeostasis and Emotions

Our internal balance can be threatened not only by the physical world but also by our emotions. Feelings and emotional upheavals disrupt homeostasis by changing our brain chemistry. These emotional fluctuations play a central role in the disease of addiction.

The homeostatic process can usually handle minor emotional disappointments and hurts, but a large dose of stress fuels a roller coaster of emotion that wreaks havoc with equilibrium. By releasing chemicals that change our body and brain chemistries, stress applies pressure to all our systems, including the immune system, which in turn makes us vulnerable to myriad emotional and physical maladies.

In such cases, medication is often needed to restore homeostasis.

THE ROLE OF GENETICS

You hear it all the time:

"She's got her mother's eyes."
"Poor kid, he's got his father's nose."
"Baldness runs in their family."

On the simplest level, genetics—the science of heredity and variation in all living things—is the medical record of family trees.

Both external (physical) and internal (chemical) features are determined by genetic traits passed down through family lines.

If your bloodlines are filled with tall and trim predecessors, chances are you will be tall and trim. Likewise, if your family has historically been short and overweight, you could develop the same physical features. However, *genetic predisposition does not translate to inevitability.* Weight, for instance, can be altered through choices about exercise and nutrition. Say a man with "trim genes" is a couch potato who swills beer and eats chips and fries. Genetics alone will not keep him trim. After years of sloth, he'll have a beer gut and 40 additional pounds.

At best, predisposition is a diagnostic tool to help prevent or treat genetically based pitfalls. If people have heart disease running through their family trees, it's advisable that they lower their cholesterol, stop smoking, and engage in regular exercise. Children of a parent with diabetes should have their blood glucose levels routinely checked and be counseled on good eating habits. These examples underscore an important point about genetics—so important that it's worth repeating: Predisposition does not translate to inevitability. With knowledge, foresight, and healthy behaviors, anyone can defy much of their genetic fingerprint.

A New View of the Family Tree

For centuries, family trees could be viewed only from the outside. Your ancestors sat at the very top of the tree, and you (or your children) were placed at the lowest level. The few genetic traits we could track at that time were external (things like hair and eye color, height, and weight) and historical (ancestors who had died of heart attacks; cancers that appeared to run through the family line).

In the past decade, research scientists have begun to map the human

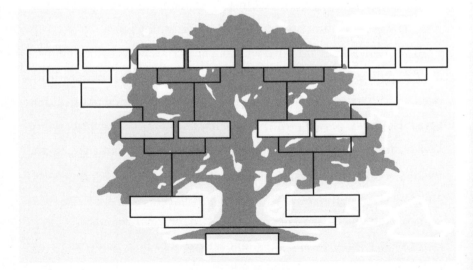

genome, which stores all our hereditary information and largely defines who we are. As scientists crack the genome code, it's as if they are cutting a cross-section of the human family tree and looking inside that slice to discover the chemical fingerprints embedded in our lines of heredity.

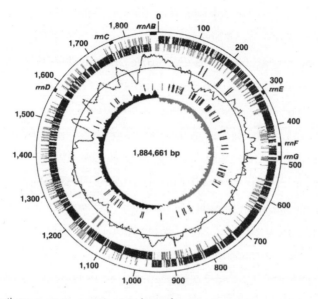

The new family tree: a cross-section readout of a gene

Thanks to this inside view, we've discovered that genetics not only transmits physical traits but also plays an important role in determining brain chemistry . . . and it shows itself in inherited behaviors like chronic depression, bipolar disorders, anxiety, hyperactivity, sleep disorders, and many other so-called psychological and behavioral conditions.

These chronic problems are created by inherited homeostatic imbalances, and these imbalances constantly affect our brain chemistry and therefore our emotions, behaviors, and everyday functioning. Even under minor stress, these imbalances can cause emotional or mental instability that directly influences addictive tendencies.

Imagine a keg of nitroglycerin, the main ingredient of dynamite. Nitroglycerin is highly unstable and extremely volatile, yet it can sit without incident for days, weeks, and years. But as time passes, it degrades bit by bit, becoming more unstable. Then, one day, it receives a shock—say, pressure or heat—and it explodes.

Now picture an inherited imbalance in brain chemistry. It, too, may be highly unstable and extremely volatile, yet it can function marginally for years, attracting little if any notice. One day, it receives a shock in the form of a major stress and detonates in an explosion of dysfunctional emotions and feelings that can trigger addiction.

Like fingerprints, brain chemistry is unique. That's why we all behave differently. Similarly, no one's brain chemistry is perfectly balanced. All of us are born with different combinations of "flaws" that reflect our individual homeostatic imbalances. These flaws can be reflected in emotional instability. The more off-balance your individual brain chemistry, the more vulnerable (or at risk) you are to addiction.

Every day, newspapers and medical journals report newly discovered genetic links to smoking, drinking, behavioral addictions, and drug abuse. With an estimated 20,000 to 30,000 genes contained in our DNA, and billions of possible combinations of those genes, new scientific studies clearly confirm the genetic influence on homeostasis and inherited diseases. Here are just a few of thousands of examples.

- Mice mutated with a defective Per2 gene drink three times more alcohol than normal.
- Nonsmokers are more likely than smokers to carry a protec-

tive gene, CYP2A6, which causes them to feel more nausea and dizziness from smoking.

- People with two copies of the ALDH*2 gene variation rarely drink alcohol and more rarely develop alcoholism.
- In a study at the University of Southern Florida, 95 percent of the participants who abused alcohol and illicit drugs and smoked shared a double A variation of the mu-opioid gene.

As the human genome is mapped precisely, more genetic links to addiction will be confirmed.

But let's be clear: *No one has discovered any single gene for addiction.* Rather, addiction is the result of combinations of genes that, when stressed, cause myriad destructive homeostatic imbalances.

The chemical imbalances that lead to addiction are not discernable through casual observation. You cannot spot an addict by his or her physical features (although physical *behaviors*—like raiding a medicine cabinet at a house party—are telling). Instead, the hereditary imbalances that cause addiction are found in the brain and its chemistry.

Of course, some genetic traits are more clearly expressed than others within different family trees, so degrees of vulnerability to addiction vary widely. That's all the more reason you should research and review your own family history. If it's filled with addiction and alcoholism, you can take steps to avoid the land mines that may trigger the disease, just as you would take precautions if you were predisposed to another disease.

Genetically speaking, your addiction may not be your fault, but from both a social and human perspective, prevention and treatment is *your* responsibility.

Environment, Imprinting, Stress, and Addiction Risk

In addiction medicine, *environment* is defined simply as the world in which you live. It has little to do with climate change and a lot to do with the people close to you who may put you at risk of addiction by adding to your stress. These relationships are grouped in four categories.

Community environment. In terms of addiction risk, does it make a difference whether you live in a small town or a big city? Not really. What is important is the cohesiveness of your community (or lack of it) and how you connect (or don't) to it.

A dysfunctional community poses a greater risk to addiction than a community that operates harmoniously. If your community has favorable or lax views of drug use, you've got a better than average chance of trying drugs. Statistically, if your town or city has positive or lax views on firearms and crime, your risk of addiction is raised.

If your town or city has a healthy ambience but you don't fit in, or you withdraw or detach yourself from the community, then you run a greater risk of addiction. Conversely, if you are an active participant in a robust, well-organized, and welcoming community, your risk for addiction is decreased.

Family environment. Through a process called imprinting, infants and toddlers learn and establish patterns of behavior by observing and imitating those closest to them. At that early stage, their central nervous systems soak up almost every stimulus within reach. This "imprinted data" is expressed years later as feelings and behaviors, both good and bad, when events in our lives reflexively recall these imprinted messages. For that reason alone, families—their interactions, cohesiveness, and attitudes—have the earliest and most lasting impact on children. In terms of preventing addiction, the importance of a good, stable family environment cannot be overstated.

If the family is conflicted or dysfunctional, the risk of addiction is increased. The greater and more hurtful the conflict, the greater at risk the children are for future addiction. Divorce harms children on many levels by creating fierce conflict within a dysfunctional family environment. Physical, psychological, and sexual abuse place children at risk for addiction in their later lives. Parental alcoholism and drug abuse put children in harm's way of the same afflictions as they grow older. A favorable or lax attitude toward drugs and alcohol abuse by parents or siblings contributes to the risk of addiction.

Studies show that a corrosive family atmosphere places adopted children—those without genetic ties to the family—at an almost equal risk of addiction as bloodline children.

Friends and peer environment. Among teens and young adults, peer pressure and "group think" are major contributing factors to addiction risk. Having friends who take drugs increases the risk of addiction. Being part of a group that intentionally stands apart from the community and its values raises the risk of addiction. Friends who engage in non-drug-related petty, misdemeanor, or felony behaviors increase your risk of addiction, even if you don't take part in their criminal activities.

For recovering addicts, the most difficult part of sobriety is staying away from friends who were part of their past and finding new friends who will become part of a new and healthy living environment.

School and work environment. We spend about a third of our lives at school or work, so this environment can affect anyone's at-risk profile.

In either setting, the difference between involved and detached personal performance, participation, and commitment to shared goals marks a clear line between healthy and at-risk environments.

STRESS: THE ADDICTION TRIGGER

A sign in a Southern California bakery window proclaims: Stressed spelled backward is Desserts!

If only reversing stress were that easy. Yet the sentiment reflects the most common misunderstanding about stress. Most people think of stress as something caused by "bad" feelings and events that are fixed only by "good" feelings and events—like eating a tasty dessert.

In reality, stress is *any* change—good or bad—to the body's physical or emotional norm . . . to its homeostasis. And as we've seen, disrupting homeostasis can invite trouble.

Stress can be obvious, subtle, acute, or chronic. It can come from anxiety about a first date, interviewing for a job, or running into your ex-lover; it can manifest in feelings created by caring for a sick parent or child. It's stressful if you get fired or flunk a major exam. It's also stressful when you move into a bigger and better apartment or house. Good stress or bad stress, it's all stress . . . for at the center of these occurrences is a change you must adjust to, and that adaptation is itself stressful because your homeostasis is challenged.

Generally speaking, stress falls into two categories: physical and emotional. Physical stress triggers an immediate reflex in the autonomic nervous system. (Think of this merely as your body's "automatic" system: Something happens, and the nervous system "automatically" reacts.) It's a primal reflex, like pulling a finger away from a flame or hot surface, that almost everyone processes the same way.

Emotional stress is more subtle and diverse and involves grief, anxiety, disappointment, depression, and other feelings on the human spectrum of emotions. Stress can arise from the mere *anticipation* of emotions. These feelings affect and are affected by brain chemistry along with other factors such as memory, physical and emotional stability, learning, sleep deprivation, and other brain functions. Each person processes emotional stress differently, based on his or her individualized brain chemistry.

Feelings like grief and anxiety do not appear and vanish in a millisecond. Because feelings linger, managing emotional stress requires a longer, more open-ended timetable than the response to physical stress. Balancing emotional stress may involve a small or large remixing of brain chemistry.

The degree of any specific brain chemistry imbalance is the hand each of us has been dealt by genetics and, not coincidentally, defines our individualized norm. Yet we've survived since birth by learning to adapt to a wide range of situations, circumstances, and feelings. While each of us is better in some areas than others, we're all basically functional.

But if you add a big dose of stress to the mixture, it's like throwing your inherent imbalance into a Cuisinart and processing it at top speed. The result? An ugly puree of chemistry that throws your balance so far out of whack that you feel lousy, your ability to adapt collapses, and you lose the ability to function.

Learning to manage stress is critical to managing addiction.

Once stress hits, you have two ways to respond: constructively (through good choices) or destructively (through bad choices). Good choices not only resolve bad feelings much faster, they go a long way toward ensuring overall health. The more you practice good choices, the more they are reinforced. Conversely, bad choices only perpetuate and intensify bad feelings, ultimately destroying your overall health.

So what tools do you need to make good choices?

To begin, you need an understanding of the biology (brain chemistry) that creates those bad feelings in the first place. You'll need human resources to counsel you through the pain. You'll need to eat nutritiously, sleep well, and exercise regularly so that you feel your physical best. All of these behavioral modifications will help you consistently make and follow through on good choices.

Let's say your lover breaks up with you. That hurts a lot and is the source of ongoing stress (in the form of bad feelings) for quite a while. You could fly into rages, obsess to the point of stalking, sink into depression, drink way too much, shoot heroin, do a line of coke, smoke some methamphetamine (meth), or blunder into any number of other bad choices.

Or you could spend time with family and friends who will advise and comfort you. You could go to the gym to pump up those all-important endorphins that make you feel better. You could see a therapist to work out your feelings. You could, when appropriate, consider short-term medication to relieve anxiety and sadness—meds that restore and maintain the balance of your brain chemistry and thus your emotions. This rebalancing not only makes you feel better, it also helps you make consistently good choices.

A lot of stress in life is predictable, so it's wise to anticipate the effect of bad feelings and have a plan in place that does not involve bad choices. For instance, picture going to a party where you know few people. You're anxious because you want to have fun and make a good impression. You could indulge in any number of bad choices—down a couple of martinis beforehand to relax, smoke a joint, take a Valium, or snort a line of coke.

Or you could have a plan in place. Perhaps you go jogging before the party to burn off steam, or maybe you bring a friend along to buffer the social anxiety. You could dress your best to give yourself confidence. You could plan to leave at a specific time but have a backup option to stay longer if you meet someone interesting. One of these and other good choices can manage the stress created by anxiety.

We cannot "cure" stress, but we can manage it responsibly. Until we learn to manage this inevitable force of nature, those of us with genetic predispositions will remain vulnerable to addictive behaviors. But we won't need addictive substances if we fill our emotional toolbox with smart choices and gain a fundamental understanding of brain chemistry.

SELF-MEDICATION AND HOMEOSTASIS

Self-medication is a conscious response to an actual or a potential homeostatic imbalance. In layman's terms, self-medication simply means acting on your own—without a doctor's consultation or prescription—to make yourself feel better.

Cut your finger? Put some Neosporin and an adhesive bandage on the cut.

Bothered by a nasty rash? Apply hydrocortisone or another salve.

Feeling a cold or flu coming on? Take oscillococcinum or Theraflu . . . or maybe have some chicken soup.

We all self-medicate, and we do it without a second thought, almost on autopilot.

In most cases, it's a protective, efficient, and even smart reaction because it treats problems immediately. Otherwise, the finger would keep bleeding, the rash could spread, and the flu could develop into pneumonia.

Problems with addiction, however, tend to start when you self-medicate intangible maladies (things that can't be seen, fully understood, or accurately self-diagnosed), *particularly vague feelings and/or specific emotions that make people feel bad.*

When depressed, some people might go see an Albert Brooks comedy at the movie theater or stay home and watch *The Simpsons.* Or they might keep themselves so busy that they don't have time to dwell on their depression. Or they do any one of a thousand things to avoid feeling bad, including taking a drink of good wine, smooth scotch, designer vodka, or even rotgut rye. But whatever action they take, the aim is the same: to feel better.

Self-medication with alcohol and/or drugs can be viewed as a biological, primal response: You feel awful and want to feel better *immediately.*

Inasmuch as it is an attempt merely to "feel better," addictive behavior is inextricably linked to self-medication and survival. Like everyone else, when addicts feel bad, they self-medicate. Indeed, scientists have recently confirmed that for addicts, self-medication is merely an attempt to restore specific imbalances in their brains.

So it's vital we learn about the imbalances that make addicts feel bad in the first place.

Ask the Doctor

My cousin won the lottery and became an instant millionaire, and then he started smoking marijuana and drinking alcohol every day. How does that kind of addictive behavior happen when you're on easy street?

Stress is *any* change in our daily routine . . . and the bigger the change, the bigger the stress. The dramatic change in your cousin's finances represents a potential disaster in his new life. In fact, people's lives become more stressful with the huge change in their lives created by an income jump.

Furthermore, people with a lot of money have stress from dealing with family and friends, receiving requests for financial support from strangers (and relatives), giving up their jobs and their professional identities, and dealing with less structure in their lives.

At what age should we first talk to our children about drugs, and what should we tell them?

Talking to kids about drugs is like talking to them about sex. The discussion occurs when they are old enough to ask questions, which can start as early as age 4. Answer their questions truthfully but simply. When kids get answers, they will move on.

Ask your children what they have heard about drugs, what scares them, and how they think drugs may affect them. Check with school counselors and teachers to see what is being taught in school—it may not reflect the truth or the new medical paradigm, and it may be fraught with judgment.

As your children reach preadolescence, begin the dialogue in more detail, directing the discussion to their genetics and environmental predispositions. Here's the important part: Let children know that drug addiction is primarily a medical disease that should be caught as early as possible to ensure its best treatment. It is *not* a behavioral malady.

Once these discussions begin, accept your responsibility to create the right environment to prevent substance abuse in the home. Always keep the door open, try not to be judgmental, and

(continued)

⌐ Ask the Doctor (cont.)

let kids know that everyone has these questions, not just them. Sex and drugs need to be broached carefully, whereas rock 'n' roll needs no introduction.

What effects do various abused substances have on a fetus?

The hard truth is that no fetus gets away clean. The answers and possible damage depend upon the substances abused, the general health of the mother, and the trimester in which the abuse takes place.

The first trimester is the riskiest period. Organs form during the first 3 months, making the fetus especially vulnerable to serious problems—even its survival.

As a pregnancy proceeds toward term, the fetus has progressively more integrity, but certain substances (like opiates) can cross the placental barrier and create dependencies in the fetus. The baby is then born addicted and goes through withdrawal at birth. A mother's stimulant addiction can cause smaller infants, long-term cognitive problems, and developmental issues in the child's heart, lungs, brain, and kidneys.

Often, a mother who is addicted to one substance is cross-addicted to another (cocaine and nicotine, for instance). This compromises her general health, giving rise to any number of birth defects and maternal complications at delivery.

Fetal alcohol syndrome is a condition that occurs with maternal alcohol abuse and is characterized by devastating mental, physical, and developmental birth defects, all of which are completely preventable if a woman simply does not consume alcohol during pregnancy. Indeed, the Centers for Disease Control and Prevention states categorically that there is no "safe" time, amount, or kind of alcohol an expectant mother can drink without potential harm to the fetus.

Some studies also indicate that fetal exposure to addictive substances renders the child more susceptible to addictions later in life.

Brain Chemistry

In the past decades, hundreds of books and technical papers have been published on the subject of neurochemistry; scientific developments have vastly improved our fundamental understanding of how the brain works. No matter how much we know about the mind, countless mysteries remain. But this much is clear: Research has indelibly linked the causes and effects of addiction to chemical interactions in the brain and our bodies' responses to those changes.

The brain is a vast matrix that creates and controls emotions and behaviors by sending chemical signals along a complex electrical circuitry. In keeping with the homeostatic principle, the purpose of these electrochemical interactions is to promote well-being by reacting to and defending against changes that might threaten the normal range of balance.

Addiction stems primarily from emotional threats to the internal milieu. When feelings escalate (perhaps fear becomes paranoia, or sadness becomes depression, or happiness becomes mania), they can cause homeostatic chaos in brain chemistry that dumps someone at addiction's front door.

How and why these emotional balances are upset and then restored is the central focus of the new paradigm in addiction medicine.

NEUROTRANSMITTERS AND RECEPTORS

Whenever an event or feeling happens, the body responds to restore or maintain homeostasis. In this frontline defense, neurotransmitters and receptors are the brain's foot soldiers, constantly reacting to every change with adjustments or adaptations that keep the body stabilized.

Neurotransmitters are nerve cells that relay news of physical and emotional occurrences that need attention—perceived threats or challenges to homeostasis that must be met and favorably resolved. These chemical signals are received by protein molecules called receptors.

Think of the interaction of a neurotransmitter and a receptor as a brief electrical hookup. The neurotransmitter approaches and then connects with the receptor, like a plug fitting into a socket.

In the same way that connecting a plug to a socket allows electricity to light a bulb, the chemical link of neurotransmitter and receptor pumps in the juice that turns on your emotions.

Three types of neurotransmitters are directly responsible for addiction: dopamine (the pleasure and reward chemical), noradrenalin (the readiness-response chemical), and serotonin (the mood-regulating chemical). A few others—such as GABA (gamma-aminobutyric acid), glutamate, and the opioids—come into play, but they serve primarily as assistants to the big three.

Different types of neurotransmitters match specific receptor types. Picture a dopamine neurotransmitter and its matching receptor as a regular two-prong plug and socket.

A noradrenalin neurotransmitter and its corresponding receptor is depicted as a three-prong plug and socket.

Now imagine a serotonin neurotransmitter and its corresponding receptor as a USB plug and its port.

If you place all three connections side by side, their differences are clear. It's obvious that dopamine neurotransmitters cannot fit into noradrenalin or serotonin receptors, nor can noradrenalin neurotransmitters connect with dopamine or serotonin transmitters. Each type of neurotransmitter fits only with its corresponding receptor.

Just as all plug and socket connections complete an electrical circuit to power an appliance, all neurotransmitter-receptor interactions serve one overall purpose: to restore and/or maintain homeostasis by making you feel better.

Under this umbrella of common purpose, each of the three neurotransmitter-receptor connections has its own unique and separate task. It's as if the two-prong plug and socket were used only to start coffeemakers, or the three-prong plug and socket were made only for alarm bells, or the USB pair was designed for use solely with lava lamps.

Of course, coffeemakers provide stimulants . . . and that's pretty much what dopamine does. Dopamine can make you feel good. It works with the memory and learning functions of the brain to oversee the pleasures we take from such actions as eating and sex. In excess, however, dopamine manifests in symptoms ranging from a subtle lack of focus to sheer mania.

In the same way that alarm bells alert us to dangers or perceived threats, noradrenalin puts us on alert by arousing awareness and kick-starting readiness. Too much (or imbalanced) noradrenalin can turn anxiety into panic.

Lava lamps display moods in moving shapes and colors, from the darkest to the brightest shades. Serotonin similarly regulates all human moods, from contentment to the deepest depressions.

A connection of plug and socket provides power to an appliance. In biochemistry, when a neurotransmitter connects to a receptor, the neurotransmitter actually pours its specific chemical (dopamine, noradrenalin, or serotonin) into the receptor, heightening or lessening the amount of the original chemical in the brain. This change in concentration changes homeostasis, and that alone creates new feelings or modifies old ones.

Let's look more closely at each of our "big three" neurotransmitters. While their functions sometimes overlap, each has a distinct profile.

Dopamine

As the chemical responsible for making you feel good, dopamine stimulates and arouses. It can make you absolutely euphoric. It gives pleasurable responses to experiences such as eating good food, enjoying sex, winning a game, playing with your dog, and countless other activities and satisfactions. In this capacity, it feeds and controls the brain's *reward center.*

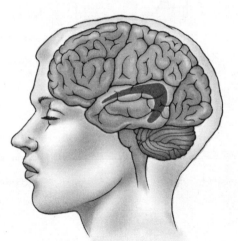

The reward center, located almost exactly midbrain, is the clearinghouse for good feelings.

Imagine eating a piece of lemon meringue pie. You taste it, savor it, and glory in its silky smoothness. Each single pleasurable sensation of taste, smell, and texture releases dopamine into the reward center. Or imagine having great sex. At orgasm, a veritable flood of dopamine is released in the reward center, making you feel terrific.

Dopamine doesn't take onetime pleasures for granted. As soon as a reward is registered in the reward center, a chemical notice of it travels via the *reward highway* to the frontal lobe of the brain. Once there, dopamine delivers this "teaching message" to the *memory center*. In response, memory motivates the *behavior center* to repeat both experiences. In essence, dopamine reinforces those specific feelings of pleasure by giving you access to them in both memory and behavior.

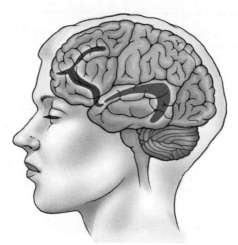

A nonstop expressway from the reward center to memory and behavior in the frontal lobe

Dopamine also plants data in the frontal lobe to prioritize rewards; the more pleasurable a reward, the more you will want it and the higher priority it will receive. That's how nature teaches us to repeat behaviors that lead to rewards: Anything you do that makes you feel good—or at least better—creates a memory. The better the behavior makes you feel, the more memory will cue behavior to repeat it.

This perfectly natural drive motivates us to seek and work for the things that give us pleasure.

Noradrenalin

Taking center stage in the readiness response is the neurotransmitter noradrenalin, sometimes called norepinephrine. Whenever you are faced with a crisis, challenge, or anything that threatens your status quo, noradrenalin is released to prepare you to either confront or withdraw from the physical or emotional threat. As such, noradrenalin is the primary chemical in the fight-or-flight response, a fundamental survival impulse.

Imagine you're walking on a deserted sidewalk late at night and you approach a dark alley. Noradrenalin relays the signal of potential threat. Suddenly, you're alert and almost tingling with awareness. You cross the front of the alley cautiously . . . or you walk to the other side of the street to avoid it. Your fight-or-flight response kicks in when your feelings—in this case, a sense of a perceived danger—are heightened by noradrenalin.

Serotonin

Serotonin is the chemical neurotransmitter that largely regulates moods. It exerts a huge influence in the areas of sleep, anger, aggression, appetite, and sexuality.

Serotonin was first identified in 1948 not as a neurotransmitter but as a substance in blood serum that narrowed the openings of blood vessels—hence the name *sero,* for a serum agent, and *tonin*, meaning vascular tone. Almost 20 years later, it was recognized as a neurotransmitter that plays a vital role in brain chemistry.

BALANCE AND IMBALANCE

When brain chemistry is within the normal range of homeostatic balance, the big three neurotransmitters augment our lives in immeasurable and important ways. Dopamine gives us the inherent good feeling, or the rush, of successfully surfing a particularly awesome wave. Noradrenalin protects us by alerting us to a change in the waves that might threaten our ride. And serotonin provides a variety of moods that enhance the journey to shore.

Of course, no one has perfectly balanced brain chemistry. We all have eccentricities, behavioral quirks, and emotional frailties, and most of them stem from a relatively small degree of imbalance in the neurotransmitter-receptor connections. But larger imbalances pose a problem. Depending on the degree of the imbalance, emotions can express themselves in a number of ways, some good, some not so good. Anxiety can turn calm into panic, sadness can intensify into despair, anger can explode into rage, happiness can flip to discontent in the blink of an eye . . . and on and on, each emotion changing as it is either intensified or soothed by its own neurotransmitter-receptor interaction. As the concentration levels of neurotransmitters change, emotions and behaviors change.

Inherited imbalances in brain chemistry create a constant need to restore homeostasis. Through these neurotransmitters, the brain automatically senses what chemicals it has either in excess or deficit and tries to restore the proper amounts (or concentration) needed to function at an optimal level. Accordingly, it seeks what it needs to balance the neurotransmitter. The more severe the imbalance, the greater the need, and the more relentless the seeking.

In medicine, this seeking is called a *wanting*. It expresses itself not as a vague or generalized desire but as an insatiable yearning for the specific substance or chemical that will balance the connection and make us feel better.

This is not like wanting a new car or *really* wanting a giant flat-panel

TV. It is, instead, a desire deeply rooted in brain chemistry that has nothing to do with rational thought processes and everything to do with primal instinct. The wanting for the specific substance is so intense that you feel you will die if it is not fulfilled.

Both diabetics and addicts suffer from chronic homeostatic imbalances. Both have specific wantings that need to be fixed instantaneously. A diabetic person has a chronic physiological imbalance that causes a survival need—a wanting for insulin. If the pancreas cannot produce enough insulin to maintain the normal level of blood sugar, insulin must be supplied externally (often by injection).

In the same way, an addict has a chronic imbalance that initiates a wanting. For example, if someone feels depressed all the time, it is likely due to a neurotransmitter imbalance. The body cannot produce enough serotonin to restore homeostasis, so serotonin must be supplied from outside. This restoration of balance may come in the form of self-medication or through pharmacological treatment.

To understand addiction, it's vital to understand the idea of immediate gratification, or instantaneous reaction. The goal of all neurotransmitter-receptor interactions is to fix whatever imbalance occurs and make the person feel better *right now*. Not in an hour or a day, but *immediately*. And, as we all know from experience, urgent fixes are not always the best options.

So let's examine how different levels of imbalance impact each of the big three neurotransmitters.

Dopamine Imbalance

Dopamine regulates our reward and pleasure centers. As extraordinary as dopamine can make each of us feel, problems are almost inevitable if we are born with a hereditary imbalance. An excess of dopamine in children incites behaviors like ADD (attention deficit disorder) and ADHD (attention deficit hyperactivity disorder). In adults and adolescents, excess dopamine can create mania and bipolar disorders.

As you recall, dopamine drives the reward highway in the brain,

RED LIGHT, GREEN LIGHT

To understand brain chemistry's relation to stress and addiction, simply think of a traffic signal.

The green light represents a perfectly balanced neurotransmitter system, known as homeostasis. This signal means the road ahead is safe to travel.

The yellow light goes off when your brain chemistry is slightly unbalanced. (We all have some inherited imbalance in at least one of the three major brain chemicals associated with addiction: serotonin, noradrenalin, and dopamine.) This slight imbalance is a signal that means: Drive with caution to avoid losing control.

The red light goes off when you add stress to your life, which throws your minor chemical imbalance into a major one. This chemical change causes an influx of bad feelings begging to be soothed. Self-medication (commonly through substances) initially eases those anxieties. The instinct to compensate for the brain's imbalance is normal (and primal). But this coping mechanism, along with unhealthy choices, can result in addiction.

The goal of the neurotransmitter stabilization is to rebalance the brain chemistry and attain homeostasis—at least to get as close as is humanly possible. Rebalancing brain chemistry to regain homeostasis, essentially getting from the red light to the green light, is the core concept behind *The Addiction Solution*.

which communicates with the memory center to create a wanting for more dopamine. This conditions the brain to "want" dopamine . . . and the more this highway is reinforced, the more the brain wants dopamine. For those with dopamine imbalances, trouble can start if a reward is withdrawn unexpectedly. When that happens, the dopamine cells signal wanting the reward again.

A mild dopamine excess that manifests itself as hyperactivity and lack of focus can be converted by a dose of stress into agitation and mania. Dopamine's specific wanting can be satisfied by stimulants that mimic the action of dopamine on the receptor: coffee, nicotine, cocaine, and methamphetamine (meth). These stimulants not only fulfill the wanting by calming agitation and refocusing energies, they make the user better able to function.

When the stimulants wear off, however, agitation returns, and dopamine predictably signals another wanting. Your stored memory then triggers behavior, motivating you to acquire the reward again and again. Each time you satisfy the wanting, your prefrontal cortex is damaged, so your judgment evaporates a little more, suppressed by both the reward substance and the wanting.

Noradrenalin Imbalance

Noradrenalin alerts us to potential threats. But if you have inherited even a mild overabundance or experience a sudden surge of too much noradrenalin, you may feel anxious even when facing petty nuisances. Add stress, and this slight excess, or imbalance, can cause extreme anxiety and even panic. If you are born with too much noradrenalin, you are prone to frequent anxiety or panic from the smallest dose of stress.

Noradrenalin may spur you to readiness in dangerous situations. When it's out of balance, you may be motivated to prepare yourself, but it's just as likely that you will panic or withdraw. Let's say, for example, that a woman steps off the sidewalk into the path of an oncoming bus. Balanced noradrenalin allows her to make the right choice—in this case, "flight"—and she steps back on the curb. But an imbalance complicates the choices: She might step back, or she might panic and freeze like a deer in headlights. The fight response is never a wise reaction to an oncoming bus, but by diminishing judgment, a noradrenalin imbalance lessens her capacity to act in her best interests.

Compound a chronic noradrenalin imbalance with stress and what was once functional anxiety turns into dysfunction. Walter Cannon (the American who gave homeostasis its name) reflected that addictive imbalances overwhelmingly led to flight instead of fight, to withdrawal (often into drugs) rather than confrontation. Subsequent research has backed his theory. Dependence on antianxiety drugs like Valium, Xanax, Ativan, Klonopin, marijuana, or nicotine (among others) is an all-too-common withdrawal response to feeling overwhelmed by almost everything. The neurotransmitter imbalance sends out a wanting signal, and antianxiety drugs satisfy the need.

An overabundance of noradrenalin also plays an important role in sleep disorders, which are often accurate predictors of later substance abuse. (We'll touch on sleep disorders in Chapter 3.)

Serotonin Imbalance

If your serotonin balance falls within the normal range, you'll experience a standard array of moods, both good and bad. But if you have an inherited imbalance of too little serotonin, you can easily fall into depression and/or obsessive thoughts or behavior. The greater the degree of imbalance, the deeper the depression and the more obsessive the behavior. Many scientists consider serotonin the dark twin of dopamine: While excess dopamine enhances pleasure and reward, insufficient serotonin can lead to the blackest of depressions. Add even a small amount of stress to the equation and a depression can turn suicidal.

A serotonin imbalance immediately signals a wanting. Consider a man who is depressed. The sudden drop in his serotonin sends out the wanting message. So he drinks a martini or a beer (anything alcoholic), and the first buzz starts to lighten his mood. He has another drink and another and he feels better and better . . . until he goes to sleep or passes out. In the morning, his depression returns, and serotonin again signals a wanting, which he may answer with another alcoholic drink.

Or let's say a woman is in pain and wants to feel better. She takes an OxyContin or Vicodin and her pain eases or disappears as these opiates—so named because they contain constituents or derivatives of constituents found in opium—increase her serotonin production. When the effect of the drug wears off, her serotonin level drops and the pain returns, so she pops another Oxy or Vike. Or she shoots some heroin, another bad choice for pain relief (or depression).

Both depression and pain cause stress. The greater the pain or depression, the greater the stress, tilting the serotonin neurotransmitter even more out of balance and causing both more urgent and greater wantings. In these two instances, self-medicating with drugs is all about numbing bad feelings.

SELF-MEDICATION AND NEUROCHEMICAL IMBALANCES

In Chapter 1, self-medication was defined as your own effort to restore homeostasis. You might bandage a cut, take an antacid for a burning stomach, or put salve on a rash.

The same principles and reasons for self-medicating physical problems hold true for neurochemical imbalances. It's really pretty basic: If you feel bad—physically or emotionally—you strive to make yourself feel better. You do your best to fill any need or biochemical wanting as

---

GABA AND GLUTAMATE

Earlier we mentioned that two neurotransmitters serve as assistants to the big three (dopamine, noradrenalin, and serotonin). Actually, GABA (gamma-aminobutyric acid) and glutamate are two amino acids that *act* as neurotransmitters during the addiction process.

Simply explained, glutamate is the brain's major agitator, whereas GABA is its most effective pacifier. They are polar opposites: Think of glutamate as heavy metal played full blast and GABA as elevator music.

When an abused substance is abruptly withdrawn, glutamate levels instantly rise, agitating the entire nervous system and making us extremely anxious and unstable. To combat this, GABA-ergic meds (like Neurontin) are administered to counteract the frenetic intensity created by glutamate, making withdrawal a safe and comfortable experience.

Without these GABAergic medications, withdrawal becomes the classic, torturous, cold-turkey scenario that has killed tens of thousands of addicts over the past century.

soon as possible, whether that means taking insulin or a stimulant like cocaine.

So how do you choose your brand of self-medication? How do you know to treat a cold with chicken soup? How do you choose between aspirin and ibuprofen for a headache? In other words, how do you find what works for you?

People seek and find their self-medications mostly through trial and error.

Say you're coming down with a cold. You try chicken soup because your grandmother swore it was the best remedy, but it doesn't ease your symptoms. So you go to the drugstore and get Sudafed. Maybe that works—or maybe you have to try Contac or Theraflu or any number of cold medicines until you find the one that's right for you. Once you do, you remain loyal to that solution *because it works best for you.* It makes you feel better than any of the others did.

Now let's say you're depressed. You watch a comedy on TV or at the movies. It's a funny flick, but after it's over, you're still depressed. You feel so down you keep trying one thing after another, but nothing really lifts your spirits. One day you have a good stiff drink and it makes you feel better. A second drink and the dark fog starts to dissipate. A third makes you almost carefree—you actually feel good. So whenever you're in a funk, you take out the bottle and have a couple of pulls because alcohol makes you feel better than anything else did.

The aim of self-medication is to feel better. If you're depressed, a cocktail may make you feel better. If you're as anxious as a skittish cat, a Valium may make you feel better. If you're unfocused and a little hyper before going out to a party, a hit of cocaine may make you feel better.

Nobody ever got addicted because self-medicating substances made them feel worse. Indeed, one of the things you become addicted to is *feeling better.* And why not? It's better than feeling bad all the time.

Forrest Gump famously declared that "life is like a box of chocolates." Addiction is a box of many and assorted "candies," with a variety of self-medications from which to pick and choose. You can't know which you'll like until you try them. When you discover one that makes you feel better than any candy you ever even imagined, it becomes your absolute favorite. No more assorted samplers for you. From now on, you're buying only boxes loaded with your number one favorite, which then becomes your self-medication of choice.

But it's *not* your choice, not really. Your specific neurotransmitter imbalance signals a wanting for a specific substance, and you sample your way through a menu of self-medications until you find the one that satisfies you better and faster than the others. It is actually no more your choice than the biochemical demand for insulin is a "choice" for a diabetic person.

So, in addiction terms, self-medication is merely a personal search to gratify the specific biochemical need of a neurotransmitter imbalance.

Access, cost, availability, and environment all play a part in self-medication, but this much is true: Every neurotransmitter imbalance will signal a wanting until its specific need is filled.

NEUROTRANSMITTER MIMICS

We stated earlier that types of neurotransmitters could be received only by their designated receptors. How, then, are substances like cocaine, meth, opiates, heroin, and alcohol able to connect with the receptor?

The answer is simple. The chemical composition of certain drugs *mimics* the specific neurotransmitter that signals a wanting. Cocaine and meth mimic the dopamine type of neurotransmitter. Alcohol and heroin imitate serotonin. Valium, Xanax, and the rest of the class of drugs known as benzodiazepines (benzos) impersonate the noradrenalin neurotransmitter. In each case, the chemicals in the drug look and act like its correlating neurotransmitter, with only minor variations. In a sense, the drug tricks the receptor into accepting it as the real thing—perhaps only for an instant, but that's all the time it takes for a connection.

Once they connect, the alcohol or drugs coat the receptors with counterfeit chemicals that closely mimic the real neurotransmitters and actually block, or prevent, the real neurotransmitters from attaching to the receptors. When the effects of these substances start to wane, a wanting is signaled, and the receptor seeks these same substances to relieve the wanting.

The fact is, receptors can choose the chemicals with which they interact.

Receptors prioritize their chemical hookups, preferring those that promise the fastest path to restoring lost balance (homeostasis). The counterfeit options provide rapid fixes, and they really do defend against neurotransmitter imbalance by making the user feel good. Of course, it's usually a temporary fix—a sort of an "it seemed like a good idea at the time" moment for the receptor—but brain chemistry reacts to the first *appearance* of a solution and not always to the healthiest and best solution.

The favored choice of noradrenalin receptors is endorphins, chemicals that are manufactured during rigorous exercise. An endorphin rush, also known as a runner's high, helps soothe pain and support feelings of calm or exhilaration. In the past decade, medical studies have confirmed both the benefits of endorphins and their preferential interactions with receptors in the brain. It's also been shown that acupuncture can trigger the production of endorphins.

The second choice for noradrenalin receptors are mild stimulants like nicotine and caffeine, followed by riskier antianxiety medications like marijuana, and the safer antiseizure medications. Last on the list of preferred choices would be the noradrenalin neurotransmitter itself.

The favored choices for dopamine receptors are caffeine (coffee, tea, and so-called energy drinks like Red Bull or Jolt) and sugar. Nicotine from cigarettes, cigars, and chewing tobacco is another preferred substance.

The secondary preferences for dopamine receptors are stimulant drugs like cocaine, meth, Dexedrine, Ritalin, and Adderall.

Last to be accepted by the dopamine receptor is the dopamine neurotransmitter itself.

The serotonin receptor has just two options. Its first choices are the chemicals found in alcohol and opiates because they quickly provoke a rise in serotonin level that makes you feel better. Only secondarily does the receptor accept the natural serotonin neurotransmitter.

Neurotransmitter Preferences

Receptor	First Choice	Second Choice	Third Choice
Noradrenalin	Endorphins	Mild stimulants: nicotine, tea, coffee Antianxiety meds: Valium, Xanax, Ativan, etc. Antiseizure meds: Neurontin, etc.	Noradrenalin neurotransmitter
Dopamine	Caffeine, nicotine, sugar	Cocaine, Dexedrine, Ritalin, Adderall, methamphetamine	Dopamine neurotransmitter
Serotonin	Alcohol and opiates	Serotonin neurotransmitter	No third choice

Why are the natural neurotransmitters the last to be accepted by their designated receptors? It's because the receptors already "know" from experience that their matching neurotransmitters are imbalanced and incapable of easing bad feelings (especially since they are directly causing the bad feelings). So, in an attempt to restore homeostasis, the receptor searches for other solutions—anything that makes you feel better—and it accepts a natural neurotransmitter only if the quick-fix options aren't at the front of the line.

While each receptor has its preferred connections, no one is powerless to change those preferences. As we learn how neurotransmitter receptor connections work, all of us can make smarter choices.

CONNECTING THE DOTS

From birth, we all have some degree of genetic imbalances in dopamine, noradrenalin, and/or serotonin neurotransmitters. It's the severity of those imbalances and the impact of stress on them that neurochemically distinguishes addicts from nonaddicts.

Because each imbalance seeks what it needs, addiction specialists should be able to identify the specific imbalance by knowing what substance the addict abused.

Most of the time, cocaine or meth abuse indicates a severe dopamine imbalance. An addiction to prescription drugs like Valium strongly points to an exaggerated noradrenalin imbalance. Alcoholism is almost always driven by significantly low levels of serotonin. Abuse of heroin and other opiates like OxyContin and Vicodin also arises from substantial serotonin deficits.

Behavior is another indicator of specific neurotransmitter imbalances

(continued on page 42)

Your Addiction Prediction

We don't choose the drugs we abuse, they choose us.

When someone comes to my office for treatment, I can actually predict the biochemical cause of their addiction based simply on the substance he or she abuses.

We're all born with individualized neurochemical imbalances that, when impacted by stress, can trigger addictions. Identifying these specific imbalanced chemicals, or neurotransmitters, allows us to accurately predict the specific substances that will choose us.

When severely out of balance, the three major neurotransmitters—dopamine, serotonin, and noradrenalin—create uncomfortable feelings and behaviors that we often fix by self-medicating. When we're depressed, we need serotonin . . . and the opiates and alcohol give us a quick fix. Overwhelming anxiety and panic arise from a surge in noradrenalin, and drugs like Valium and Xanax almost immediately calm this discomfort. Cocaine and methamphetamine addicts abuse their substances to quiet the mania and severe agitation that stem from an overload of dopamine in their brains.

These drugs interact with each specific neurotransmitter's receptors by blocking the otherwise discomforting effects of each specific imbalance. So show me your drug, and I'll show you the neurotransmitter that needs balancing.

Your Addiction Prediction, a simple 15-question test, sorts out which of your neurotransmitters are likely to be imbalanced.

After you've answered all the questions, see which sector most of your answers land in. This will be the neurotransmitter that is most likely out of balance.

Unlike the new medical paradigm, Your Addiction Prediction is not scientifically tested, but over my twenty years of clinical experience, it has proven to be an extremely reliable if simple tool to connect the dots between someone's addiction and their imbalanced brain chemistry. In so doing, it allows us to guide both short-term and long-term recovery by offering an alternative menu of nonaddicting options to medically treat individual neurochemical imbalances.

YOUR ADDICTION PREDICTION

Fill in the circled numbers that apply to you

1. I can sometimes stay awake for days without sleeping
2. I often get depressed or sad
3. I sometimes get heart palpitations or chest pains
4. I have alcoholism in my family
5. I often start projects and never complete them
6. I am often constipated or have diarrhea, and sometimes both
7. Reading is hard for me because I often lose track of what I've read
8. I've had panic attacks where I can feel scared, my heart races, I have trouble breathing, and I can feel dizzy
9. I sometimes have obsessive behaviors or thoughts
10. I have trouble falling asleep
11. I had trouble focusing when I was younger and couldn't sit still in class
12. I took antidepressants like Prozac, Zoloft, and Lexapro, but they didn't really help me
13. I avoid social situations with people I don't know
14. Sometimes I can stay in bed and sleep all day
15. One of my relatives was depressed

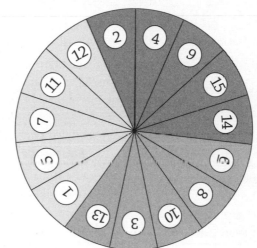

The shade where you find most of your answers indicates your major imbalance and predicts the substances you are most likely to abuse.

NEUROTRANSMITTER IMBALANCE	ABUSED SUBSTANCE
DOPAMINE	COCAINE/METH
NORADRENALIN	VALIUM/XANAX/ATIVAN/KLONOPIN
SEROTONIN	OPIATES/ALCOHOL

and an accurate and early barometer of a specific imbalance that may someday lead to addiction.

If you're hyper, manic, or unfocused, it's a good bet that you suffer from a dopamine excess. If you're usually anxious, worried, or prone to panic, you've probably got too much noradrenalin in your life. Alternatively, if you're chronically depressed, obsessive, or compulsive, you are most likely the victim of seriously low serotonin levels.

Behavior	Substance	Neurotransmitter
Bipolar Lack of focus Hyper, manic ADD/ADHD	Cocaine Methamphetamine Stimulants	Dopamine
Depression Physical pain OCD	Alcohol Opiates (heroin, OxyContin)	Serotonin
Anxiety Panic	Benzos (Valium, Xanax)	Noradrenalin

This chart can work forward by projecting certain types of behavior and feelings onto the likely substances abused and then identifying the likely neurotransmitter imbalance. Or it can work backward, projecting certain types of neurotransmitter imbalances onto likely substances abused and then identifying associated behavior.

The Anxiety Anomaly

Anxiety is sometimes more complex than the chart above shows. This complexity demonstrates how different neurotransmitters can overlap.

When anxiety strikes, many patients ask their doctors for medications to help them calm down and feel better. Initially, the anxiety might look like a classic symptom of excess noradrenalin. But the physician must also consider that the noradrenalin excess could actually be the result of a serotonin deficit.

Remember: Serotonin deficits often cause obsessive and/or compulsive behaviors that demand perfection. Of course, perfection is unattainable, and the frustrating and constant failure to achieve perfection raises the person's noradrenalin levels, resulting in anxiety. The primary cause of this type of anxiety is not noradrenalin but the serotonin deficit that kick-started the behaviors that led to the anxiety (or increase in noradrenalin). Treating this obsession-driven anxiety with benzodiazepines (Valium, Xanax, Ativan, etc.), which target noradrenalin, will offer only temporary help. It's an example of "calming the symptom without treating the cause." Not to mention that benzos themselves are habit forming and create another addiction.

In cases like these, physicians might instead prescribe SNRIs (serotonin and noradrenalin reuptake inhibitors) like Effexor, Pristiq, Savella, and Cymbalta that increase serotonin while diminishing the effect of noradrenalin.

CHEMICAL AND MOLECULAR SIMILARITIES

The big three neurotransmitters primarily responsible for addiction share similarities in structure, shape, and makeup not only to each other but also to the abused substances that mimic them.

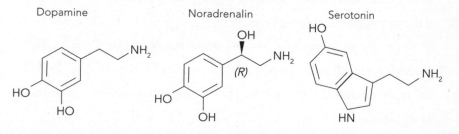

Dopamine   Noradrenalin   Serotonin

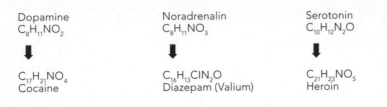

Dopamine
$C_8H_{11}NO_2$

↓

$C_{17}H_{21}NO_4$
Cocaine

Noradrenalin
$C_8H_{11}NO_3$

↓

$C_{16}H_{13}ClN_2O$
Diazepam (Valium)

Serotonin
$C_{10}H_{12}N_2O$

↓

$C_{21}H_{23}NO_5$
Heroin

Just one molecule separates the chemical formula of dopamine from noradrenalin. Serotonin has just slightly more carbon and hydrogen, with similar levels of nitrogen and oxygen.

Now compare the neurotransmitter formulas with their corresponding abused substances. Cocaine is merely an amped-up version of dopamine. Notice the similarities between noradrenalin and diazepam (the generic form of Valium) and between serotonin and heroin. In each comparison, the chemical formula of the abused substance is a revved-up version of the original neurotransmitter.

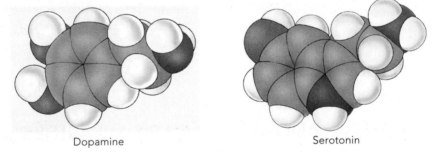

Dopamine   Serotonin

Even the structures of the big three neurotransmitters are similar, with the same types of molecules at their centers and ends. They also bond in like manner. Only their shapes slightly differ, as if modified by a single twist and pull of genetics.

Is it any wonder these abused substances so easily mimic their matching neurotransmitters? On a microscopic level, it's almost as if the big three neurotransmitters and their analogous substances make up a truly nuclear family.

Your Unique Neurochemical Imbalance

The seed of addiction resides in imbalanced brain chemistry. We've also learned that these imbalances are determined by genetics—the hereditary hand each of us is dealt, for good or ill.

Your inherited neurotransmitter imbalance (either serotonin, dopamine, or noradrenalin) is like a fingerprint that defines your unique neurochemical imbalance. Your vulnerability to addiction is related to the severity of your imbalance.

If your inherited imbalance varies only slightly from true homeostasis, you'll weather most storms safely and effectively. However, if your imbalance is more severe, your ability to handle those storms will be compromised. The more severe the imbalance in your brain chemistry, the more trouble you'll have coping with the stress of your everyday life—and the more susceptible you will be to addiction.

An increase of stress in your life, either physical or mental, can dramatically tilt your natural imbalance, causing uncomfortable mood swings and severe anxiety. These unstable feelings can encourage self-medication—a natural instinct to rebalance your chemistry—that would be helpful if the "medication" of choice was not an addictive substance.

Once you are addicted, detoxification will begin a rebalancing act of your brain chemistry with the goal of adjusting these neurotransmitters toward homeostasis. The closer you get to this perfect balance and, most important, the longer it's maintained, the less vulnerable you are to relapse.

IN SUMMARY

Let's review what we've learned about brain chemistry.

The brain controls our emotions and behaviors by sending chemical messages along a complex electrical circuitry. These signals are carried by neurotransmitters that connect with designated receptors to restore or maintain homeostasis to make us feel better. Three types of neurotransmitters are largely responsible for addiction: dopamine, the pleasure and reward chemical; noradrenalin, the readiness-response chemical; and serotonin, the mood-regulating chemical.

If all these neurotransmitters are in balance—and that is extremely rare—we should be able navigate life's storms without serious incident. However, inherited imbalances in any or all of these three neurotransmitters create a constant and turbulent need to restore homeostasis. This biochemical need expresses itself as a palpable "wanting" for the specific substance that will restore balance. The more serious the imbalance, the greater the wanting. Once stress hits an imbalanced system, a tidal wave of bad feelings and bad behaviors crashes on the shore, creating a perfect storm for substance abuse. Accordingly, addiction is about the severity of neurotransmitter imbalances and the impact of stress upon them.

Abused substances usually offer the fastest relief to imbalanced neurotransmitters because they both mimic and block natural neurotransmitters from connecting with their receptors. Once abused substances reinforce themselves by traveling to the reward center (with side trips to the memory and behavior centers in the brain), addiction settles in.

Arising as it does from an inherited imbalance of neurotransmitters in the brain, addiction is clearly not a social or character malady. Addiction is a medical disease requiring medical treatment.

Always remember:

Addiction
Originates in brain chemistry,
Is determined by genetics,
And is triggered by stress.

Ask the Doctor

My uncle has Parkinson's disease, and my aunt says this is from a problem with his dopamine. Does this mean he also has a potential drug problem?

Dopamine has three major pathways in the brain that control motor function, cognition, and feelings of pleasure (the latter through the reward pathway). Additionally, the expression of each pathway is influenced by 14 serotonin pathways in the brain.

Your uncle's Parkinson's is a result of the dopamine pathway that controls motor function, not a pathway connected to pleasure/reward/addiction.

Six weeks ago my husband lost his job—the company called it downsizing. Since then, he's done very little but sleep and lie on the living room couch watching TV and drinking beer. I'm seriously worried. He shows no motivation at all, and his sex drive has plummeted to zero. When I try to talk to him about it, he says he just needs some time to regroup. What should I do?

Your husband is suffering from a situational depression. If not handled correctly, it can lead to bigger problems, including addiction.

Many people, especially men, invest a great deal of their identity in their work. When that work or job is lost, part of their identity and self-esteem goes with it. The suddenly unemployed become understandably confused and unable to relate to the world in the familiar ways they have relied on for years, and this affects both their relationships and their health.

The first thing I would do is find a psychiatrist or psychologist well versed in depression to guide your husband through these uncomfortable waters.

You can help him solidify the meaningful relationships in his life; concentrate on hobbies and interests that stimulated him in the past; and focus on healthy lifestyle choices such as eating

(continued)

⌐ Ask the Doctor (cont.)

well (meaning a balanced diet), getting adequate sleep, and exercising daily.

Medically, both the serotonin and noradrenalin neurotransmitters (the brain chemicals responsible for depression and anxiety, respectively) will be challenged during this period. Serotonin changes or imbalances are tied to potential abuse of alcohol and opiate medications, so be sure he avoids exposure to these substances. Noradrenalin changes or imbalances correlate to potential abuse of benzodiazepines like Valium, Xanax, Ativan, and Klonopin, so he should steer clear of these medications as well.

Once lifestyle adjustments have been made, your doctor can suggest healthier options from your medicine cabinet that will not further complicate your husband's situational problem. These include SSRIs like Prozac, Zoloft, Celexa, and Lexapro and SNRIs such as Effexor, Cymbalta, Pristiq, and Savella.

Nonaddictive anxiety medications like beta-blockers (Inderal) and antiseizure drugs (Neurontin) may also be helpful for short-term relief of his anxiety.

One more thing. After dinner, if time permits, take your husband for a walk. The additional exercise is good, but the quality time is better. Showing your support will mean a lot to him.

Who is at greater risk for addiction, men or women?

Overall, women. This is mainly because more women are addicted to nicotine, which is closely associated with long-term addiction.

However, the statistics change for each abused substance. Men win the race in addiction to alcohol and stimulants like cocaine and meth; women reign in the arena of prescription drugs like Valium and Xanax.

If you include behavioral addictions like food addictions and anorexia, women again take the lead, even as men are more likely to have gambling and sex addictions.

The Medical Treatment of Addiction

Up to this point, our focus has been on the actual disease of addiction—its origins (genetics), how it's triggered (stress), and where it manifests (in imbalanced brain chemistry). The underlying theme throughout has been that addiction is a *medical* disease . . . and it follows that as a medical disease, addiction must receive *medical* treatment.

DUAL DIAGNOSIS

The new paradigm for addiction treatment is based on the concept of dual diagnosis, which identifies and treats the *primary disease* (the imbalance in brain chemistry) in order to correct the *secondary disease* (the addiction and its symptoms or behaviors). Simply stated, imbalanced brain chemistry is the primary disease that gives rise to the secondary disease of addiction.

Of course, imbalanced brain chemistry has its own symptoms, reflected largely in behavioral disorders like depression, mania, obsessive compulsive disorder (OCD), sleep disorders, hyperactivity, anxiety, and other acute and chronic emotional states. As we have learned, those behaviors define the patient's norm. When stress is added to this volatile mix, the predisposed are driven to addiction merely to immediately feel better so they can function and survive.

According to the dual diagnosis model, *the physician must treat both diseases,* not just the more visible secondary behaviors.

In the case of addiction, that means the doctor must first identify (diagnose) the patient's imbalanced brain chemistry, which reveals the patient's drive toward specific substances that take away her bad feelings. In addiction medicine, doctors can't just treat the addiction, they must address the underlying chemical imbalances (the primary disease) as well. Unless the imbalanced brain chemistry is treated, an addict may quit for a time but will most likely be driven back to substance abuse by the same chronic imbalances that initially triggered the addiction. This is the single biggest reason that the traditional method of treatment and its conventional 28-day inpatient programs have a failure rate of over 90 percent.

Dual diagnosis requires a duality of treatment. The first stage eliminates the biochemical "wanting" by restoring and then stabilizing imbalances in the neurotransmitter-receptor connections. The second phase corrects dysfunctional behaviors central to an addictive identity and teaches the skills to maintain good habits and make healthy choices. This phase includes many familiar therapies that help patients sustain wellness throughout their lives, including support teams, 12-step programs, nutrition plans, group and individual counseling, homeopathy, stress management, and the like.

Only when the primary disease is medically treated, and a personalized toolbox of behavioral therapies is created to address the secondary addictive behaviors, can addicts finally move toward long-term, successful management of their disease.

Duality of Treatment Model

	Removes	Creates
Medical Treatment	Biochemical "wanting"	Homeostatic balance
Behavioral Treatment	Bad habits Lack of self-control	Good habits Healthy choices

Let's look now at the broad guidelines of both treatment and management of addiction. While every treatment should fit within these parameters, each plan must be tailored to each individual.

The third part of this book will examine case studies that emphasize personalized treatment plans. What follows in this chapter is the blueprint from which those treatments were created.

THE MEDICAL DETOX

Traditionally, detoxification (detox) refers to a process by which toxins (in this case, addictive substances) are eliminated from the brain and body chemistry. Until fairly recently, detox from drugs and alcohol entailed torturous withdrawal lasting days or weeks. Going "cold turkey"—in which an addict's drug or alcohol was abruptly cut off—led to dangerous symptoms of sudden withdrawal. Those included convulsions, high fevers, cold sweats, seizures, delirium, and a host of potentially lethal reactions.

If the addict survived—and many did not—he'd be pronounced "clean and sober." But the addict's palpably strong wanting (craving) for drugs or alcohol remained hidden within his inherited and imbalanced brain chemistry. Eventually, the addict almost always returned to substance abuse.

We now know that addiction springs from a dysfunctional interaction in the brain's neurotransmitters and receptors. It follows that any lasting solution must not only rid the system of toxins but also fix the neurotransmitter imbalance that caused the addiction.

Two main categories of prescription medications can help normalize the neurotransmitter imbalances specific to an addiction:

Detox medications safely, effectively, and comfortably withdraw patients from their addictions, sometimes in just a matter of minutes.

Stabilizing medications treat the primary diagnosis—the underlying neurotransmitter problem—in a safe and controlled fashion. By creating a new and stronger baseline balance, these meds remove the craving for the abused substance.

Detox meds are always administered first to alter the neurotransmitter imbalances and quickly restore homeostasis. They're followed by stabilizing meds that create and maintain a healthy balance, which cements the changes.

Addicts take detox meds only during the actual detoxification process, but they often remain on stabilizing meds for the rest of their lives to maintain homeostasis. It's similar to the way that people with type 1 diabetes take insulin throughout their lives to maintain glucose balance.

Detox and stabilizing meds treat the neurotransmitter imbalances that drive addiction in several different ways.

1. Some of these meds mimic the abused substance at the receptor areas in the brain, acting like the abused substance but without causing the harmful side effects. These "substance impostors" include Librium, Xanax, Valium, Ativan, Klonopin, phenobarbital, Neurontin, and buprenorphrine (Subutex, Suboxone).

2. Anticraving agents (like Zyban and Wellbutrin) target the areas in the brain that create the wantings that drive addiction.

3. Antianxiety agents that target noradrenalin imbalances provide relief for the anxiety that is always present during detox. Xanax, Klonopin, Valium, Ativan, and Librium (the benzos) and Neurontin are effective examples. Unlike the benzos, antiseizure drugs like Neurontin can be used without the accompanying dependency issues.

4. Antidepression agents—medications such as Prozac, Zoloft, Paxil, Lexapro, Cymbalta, Effexor, Pristiq, Savella, and Wellbutrin—balance serotonin levels, thereby relieving depression. (Because of their proven effectiveness in boosting serotonin, these same meds also diminish OCD behaviors that trigger irritability in the noradrenalin receptors that lead to anxiety and sleep disorders.)

5. Stimulant agents target dopamine receptors to help ease hyperactive (mania, agitation) and bipolar states. This category includes medications such as Wellbutrin, Dexedrine, Ritalin, Strattera, Concerta, Adderall, and Provigil.

In each instance, the medications deliver to the receptor the same message sent by the abused substance. In other words, they mimic or replicate the message but do so via a safer and different messenger. By rebalancing the neurotransmitters in a safe manner, these meds prevent a withdrawal that would otherwise create cravings and keep the patient in the cycle of addiction.

As noted previously, receptors can make choices between their matched neurotransmitters and any so-called impostors.

Detox and Stabilizing Medications

Abused Substance	Detox Meds (Short Term)		Stabilizing Meds
The Opiates OXYCONTIN VICODIN HEROIN	For opiate withdrawal	Buprenorphine (Subutex and/or Suboxone)	SSRIs: Prozac, Zoloft, Lexapro, Celexa, Paxil SNRIs: Pristiq, Savella, Effexor, Cymbalta
	For anxiety	Benzos: Klonopin, Ativan, Xanax Neurontin, Seroquel	
	For sleep	Hypnotics: Ambien, Lunesta, Sonata Antihistamines: Vistaril, Benadryl	
Alcohol	Neurontin, Lyrica; Benzos: Xanax, Klonopin, Ativan, Librium		
The Stimulants COCAINE METH	Neurontin, Klonopin, Xanax, Valium, Seroquel, Zyprexa, Depakote		Stabilizes if ADHD: Adderall, Ritalin, Dexedrine, Concerta, Provigil, Strattera, Vyvanse, Wellbutrin
			Stabilizes if bipolar disorder: Zyprexa, Seroquel, Abilify, Lamactil
The Benzos VALIUM XANAX ATIVAN KLONOPIN	Phenobarbital or slowly taper down the abused benzo		SSRIs (see above) SNRIs (see above) Beta-blockers (Inderal) Lyrica, Neurontin, Seroquel

This chart lists the medications used for both detox and stabilization of the neurotransmitter imbalances associated with each specific substance of abuse. Anxiety is to be expected in every withdrawal, so benzos, Neurontin, and Seroquel could be given for detox in almost every instance. The same goes for sleep disorders and their medications.

Note: This menu varies from patient to patient. Dosage is not listed since it is dependent on individual patient issues.

Treating Complicated Conditions

During detoxification, conditions that complicate and perpetuate addiction, such as sleep disorders and pain syndromes, can be treated with appropriate and nonaddictive prescription drugs (like Ambien for sleep, Lyrica for pain, and Neurontin and Cymbalta for anxiety).

Sleep problems can also be addressed by restoring noradrenalin balance through daily 30-minute sessions of moderate cardiovascular exercise (which creates endorphins to calm anxiety), by learning relaxation techniques, or by taking nonaddictive prescription meds like Benadryl, Ambien, Neurontin, trazodone, or Seroquel. Supplements like kava-kava, melatonin, and valerian may also aid in the quest for a good night's sleep.

While all addictions involve sleep disorders, not all sleep disorders lead to addiction—particularly if sleep disorders are addressed early and the responsible neurotransmitters rebalanced properly. Sleep apnea, a common cause of sleep disorders, is best treated by providing the patient with oxygen during sleep—either with a CPAP (Continuous Positive Airway Pressure) or BiPAP (Bilevel Positive Airway Pressure) device—instead of creating a dependency on benzodiazepines.

Addictive behavior often leads to metabolic disorders. For example, alcoholism can cause a vitamin B deficiency, while cocaine abuse can lead to malnutrition. In such cases, you must restore the lost vitamins and redress nutritional needs before you can regain homeostasis.

Detox and Stabilization Timeline

As we have seen, the new model for treating addiction calls for medical detoxification first, followed by the use of stabilizing medications.

While patients should feel comfortable (even good) during detox and stabilization, safely rebalancing brain chemistry to achieve homeostasis

(continued on page 58)

A Note on Sleep Disorders

All addictions involve at least some disturbance of sleep, such as insomnia, too much sleep, or lack of REM (rapid eye movement) sleep. In fact, sleep disorders are often early predictors of the exact type of neurotransmitter imbalances that lead to addiction, so restoring normal sleep patterns is essential to regaining homeostasis and good general health.

A normal sleep cycle (your circadian rhythm) includes light sleep (stages 1 and 2) leading into deep sleep (stages 3 and 4 and, finally, REM, or dreaming sleep). This sequence requires normal homeostatic balances of the dopamine, noradrenalin, serotonin, and GABA neurotransmitters—the same neurotransmitters responsible for addiction. When chronic or inherited imbalances exist in these neurotransmitters, sleep disorders follow.

For instance, almost all sleep disorders are closely related to anxiety. As we've seen, a root cause of chronic anxiety is a serotonin deficit often expressed by depression or obsessive compulsive behavior, which in turn creates excess levels of noradrenalin, resulting in poor sleep. So the sleep-deprived person spends her waking hours drinking lots of coffee (caffeine), smoking (nicotine), or consuming other substances like sugar to stay awake.

Lack of sleep lures tired folks into taking antianxiety meds like Valium or Xanax (both benzodiazepines) that will help them sleep. Unfortunately, when these benzos are stopped, they can create a rebound insomnia, bringing forth a harmful dependency—or a tolerance develops that creates the need for higher and more continued dosage. These benzos also induce light sleep (stages 1 and 2) but do not promote deeper sleep (stages 3, 4, and REM), and ultimately result in sleep deprivation. Other people turn to sedatives like Dalmane as sleeping pills. But while allowing you to quickly enter stage 1 and 2 sleep, sedatives inhibit (or block) stage 3 or 4 and REM sleep, the restorative stages you need for healthy functioning.

Hypnotics like Ambien, Lunesta, and Sonata provide a good night's sleep by fast-forwarding you to REM sleep. On the downside, some people taking hypnotics may experience fully functional somnambulism—that is, driving, eating, watching TV, or cooking a complicated meal without any memory of it. Hypnotics wipe out sleep memory and, in some patients, can lead to dangerous behavior.

Beyond the addict's predisposition to sleep disorders, abused substances themselves can directly affect sleep. Abused stimulants (cocaine and meth) block the reuptake of dopamine, noradrenalin, and serotonin and keep you awake. Nicotine and caffeine—often taken to self-medicate anxiety and fatigue—do the same thing to a lesser extent. Opiates (heroin, OxyContin, etc.) decrease the amount of REM sleep; withdrawal from opiates increases the length of time in sleep stages 1 and 2 and steals time from REM sleep.

Heavy drinkers generally sink into sleep rapidly, but their sleep is usually short and mostly consists of non-REM sleep. Depending on the amount consumed, alcohol suppresses REM sleep, and alcohol withdrawal creates a REM rebound that can manifest as hallucinations (the intrusion of REM sleep into waking).

Sleep disorders wreak havoc with overall health and reinforce addiction. Addicts go through days, weeks, months, and even years of insufficient sleep. When people don't sleep, a sleep deficit accrues. The sleep disorder must be corrected and the sleep debt repaid before successful behavioral rehabilitation can begin. That's why many patients sleep so much during the first days and weeks in detox. As the healing processes bring the body back into its normal homeostatic balance, the odds of addiction and relapse greatly decrease.

can take weeks or months, depending on the individual. The process cannot be rushed to fit into a 28-day program. Each patient must take as much time as needed, because the next behavioral and psychological phase of treatment (recovery) cannot begin before medical stabilization.

During medical detox, the patient undergoes daily drug testing. This ensures trust between all parties—patient, recovery team, family, and friends. It's a small price to pay when considering that without detox and stabilizing meds, an addict's only recourse is to go cold turkey. Even when that kind of withdrawal is successful, the addicts may have kicked their substance addiction but be left with their inherited and severely imbalanced brain chemistry.

For example, a depressed man who turns to alcohol may kick his substance abuse cold turkey and be pronounced "sober." But without the stabilizing meds, he still suffers from the depression that triggered his alcoholism. In Alcoholics Anonymous (AA) parlance, he's a "dry drunk"—sober but miserable, every minute clinging to his sobriety with white knuckles. The odds are overwhelming that his primary disease of depression will lead him back to alcohol.

Balancing brain chemistry is only the critical first step—the foundation necessary to build new, sustainable, and healthier behaviors. In a sense, medical detox and stabilization are merely the beginning of a lifelong road to total recovery. The next crucial steps are rehab and recovery.

REHAB AND RECOVERY

In the old, traditional treatment method, rehab and recovery were nearly indivisible parts of the 28-day treatment program. "He's in rehab" meant that a patient was more or less incarcerated in an addiction facility/drug rehab center.

The new paradigm of addiction medicine draws more distinctions between rehabilitation and recovery. And in most cases, both phases can be accomplished on an outpatient basis.

Rehab begins immediately upon surrendering to treatment. It continues through the detoxification and stabilizing processes that eliminate toxins from the body and rebalance brain chemistry. Rehab is measured in weeks or months.

Rehab can and should be a period of self-discovery in which patients learn the impact of addiction on their general behavior and well-being and commit to a total program centered on good health, not simply on abstinence.

Rehab is the moment to gather the resources needed to move ahead—specifically, a doctor who both understands addiction and has the professional resources to assemble a winning team of therapists, family and addiction counselors, nutritionists, and others, depending on each patient's needs. Think of the doctor as a general contractor for addiction treatment.

Recovery is a lifelong process, colored by empowerment and incorporating the maintenance of brain chemistry through neurotransmitter stabilization, behavioral modification, and a preventive medical health plan.

If rehab is a sprint, recovery is a marathon. Recovery is not measured in number of days but in the many benefits of *ways*—the way we behave, the way we stay on course, the way we get back on the wagon when we fall off, the way we repair relationships, and the way we allow ourselves to be guided by professionals and those who love us.

During recovery, the treatment team guides the patient through 12-step participation; nutritional support; medical and psychiatric care; lifestyle changes; personal and family counseling; an enjoyable (and gradual) exercise regimen of at least 30 minutes a day; and educational, career, or professional counseling.

Underlying and associated problems—like sleep disturbances and behavioral and/or mood disorders—are investigated, recognized, and treated in this phase. It is imperative to recognize the link between stress and addictive behaviors and to develop plans to deal with stressors proactively, not reactively.

Recovery is the time to set both short- and long-term goals that are achievable and that reinforce the triumphant feeling of the experience.

The word *rehabilitation* comes from the Greek root *habilis*. Roughly translated, it means "to invest again with dignity."

Rehab and recovery are never easy. Human beings are inherently imperfect, and relapse and setbacks are part of the journey. But with an intact support team, addicts can't fall too far before they are pulled back. They must be approached not with punitive measures but with understanding and compassion. A large part of that comes in protecting the addict's rights as a medical patient. As addicts take the responsibility of moving forward through the phases of recovery, so must caregivers take the responsibility of preserving patients' rights.

First among these rights is anonymity. Bill W. got it right when he named his budding group Alcoholics Anonymous. Anonymity breeds trust in the process . . . and trust begets treatment . . . and treatment eventually restores dignity.

Without this protection, the shame that all addicts feel creates deeper feelings of inadequacy and low self-esteem.

The Cost of Care

"I'm willing to change, but I can't afford treatment. Everybody knows rehab costs a fortune!"

That was true once. High-profile drug and alcohol treatment centers, where patients checked in for 28 days, cost from $50,000 to $100,000 per month. Even the low-end centers and clinics cost dearly, from $2,500 to $5,000 per week and up.

But those "special treatment" facilities define the old paradigm, and, as we have seen, the old methods had a high failure rate. The new paradigm not only works, it does so at a fraction of the cost of the more prominent facilities.

And there's good news for people whose group health plans offer coverage for mental health and substance abuse: Thanks to the federal Mental Health Parity and Addiction Act of 2008 (effective January 2010), limits on mental health and substance abuse payments now must be equal to payment limits placed on other medical conditions.

To determine whether you are covered, check with your health carrier, your state or federal ERISA office (within the Department of Labor), or any Health and Human Services (HHS) office. Under this new act, they are required to give you information about your rights and benefits. If you still have questions, do an Internet search for "Mental Health Parity Act of 2008" and browse the Web sites offering information.

Even if you don't have insurance or aren't covered by the new law, there's hope: *The new paradigm offers a low-cost solution available to everyone,* not just the rich. All it takes is total commitment, patience, the willingness to change, and the ability to learn.

The new paradigm of addiction medicine not only restores patients' wellness, it does so in private, with compassion and dignity, and with all the protection, rights, and anonymity that addicts, their families, and their friends require to help them on the lifelong road of recovery.

IN SUMMARY

At the beginning of this book, we laid out our overall theme.

Addiction
Originates in brain chemistry,
Is determined by genetics,
And is triggered by stress.

Here's the nutshell version of Addiction 101.

Homeostasis self-regulates our internal environments by stabilizing the body's natural balance. Without homeostasis, life would be impossible to sustain. At the same time, we all have different chemical imbalances that predispose us to certain and varying medical and psychological problems.

Genetics—the outward traits and internal makeup we inherit from our biological family—determines our individualized homeostasis in each aspect of the body, especially in the hidden and imbalanced *brain chemistry* that directly relates to addiction.

In the brain, *neurotransmitters* and their specific *receptors* continually engage in a delicate balancing act. When dopamine, serotonin, and/or noradrenalin neurotransmitters are chronically imbalanced, they create bad feelings like anxiety, depression, mood swings, obsessive fixations (and behavior), and hyperactivity.

When large doses of *stress* (any change to which you have to adapt) are added to the equation, they negatively impact your inherited neurotransmitter imbalances, triggering addiction.

That's because when people feel bad, they want to feel better. Addicts are driven by their specific imbalances to *self-medicate* with substances that at least temporarily soothe their bad feelings.

Once addiction takes hold, the new scientific paradigm insists you undergo treatment that addresses both your personal medical and behavioral issues—but success comes only after you fully commit to managing your addiction.

On the medical side, *detox medications* allow a safe, comfortable withdrawal from your abused substance, while also repairing the specific homeostatic imbalances that initially targeted you for addiction. Once that imbalance is fixed, *stabilizing medications* can maintain your brain chemistry's homeostatic balance for the rest of your life.

Importantly, the concept of *dual diagnosis* allows physicians to view addiction not as a freestanding social or character problem but as a medical disease brought on by an inherited *primary disease* such as depression, anxiety, insomnia, or a host of other emotional issues created by your genetically predetermined neurotransmitter imbalances. Addiction itself is a *secondary disease* that is a very real consequence of the primary disease.

Once your medical issues are favorably resolved in *rehab,* you must address the behavioral issues of your disease and begin your long-term *recovery* through 12-step and educational programs, individual and/or group therapy, and myriad other techniques and treatments. These will guide you in managing your addictive behaviors while creating and rebuilding a supportive environment of family and friends that will help you make long-term, healthy choices.

Remember: *Your addiction may not be your fault, but it is your responsibility.*

Ask the Doctor

I've heard good things about some addiction treatments that use only dietary and holistic approaches. Do these actually work?

As we now know, the primary neurochemical imbalance that provokes addiction must be addressed to fix addiction, and that requires a medical approach. Once a patient's equilibrium is restored, adjunctive measures like dietary and holistic treatments can be extremely helpful in establishing and maintaining a healthy lifestyle. At the same time, many homeopathic remedies are unproven, and several others are not created equal due to variations in quality and ingredients among different manufacturers. Check with someone who specializes in naturopathic medicine for guidance.

I've been listening to your radio show for a few months now. Maybe I missed this, but I don't understand why you would give potentially addictive drugs to addicts during treatment. Isn't that against the law?

This is an excellent and intelligent question.

The goal of addiction treatment is to control the biochemical drive toward substances that create dependency and destructive behaviors. Substituting safer options that eliminate cravings and dangerous fluctuations in our neurotransmitters (and the associated uncomfortable feelings) allows the chemically imbalanced person to function at a much higher level. Once this chemical balancing has occurred with these prescription medications, the behavioral treatments have a chance to take hold—that is, addicts can finally understand their stressors, develop proper tools to deal with them, and develop a preventive or proactive (rather than reactive) approach to dealing with bad feelings. Once these new behaviors have become their new "habit," the prescription medications can be safely withdrawn. In some cases, long-term successful treatment depends on these medications to maintain a balanced neurochemistry that helps eliminate cravings and relapse.

The FDA has approved the use of medications like benzodiazepines (Valium, Xanax, Klonopin, Ativan) for treatment of anxiety disorders, stimulant medications (Ritalin, Adderall, Dexedrine) for hyperactive disorders, and SSRIs (Prozac, Lexapro, Zoloft) for depressive disorders—all of which work by targeting the specific neurotransmitter receptors that are otherwise satisfied by addictive and dangerous drugs of abuse.

PART 2 THE ADDICTION SOLUTION

In the best of all possible worlds, the practice of medicine embraces a responsible partnership between doctors and patients. Doctors diagnose and treat their patients' conditions with skill, knowledge, and expertise . . . and without moralistic judgment. Patients give their doctors truthful personal histories, admit to their diseases, and are committed to changing the mind-sets and lifestyles that contributed to their diseases.

If either doctor or patient is not committed to honesty and success, the other will surely fail.

If you have serious heart disease but continue smoking and eating too much and exercising too little—against your doctor's advice—your eventual outcome will be disastrous. If you have an infection and don't take the antibiotics your doctor prescribes, the infection will linger and worsen and may prove fatal.

In the same way, if you are an addict who refuses to medically treat your homeostatic imbalances or change your addictive behaviors and lifestyles, you will remain addicted.

On the other hand, if you commit to the new medical treatment and to the personal changes required to break the cycle of addiction—if in fact you are willing to change—then success in managing your addiction is practically guaranteed.

Part 2 examines some of the obstacles to treating addiction and shows how people can leap those hurdles by following the new medical paradigm.

Overcoming the Obstacles

Change is good—especially when the old methods of treating addiction clearly don't work.

But while change is easier said than done, thanks to the new paradigm of addiction medicine, there is hope and a path to a sustainable new life.

FACING THE PERSONAL OBSTACLES

Personal obstacles too often stand in the way of addicts' committing to treatment. These include:

Low self-esteem. Society portrays addicts as weak-willed, low-life characters, even as their own failed attempts to kick their addictions have left them in despair. So addicts don't feel good about themselves. While no one can change brain chemistry by just saying no, once addicts understand that the root cause of addiction is an inherited, chemical imbalance and that addiction is a controllable disease, they can seize the real opportunity to beat their disease and show a depth of character long lost within the netherworld of addiction.

Denial. We've all witnessed denial (and even used it). The heavy drinker who loses his wife, his kids, his job, and his money and still refuses to admit he has a problem is a classic and obvious example.

Denial is pervasive and pernicious. It's the Big Lie told often enough that addicts themselves come to believe it. "I can quit anytime I want" and "I don't have a problem" are obvious examples.

But denial also works on more subtle levels.

One is the disinhibition factor. Under the influence of certain substances, we lose our natural inhibitions: The shy become gregarious, the meek become bold, the fearful become fearless. Indeed, disinhibition is the reason many people take drugs in the first place. This newfound freedom of expression can be very seductive. Suddenly, addicts find themselves uncensored in thought, word, and deed—and the life of any party. So what if their drug use is wreaking havoc at home and

ADDICTION AND FUNCTIONAL INTELLIGENCE

Families and friends of addicts typically ask: How can people so smart not understand that they're addicted? One answer, revealed through the new scientific tool of brain mapping, is that addiction itself lowers a form of intelligence known as functional IQ.

Take a woman with an IQ of 132: When on drugs or alcohol, she functions at an IQ closer to 80, a clear indication that substance abuse impacts both short-term intelligence and judgment.

The good news is that most brain function can be restored by proper management of brain chemistry. The glaring exception is damage caused by methamphetamines, which can directly impact and often permanently impair the prefrontal cortex, the area of the brain that controls reasoning and judgment.

work? They're having a blast . . . and momentarily feeling good about themselves.

Of course, pleasure is ultimately most satisfying when it is balanced with responsibility. Even addicts know on some level that avoiding reality is impossible and ultimately unfulfilling.

Fear of repercussion. Most addicts hide their substance abuse from family, friends, and co-workers for as long as possible. While they realize deep down that treatment is their only hope, they also know that "coming out" as an addict might carry severe repercussions at home and in the workplace. In many places, the stigma attached to addicts is just as destructive as the disease itself. So addicts become deathly afraid of exposure, as if in seeking treatment, their entire world will collapse.

Once again, fear trumps hope.

Fear of failure. Because the failure rate of traditional methods of addiction treatment has always hovered above 90 percent, many addicts question why they should risk discovery when the odds against success are that great. Other addicts weigh going through the nightmare of an antiquated, cold-turkey withdrawal program against the chances of success.

The new paradigm in addiction medicine promises a safe and comfortable withdrawal and a success rate over 90 percent. As news of the new paradigm becomes widely known, fear of failure should dissolve.

FINDING MEDICAL CARE

Ironically, finding a supportive doctor is often an addict's biggest obstacle to successful treatment.

Of the nearly one million licensed physicians in the United States, fewer than one-half of 1 percent are certified to practice addiction medicine. As a nation, we have only one addiction specialist for every 50,000 addicts—even though addiction is our country's largest health problem. The majority of medical practitioners outsource addiction to private clinics, therapists, and/or 28-day recovery centers.

Granted, few addicts go to their doctors for issues directly related to substance abuse. Most addicts show up with complaints that initially appear to have little or nothing to do with addiction. But what appears to be a sinus infection could be a problem stemming from snorting coke or meth; skin lesions could be a result of heroin addiction (heroin addicts often pick at their skin); a patient's sleep disorder might be a clue to alcoholism (which limits REM sleep). Only by asking the right questions can the doctor determine if complaints are stand-alones or issues caused by an underlying addiction. But caution must be exercised—addicts can be very convincing and well rehearsed in their initial interviews with doctors. (At the same time, the most obvious clues to a patient's potential addiction may be complaints of pain syndromes like migraines and back pain.)

How do you find a doctor who understands the relationship between addiction and brain chemistry? Approach your family doctor; if he is unable to help, he may be able to recommend a specialist or someone who is a member of the national or state societies of addiction medicine. You can also contact the American Society of Addiction Medicine for referrals. (A link to ASAM doctors is provided at the back of this book.) If you can't afford a doctor, go to a hospital clinic associated with a medical school that has an addiction medicine program and ask for help. Once there, you'll be treated by a team of doctors—interns, residents, and addiction specialists—

all working together within the new medical paradigm.

Chapters 5 and 6 examine the steps toward treatment in more detail. But for now, understand that your doctor or team will create a blueprint that plans your medical detox and "rebalancing" act, plots your medical stabilizing course, and helps with associated issues based on your individual needs—improving sleep and nutrition, managing pain, building a support group, reestablishing personal and career goals, and so on.

The next step is to strategize the lifestyle changes you need (structured schedules, daily exercise) and learning to manage your stress. This phase usually involves reconnecting with family members and trusted friends who have been lost or marginalized due to your addiction. Explore hobbies or interests that you shelved during your drug experience. Set *attainable* short-term and long-term goals. Examine your life and your choices to help identify and eliminate your self-destructive behaviors.

If you can't afford a nutritionist, use common sense in planning your meals. Start a well-balanced dietary plan that includes all food groups, and read labels for salt and fat content and calories. Of course, you can treat yourself every once in a while—your ultimate goal is to give up substance abuse, not ice cream. But *moderation* should be the key word for all behaviors in your new health paradigm.

If you can't afford a personal trainer, join a gym to exercise and increase production of endorphins. If that is too costly, walk or jog a couple of miles a day. Or swim laps. Or walk briskly up and down stairs. Whatever exercise is available to you, just take it gradually and build from there. Your goal should be 30 minutes a day, every day, of aerobic exercise.

What Is Sobriety?

Sobriety is a goal, not a strict definition.

Too much emphasis is placed on a single, cookie-cutter characterization of sobriety as complete abstinence from all drugs and alcohol. This view is so inflexible that it is often counterproductive. Abstinence works for some people, but it's not a panacea for addiction.

Take a longtime cocaine user who no longer takes drugs but has an occasional glass of wine to no harmful effect. Should she still be considered an addict? Or should she be viewed as someone who has found a way to live productively in her community?

Complete abstinence doesn't address the root of addiction: the primary biochemical imbalance. And unless medical professionals and patients address the primary illness, they leave the door open for other self-destructive (and even addictive) behaviors: gambling, sex, eating disorders, and many others. So you wind up with "sober" but depressed alcoholics who still can't get their acts together, or "clean" but self-loathing drug addicts on the verge of suicide because they can't take any more pain and depression.

Perhaps the better definition of sobriety focuses on the word *abuse:* An ex-addict is someone who no longer *abuses* drugs.

Sobriety must be approached as a multidimensional concept of positive and real possibilities that aid each addict's unique circumstance and overall wellness. This personalized and evolving approach moves forward, one attainable step after another, reaching one level (or concept) of sobriety while seeking to attain another level of wellness. It sets a plan to keep isolated relapses from spiraling the recovering addict into failure or self-defeat.

The new addiction medicine paradigm goes beyond "clean and sober" to help addicts achieve, nourish, and nurture their overall states of wellness.

So . . . what is sobriety? Just this: Clean, sober . . . and well.

If you can't afford stress management counseling, go to the library and check out one of the many books about managing stress. Try different methods to see which ones work for you.

Build a safety net of support—family members and/or friends who will be there when you need them and who can help you build a personal toolbox for small and large crises. You may choose to attend Alcoholics Anonymous meetings (or those of another support group) and use their behavioral programs alongside your own medical plan. AA is free of charge and also a sincere model for the behavioral modification piece of your treatment. It will help greatly *as long as you continue your medical treatment.*

Remember that your success depends on restoring and maintaining the chemical balance in your brain. If a counselor, meeting, or group demands that you abandon your prescribed medication, find another meeting or group. Uninformed and negative peer pressure, no matter how well intentioned, can undo your progress. Just as all the goodwill and earnest behavioral work in the world will not help a person with diabetes who refuses to take her insulin, so it is with addiction. Without the medication needed to rebalance your neurotransmitters, your odds of success are low.

Look to the future and work toward achievable goals. Talk to friends, family, and counselors about how best to reenter the world in which you want to live and participate. Start to work toward that end.

Above all, continue the medical treatment that stabilizes the homeo-static imbalance in your brain chemistry for as long as you need . . . and that could well be the rest of your life.

Ask the Doctor

My wife started menopause last year when she was 52. Since then, she's been popping some kind of pills like there's no tomorrow, saying they calm her down. Should I be concerned?

You should be concerned, but you can also be quite helpful.

Your wife has entered a natural biological period in which her female hormones (estrogen and progesterone) have sharply declined, and she is experiencing some negative effects from this change. Specifically, it sounds like she is feeling anxious, especially if the pills she is popping are "calming her down."

Anxiety is common with menopause, as are weight gain, hot flashes, loss of libido, vaginal dryness, sleep disorders, joint aches, and an increased predisposition to heart disease and osteoporosis. With all this, who wouldn't be anxious?

The neurotransmitters responsible for her anxiety include noradrenalin and glutamate, which have been released by her body as a response to the drop in estrogen. Increases in both of these neurochemicals cause anxiety and/or agitation.

To counteract her agitation, she may be taking pills in the benzodiazepine family (Valium, Xanax, Klonopin, and Ativan). These could be dangerous and create addictions if not monitored carefully or taken consistently over several months.

I would simply ask your wife what she is taking. If the pills are on that list of benzos, help her by soliciting the guidance of a doctor (like a neuropharmacologist) who knows how to prescribe and monitor their use.

There are alternative medications to benzos that don't have addiction potential. Some of these are beta-blockers such as Inderal and certain seizure medications like Neurontin and Lyrica. Low-dose hormone replacement is helpful in addressing menopausal symptoms, but, given certain predispositions to female cancers, caution must be taken. Her gynecologist should address these issues with her.

You can help ease her anxieties with lifestyle therapies like exercise, improved sleep patterns, and a well-balanced diet. Most important, go out of your way to provide a little emotional support for her journey—it's the best medicine you can give.

While I abused cocaine in college, I've been clean for just over 10 years. But I still smoke cigarettes, drink way too much coffee, and, when stressed-out, bite my nails. Obviously, I had (or have) a dopamine issue. But here's my question: Since alcoholism is a serotonin-based disease, when I watch football with my buddies, can I have a few beers without risking addiction to alcohol?

You're right about cocaine and alcohol being driven by different neurotransmitter imbalances, and I can see why you'd be tempted to throw back a drink with your buddies. But there's a catch—actually, two catches.

The first is that alcohol famously impairs judgment. If you are already predisposed to a cocaine problem, it may resurface after your blood alcohol level reaches a critical threshold—usually on your third drink, when control deteriorates to "What the hell?"

Secondly, dopamine pathways in the reward center are stimulated by alcohol, so your natural dopamine imbalance—the one that created your predisposition to cocaine—is further impaired, which leads to a biochemical wanting for this stimulant. So while you probably would not be risking an addiction to serotonin-driven alcohol, you would put yourself at risk for a cocaine relapse.

Enjoy the games . . . but take a pass on the beer.

(continued)

ASK THE DOCTOR (CONT.)

I've tried quitting smoking so many times with so many different gimmicks. On your radio show, you talk about how brain chemistry is the answer to all these addictions. I want to know if there is a solution to my quitting in this new medical approach.

Good news for you and the millions who are addicted to nicotine: Addiction treatment now targets the receptors in the brain that create these addictions.

When you smoke, the nicotine attaches to the nicotine receptors, and you get a sense of calm. When the nicotine wears off, it leaves the receptors "wanting" more . . . which makes you feel anxious, so you light up another cigarette and feel better again.

The first product on the American market that directly targets the nicotine receptor is Chantix, and it is attracted to the receptor just like nicotine. Once the Chantix covers all the nicotine receptors (this takes about a week of gradually increasing the dose), your brain thinks you are in a constant state of smoking, since none of the receptors are left open, or wanting, nicotine.

This medication, a receptor blocker, is taken for 3 to 6 months until all the receptors "go underground" (much like weeds in a garden) and the biological wanting fades away. It works, and the side effects from these newer medications are minimal.

Who says you can't fool Mother Nature!

Surrenders and Interventions

One of the most destructive myths about addiction is that addicts must hit rock bottom before seeking treatment.

It's not always true.

Through the years, many people have recognized their own "substance problems" long before they could devastate their lives and before those close to them even suspected trouble.

Abuse is only the most obvious way of identifying an addiction. Some people spot red flags in less apparent ways.

- By finding evidence of addiction in their family tree
- By evaluating their imprinting and environment for risk factors
- By analyzing how they handle stress
- By identifying associated health problems in their family's history: chronic pain syndrome; sleep disorders; or depression, anxiety, mania, and bipolar illnesses linked to addiction

Those who pinpointed their addictions in one of these manners then surrendered to a doctor's care or entered treatment before their lives got out of hand.

Why does the myth of "rock bottom" endure? Perhaps because up to now, the treatment model looked something like this: Admit to the substance abuse problem, enter treatment, serve your 28 days, get out, enjoy a honeymoon until the bad feelings come back, then start using again . . . return to treatment . . . and on and on. The old model left addicts on a treadmill of ineffective treatment until they were often physically, emotionally, spiritually, and financially drained.

Of course, we now know that failure is avoidable. The genetic seed of addiction was discovered in the mid-1990s, and the root cause of addiction—specific neurotransmitter imbalances—was discovered shortly thereafter, as was the recognition of the role stress plays in brain chemistry. Effective, smart-targeting pharmaceutical therapies followed, and a new, successful medical treatment for addiction was born.

When is the right time to start treatment? From a medical point of view, anytime is a good time to begin the process—but the earlier, the better. Because addiction is a chronic medical illness, preventive measures can be taken to treat the disease before it gains a destructive foothold. Remember: Your addiction may not be your fault, but it *is* your responsibility.

How do you start? The first step is either surrender or intervention. Ideally, you would learn everything you could about your form of addiction and its medical treatment. However you embark on your journey to wellness, it must ultimately be *your* decision and *your* responsibility— because neither surrenders nor interventions can work without the addict's proactive and willing compliance.

SURRENDERS

In a surrender, a person accepts that he or she has an addiction (or the seeds of one) and initiates the process to get help.

Accepting a "problem" can be tricky. What's the difference between using and abusing drugs? When does having a relaxing martini after work begin to reflect alcoholism? At what point does a hit of recreational cocaine at a party become problematic?

There is no single correct answer. Some people are predisposed to addiction; others are not. It depends on their individual brain chemistries and the severity of neurotransmitter imbalances.

Most of the warning signs of addiction are found in feelings and behaviors: Depression, anxiety, and mania or hyperactivity are red flags. So, too, is behavior that seeks and prolongs the use of any substance— the once a week martini becomes a cocktail drunk twice or three times a week, then nightly, then during the daytime, until the need or quest for alcohol takes total control.

Most addictions reveal themselves incrementally, and subtly, before they are obvious to the outside world. A few good general indicators are:

- You begin to *depend* on a substance to get you through the day or night.
- You start to use a substance as an emotional or a behavioral crutch.
- Your functionality begins to erode.
- Your moods shift often.
- The passions and purpose in your life begin to diminish.
- The quest for a substance starts taking priority over healthier aspects of your life.

- The periods of time between your use of a substance become shorter and shorter.
- You start to neglect or abuse close relationships.
- Your personal hygiene is compromised.
- Your eating habits are noticeably disrupted.
- The quantity or quality of your sleep diminishes.
- Healthy behaviors like exercise begin to disappear from your daily routine.

Note that most of these examples contain the word *start* or *begin*. That's important, because you can nip addiction in the bud as soon as it *begins* to show itself—if you're paying attention. All it takes is honest self-awareness and the willingness to surrender to treatment.

How Do You Surrender?

The first step is to ask your doctor to coordinate your treatment—from arranging for the medical detox to gathering the professional team to lead you to wellness. If your doctor is unable or unwilling to help, you have options: Contact a local teaching hospital and ask that one of its addiction specialists guide you through treatment. Or contact the American Society of Addiction Medicine (ASAM) or your state society of addiction medicine for a referral to a specialist. Alternatively, browse through the resource guide at the end of this book to find the help you need.

Once you have selected a doctor to quarterback your care, enlist support from a family member or close friend who cares for you and will advocate for you throughout the rehab and recovery processes. This should be someone who will go with you to doctor appointments, check on you regularly to ensure compliance, and encourage you on your journey. It doesn't have to be just one person; you can enlist several friends. The more support you have, the better.

Next, sit down with your doctor and discuss the step-by-step treatment protocol (see Chapter 6).

Then give yourself up—surrender—to treatment.

INTERVENTIONS

When addicts spin out of control, driven only by their addictions, and they are in the full grip of denial, interventions are often the only entryway to treatment.

But beware, an intervention will fail if it is not planned and conducted properly.

Interventions should not be viewed as casual, spur-of-the-moment gatherings of families and friends. Interventions are high-level summits of tough love and firm resolve. There are rules to be followed, obligations to be met, and promises to keep. Interventions must be planned, organized, and even rehearsed. Potential objections and problematic areas must be addressed and resolved before meeting with the addict.

Most important, everyone should realize that the goal of an intervention is to motivate the addict to sincerely and willingly commit to treatment and the changes it will bring about.

Perhaps the only way to achieve the desired goal is to make the intervention about consequences—what will happen if the addict does not comply with treatment. It sounds like a simple stand to take, but it's not. Almost every family or group of friends contains an enabler—someone who lets the addict slide on obligations and responsibilities: a mother or father unable to enforce consequences, a friend who keeps "loaning" the addict money, a brother or sister who always gives the addict a place to crash. These acts of kindness, sympathy, empathy, or compassion unfortunately give addicts enough rope by which they can metaphorically hang themselves.

Successful interventions make addicts aware of the consequences they face if they choose to continue their destructive lifestyle. They'll lose their job. They'll lose the support of family and friends. No more money will be given to them. They will be isolated from anyone who cares about them. Those are just a few examples of the possible consequences to put forth.

It's not enough just to voice consequences; everyone at the intervention must commit to follow through with them, no matter how difficult or heartbreaking. Every family member, friend, co-worker, and employer must promise the others that he or she will toe the line in carrying through with consequences.

This readiness to apply consequences is key to a successful resolution. There can be no exceptions. If addicts find a loophole they can slip through, they will.

At the same time, remember that interventions are *not* about placing blame. Addiction is a medical disease, not a sign of bad character or loose morality. Although addicts' conduct often crosses the line, their actions are driven by chemical imbalances that cause irresistible cravings or wantings. Taking a judgmental attitude is ineffective.

Interventions are difficult. On the one hand, addicts need to feel loved and embraced and that a cocoon of support is available. On the other hand, they must see that they're walking the plank over a raging sea of disaster. It's a delicate balance, but it forces addicts to make a choice that will shape the rest of their lives.

Which option does the addict choose—the one filled with life and loving support or the one that falls into an ocean of destruction? If the intervention has been conducted correctly—and that means *by the rules*—and the options have been made clear, the addict's choice will be the healthy one.

Who Should Come to the Intervention?

Since the goal of intervention is to have the addict hear and seriously weigh the rules and consequences, the participants must be those people the addict loves and respects.

Look to people with whom the addict has (or has had) strong relationships, however tenuous the relationship at the moment. This includes close and longtime friends, family members, spiritual or religious advisors, co workers or employers, and a trusted doctor. Whenever possible, include medical support at the intervention. A family doctor, an addiction professional, or an interventionist can stress that addiction is a medical disease, not a character flaw.

Who Should Run the Intervention?

An intervention needs a leader to organize the participants, rehearse the intervention, and guide everyone through the actual event. In the ideal scenario, the leader is someone who can best objectify not just the addiction problem but the entire situation. Usually, that's the person with the most experience and credibility within the group. There is no room for sentimentality, leniency, or skewed perspective—those will be counterproductive. If a family member or close friend can be objective throughout the intervention, fine. If not, then an experienced specialist (preferably a doctor or a professional interventionist) must take the lead.

The intervention leader has three tasks.

1. To make sure everyone stays on message
2. To ensure the rules are followed in every instance
3. To guarantee that no compromises are made

Interventions can spell the difference between life and death. For that reason alone, the lead interventionist must stand firm, knowing that the addict will use everything at his or her disposal to compromise the rules.

How Do We Find an Experienced Addiction Specialist or Interventionist?

Ask your doctor for a referral, or contact ASAM or your state addiction medicine society by phone or online. Refer to the resource guide at the back of this book. Additionally, you can visit our interactive Web site at www.addictionsolution.com.

When you contact a professional or a treatment center, establish up front that you are seeking guidance within the new paradigm of addiction medicine and that dual diagnosis must be at the heart of the long-term treatment plan.

When Should the Intervention Be Held?

Once you know intervention is necessary, draft a treatment plan and gather the participants.

The next step is to hold a preliminary meeting with everyone except the addict. View this as a rehearsal at which the agenda is reviewed and set.

Once you've had the preliminary meeting, arrange for the intervention to take place as soon as possible. Be aware that you normally have only one opportunity for a successful intervention, since both the gathering and those participating lose credibility if the meeting fails.

Where Should the Intervention Be Held?

Hold the intervention in the addict's home. Failing that, hold it at the home of a family member or close friend. Select a nonthreatening space in which the addict feels comfortable.

What Should Be Brought to the Intervention?

Each participant should bring a written statement detailing three points.

1. How much the addict means to them. Start with positive statements explaining how much each person in the group loves and cares for the addict.
2. A specific example of how the addict's behavior has negatively impacted the participant's life. Tell the addict that certain thresholds of behavior—the triggers that provoked the intervention—can no longer be tolerated.
3. The certain consequences if the addict does not admit the problem, seek help, and enter treatment. Make it clear that no compromise is acceptable.

Point 3 can be made singly by each participant or stated collectively as a group. Remember, the only real ammunition any of the interventionists has is the promise to withdraw physical, emotional, or financial support. Consequences cannot be done in half measures; they must be applied totally, in all areas.

What Should Be Included in the Treatment Plan?

Interventions are about building a consensus in a closed circle of logic that the addict cannot rebut. So a treatment blueprint needs to be drawn.

It would include:

1. A doctor or medical addiction team to supervise treatment
2. A place for the addict to receive treatment—at home, through an outpatient clinic, in some type of sober living home, or, in severe cases, in an inpatient facility
3. Clearly stated rules of compliance, as well as the consequences of noncompliance
4. A set time for reevaluation at which new goals will be determined and a long-term care program will be established

What Are the "Rules of Compliance"?

Intervention rules should be simple, clear, and to the point. The addict needs first to commit fully to treatment and exhibit a sincere willingness to change.

The addict must comply with all elements of personalized treatment—detox, stabilizing medications, regular drug testing, 30 meetings in 30 days (or 60 in 60 or 90 in 90), counseling, therapies, and individualized care as needed.

When Should Treatment Start?

Right away. That's why having a plan is important. Once the addict agrees to the stipulations and commits to treatment, he or she should begin treatment immediately.

Why Do Some Interventions Fail?

Addicts aren't good at keeping appointments, and often they just don't show up. Other times, they arrive near the appointed time, realize that an intervention is about to take place, and walk out. Or they leave a few minutes into the session.

When addicts don't believe consequences will be carried out, interventions are just a lot of psychobabble. When family members and close friends function as enablers and codependents and are unwilling or unable to mete out consequences, then addicts play them like card sharks at a poker table. In some circumstances, addicts are too far gone to even care if everyone abandons them. In other instances, addicts are so emotionally wrecked by depression, sleep deprivation, and other conditions that they don't believe they could feel any worse.

If interventions take place without a plan, either for the intervention itself or the subsequent treatment, the agenda will wander aimlessly without good results.

Still, the most common reason for failed interventions (and surrenders, too) is the lack of financial resources to pay for treatment. Now that addiction is recognized as a medical disease, the burden of cost is easing. But treatment still contains the expense of doctors, therapists, drug testing, medications, and so on. So money is a factor, even as the cost of treatment has gone down dramatically in the new paradigm and even as new laws expand medical coverage.

When Are Interventions Successful?

1. When everyone adheres to the rules
2. When everyone stays on message
3. When everyone pushes the single and unified goal (and necessity) of medical treatment
4. When the addict knows the promises of consequences will be kept

Ultimately, however, surrenders and interventions work only when the treatment works. Fortunately, the new paradigm of medical treatment works.

ASK THE DOCTOR

For the last couple of years, I've been partying with my friends one weekend a month. I'm a bit shy, so snorting a couple of lines of coke makes me feel more confident and even good before we go out. It even seems to make sex better. The rest of the month I abstain . . . and I don't feel any cravings or desire to use it. Since cocaine helps me party and I don't seem to have a dependency on it, is it okay for me to keep doing it, or will the drug eventually catch up with me?

There are those of us who are predisposed to addictions in general . . . and there are some substances that will "addict" anyone in their path, independent of their genetic vulnerabilities.

In terms of genetics, several chromosomal and DNA markers predispose us to becoming addicted. More of these genetic markers are being discovered as we continue to unlock the human genome. Their associations with other inherited traits have confirmed what we always believed were rooted in our family trees. Environmental factors (such as the imprinting we get as children about drugs and the social networks we choose) and our individualized imbalances in brain chemistry can also point us down the path of addiction.

Some substances have a definite addictive potential if abused over time, like the opiates. Others create dependency only when all the other pieces of the addiction formula are present.

Your question speaks to the issue of why some people can drink or abuse drugs intermittently in social situations and others can't put on the brakes. All drugs of abuse stimulate the reward centers in the brain, which then send messages to the cognitive and memory areas that process this information. Individual brain chemistry and its imbalances provide the missing link to understanding the difference between casual use and dependency.

But if you are asking if it is okay to keep on doing cocaine since you don't seem to be one of those predisposed to addiction, my answer would still be a big no, since this drug is a lethal weapon that can create cardiovascular collapse in anyone at any time.

How can families and friends make a difference in the life of someone needing treatment?

Families and friends can make a tremendous difference with *any* disease, not just addiction. And make no mistake, addiction is a disease that, just like cancer and heart disease, requires emotional support.

But addiction is different from other illnesses in that by the time treatment begins, those closest to the addict have been lied to, stolen from, disappointed, abandoned, or embarrassed. For good reason, most friends and family members are disgusted, skeptical, and distrustful.

Right off the bat, those capable of providing support must understand that addiction is a medical disease created in brain chemistry, determined by genetics, and triggered by stress. It's difficult (even for doctors) not to blame or judge addicts for their behaviors, but being objective is a necessary first step in supporting your loved one. It's not about forgiving them, it's about understanding the disease. And it's important because at this point, family and very close friends will be the only ones left willing to even try to understand.

Once educated, family and friends should help the addict find legitimate resources and realize that treatment continues for a lifetime, with bumps in the road (relapses) as a sometimes natural part of the process. Help your loved one develop a team of professional support including doctors, therapists, 12-step programs, and lifestyle changes that, when combined with your emotional support, will help keep the recovery process alive and well.

Another unique aspect of addiction is the relationship of enablers and codependents to addicts. Ask yourself: Have you

(continued)

┌─ Ask the Doctor (cont.) ──────────────

perpetuated the addiction and the delaying of treatment by enabling or codependent behavior? Do you have a hidden agenda . . . or is a power or control issue interfering with your giving full support to successful treatment? You might be surprised to learn that many relationships—romantic, business, friendly—are shattered when addicts get clean because the dynamics of the relationships change when addicts are able to take control of their own lives.

If you are an enabler or a codependent, you should go to an Al-Anon meeting or to the bookstore to find *Codependent No More*, an excellent treatise on how we unconsciously keep addicts and their addictions afloat.

When addicts enter treatment, they are cut off from their social network of other addicts—their former drinking buddies or party friends, for example. With this sudden vacuum in their lives, they feel isolated and scared. They need someone to talk to daily. So call them, visit them, and help them establish new relationships that support their transition into a healthy life. Let your friends and loved ones know they are not alone.

Isn't the use of medications like methadone simply replacing one drug with another—in this case, methadone for heroin?

This question speaks to the direction we're taking in the new medical paradigm of treating addiction.

Yes, we are replacing one drug for another. The difference lies in the selections we make. It's a better choice to replace a safer alternative medication that has a predictable effect and is monitored by a physician for an abused drug that is not monitored and that is often life threatening. Getting an addict to score from a doctor is safer than getting drugs on the street or from the Internet. The pharmaceuticals on the physician's menu are protected by the FDA and manufacturers' standards, whereas the choices on the street have no such guarantees. For this reason, street drugs have a greater likelihood for abuse and adverse interaction with other lifestyle choices that the "unsupervised" user would make.

The better pharmaceuticals in the doctor's bag work by blocking the receptors that the abused substances seek, thus preventing their dangerous effects on the brain. Those substitute medications that have addictive potential are generally used only for short-term therapy and are monitored carefully by the doctor, so abuse or addiction is less likely.

In the case of methadone, the synthetic opiate attaches to the opiate receptor and blocks the dangerous and life-threatening effects of heroin. As an alternative for heroin or other opiate abuse, methadone has been itself replaced by an even safer product, buprenorphine.

The goal of pharmaceuticals in treating drug addictions is to improve the side-effect profile (including overdosing) and to lessen the addiction potential. As these pharmaceuticals evolve, they do so by interacting better with our neurotransmitters and receptors. Another goal for these alternative drugs is to gradually and safely withdraw them once detoxification has been completed. The new medical paradigm seeks the elimination of all these potentially addictive or dependency drugs through a supervised program of safe and gradual tapering.

Anxiety medications like the benzodiazepines (Valium, Xanax, Klonopin, and Ativan) with dependency potential and some risk can now be replaced with blocking agents like beta-blockers (Inderal) and antiseizure medications (Neurontin and Lyrica) that have no addiction potential and few side effects.

Above all, realize that trading one drug for another is not trading one addiction for another; it is trading an addiction for an addiction therapy that will eventually wean the addict off *all* abused substances.

Solving Addiction in 12 New and Easy Steps

6

■ The Treatment Protocol

When confronted with addiction in themselves or those close to them, the first question people ask is: "What can I do?"

Until recently, the only truthful answer was: "Hope and pray for the best, but expect the worst."

But now that the genetic origin, biochemical cause, and neurochemical triggers of addiction have been confirmed by science, a real and beneficial answer has arrived in the form of a checklist (or blueprint) detailing the step-by-step process of the new medical treatment.

In hospitals and clinical practices, it has been consistently demonstrated that the most effective tools health care professionals and patients have at their disposal for any number of procedures are checklists: simple records of what steps need to be taken and in what order.

Checklists guard against human error by ensuring that no one skips or forgets basic but seemingly humdrum steps. Checklists clearly articulate the steps of sometimes complicated processes that must be followed to ensure wellness.

Checklists put everything up front and in the correct order for everyone to see and follow. Therein lies their power: By putting things right from the get-go, a checklist is nothing less than a prescription for healing.

The following procedural checklist for the new medical treatment of addiction provides an effective and long-awaited answer to the question: "What can I do?"

THE ADDICTION SOLUTION IN 12 EASY STEPS

1. Begin with surrender or intervention. Either entry point should identify the patient's recognition of addiction as a medical disease and confirm his or her willingness to seek help.

2. Perform a thorough medical evaluation. This should include all patient intake forms (including a personal and family history that relates to addictive behaviors and current health problems), a physical examination, lab work, and a detailed patient interview. This examination establishes the addict's current physical and emotional status and highlights any co-occurring or contributing health problems. The primary purposes of the evaluation are to establish the evidence of addiction, to identify the specific dual diagnosis, and to confirm the patient's willingness to change.

3. Create a personalized step-by-step plan for medical rehabilitation that addresses the patient's imbalanced brain chemistry.

4. Strategize a recovery prognosis tailored to the individual's psychological and behavioral issues. This requires organizing a team of doctors and specialists who understand nutrition,

exercise, stress and pain management, support groups, neuro-pharmacology, personal and family therapy, vocational counseling, and preventive care. This comprehensive approach places the patient on a lifelong road to recovery.

5. Specify the rules and the consequences of treatment. This is necessary to ensure compliance. The rules should include regular and random drug/alcohol testing, creating a structured treatment environment, maintaining a defined treatment schedule, and regular follow-up evaluations. Delineate a "three strikes and you're out" template of consequences that result from breaking the rules. The first strike can carry reprimands like more work, more 12-step meetings (60 meetings in 30 days), and having the patient write letters to each member of the treatment team explaining the reasons for his or her noncompliance. When met with appropriate consequences, strikes can serve as teachable moments—a time to take inventory and regroup. Relapse should be a tool for getting better, not a punishment for tripping over a bumpy road. And most important, relapse is not the time to "start over" but to keep going with awareness. Consequences for a second strike need to be more severe but still in line with the program—privileges lost, even more work, and more meetings. With strike three, more draconian measures must be taken, such as placement in a lockdown facility for better monitoring.

6. Sign a contract. To ensure integrity, this contract is signed by the doctor, the patient, and all members of the treatment team.

Note: Steps 3 through 6 are clearly about setting boundaries, in which the doctor assumes the role of a parent guiding the addict's child ego through the first steps of treatment.

7. Initiate a medical detoxification. Detox can last from a few days to a few weeks. Since the medical withdrawal is now safe and comfortable, it allows patients to make up sleep deficits they accrued over the course of their addiction and reestablish their circadian rhythms while their natural neurotransmitter balance is restored.

8. Shift medical goals after detox from rebalancing the culprit neurotransmitters to permanently *stabilizing* the wayward brain chemistry. This is accomplished by an individualized pharmaceutical regimen that establishes and continually reinforces the biochemical balance, allowing the electrical and chemical pathways of the brain to heal. This new program needs constant fine-tuning, and specific courses of therapy vary from patient to patient. Herein lies the art of treatment. Some patients require just a few days or weeks to achieve a lasting balance, while others need several months. (Studies have proven that the addicted brain itself can take up to a year to heal.) Those with the most severe imbalances (and hence the most embedded addictions) may need to take stabilizing medications for their entire lives.

    Simultaneously begin behavioral treatment and lifestyle adjustments.

9. Working in myriad and personalized agendas of treatment, the doctor acts as quarterback (or general contractor), collaborating with the team of specialists participating in the individualized treatment plan. To become truly empowered, the addict must take an active partnership role and develop a personal and professional relationship with each member of the team.

10. Rebuild the fractured relationships that are a guaranteed by-product of addiction.

11. Redefine personal and professional goals. The words *future* and *goals* were not in the addict's vocabulary when he or she was in the throes of addiction. Now the addict can create the life goals that will give shape to the future. Include one fantasy that the addict always wanted to realize. And incorporate at least one goal that gives back to the community in a meaningful way.

12. Start fresh. Reengage with life by transitioning from a dysfunctional existence controlled by addiction to creating a life shining with a light of endless possibility. This can be as simple as filling in a calendar of daily activities like exercise, regular and healthy meal plans, doctor and therapy appointments, meetings, and social engagements that will ensure sobriety. Educational and vocational possibilities that will redefine the addict's place in the community should also be explored.

Even in the new paradigm, step 1—getting the addict to treatment—is by far the most difficult task to accomplish. But as word of the successful medical treatment spreads, addicts will be more willing and even eager to surrender, knowing there is a real light at the end of their previously dark tunnel. Once the patient sincerely complies and enters treatment, the rest of the steps follow a safe, comfortable, and effective medical protocol crafted with a partnership of professionals dedicated to each individual addict's need.

ASK THE DOCTOR

Can a person be too young to have problems with drug addiction and alcoholism?

Research has shown that children receive input about substance abuse issues as early as 2 years of age. This results primarily from exposure at home to family members who abuse drugs. This imprinting, along with a child's genetic predisposition to drug abuse, creates a foundation in the brain's hard wiring for future substance abuse.

The most critical period of vulnerability to substance abuse is adolescence. Studies have shown that teens who have used drugs (particularly nicotine) have a later risk of substance abuse that is nearly double the rate of teenagers who don't participate in these activities.

We now have a clear understanding of the role of the serotonin, dopamine, noradrenalin, and glutamate neurotransmitter imbalances that, when combined with stress, create the perfect formula for substance abuse. By recognizing these imbalances early in life, we are in a position to intervene and protect those predisposed to drug abuse. Combining neurotransmitter rebalancing with healthy lifestyle practices can transform the plague of addiction into a preventable disease.

How long does the medical treatment of addiction usually last?

Remember, addiction is based in brain chemistry, determined by genetics, and triggered by stress. Our brain chemistry, genetics, and stress travel with us throughout our lives, so managing these interconnections is a lifelong process. Whatever our individual neurotransmitter imbalances may be, they will influence the way we interact with our environment and the stressors that attack us.

As technology continues to perfect the pharmaceutical tools that rebalance our levels of serotonin, dopamine, noradrenalin, and glutamate, we are transforming addiction into a chronic but treatable medical disease. Combine this with personalized behavioral therapies and our success rate in treating addiction will reach 90 percent.

The new medical paradigm places addiction in the family of chronic diseases like diabetes, heart disease, and cancer. Treating any chronic medical illness is a lifelong process, and addiction is no exception.

PART 3 CASE STUDIES

The science is valid and confirmed.

The medicine is safe and effective.

But how exactly is it accomplished, this new medical paradigm of addiction?

How is the treatment implemented in real life, especially when it must be personalized to suit a wide variety of people abusing a broad spectrum of potentially lethal substances?

In the following chapters, the most commonly abused substances are described in detail, matching each with its specific neurotransmitter imbalance, and presenting the case histories of 11 diverse patients to show how the new medical treatment individually resolves addiction to each drug.

Three of these case subjects are alcoholics; one person is hooked on meth, another on cocaine, and one on heroin. Three more are addicted to different prescription drugs—OxyContin, Vicodin, and Valium. Another is cross-addicted to several substances.

The right of patient privacy and the current HIPAA (Health Insurance Portability and Accountability Act) regulations, as well as moral and ethical guidelines, forbid revealing the medical histories of real patients. For that reason, these case histories profile "composite" patients.

The dictionary defines a composite as "an entity made up of distinct components." That definition describes our composite patients. Each case history is assembled from distinct problems and circumstances experienced by several actual patients. Every event, situation, feeling, thought, and circumstance described in these histories is taken from the real world. Each is a factual reflection of the challenges faced by real-life patients. All the salient facts of addiction and its treatment have been focused and concentrated into individual portraits (without encroaching on a real patient's privacy and anonymity).

Composite case histories are the time-honored teaching method of every medical school across the country. And in truth, studying composites is more instructive, incisive, enlightening, and efficient than studying real patients, because each composite can be constructed as an almost classic textbook case that targets the facets and options of both the illness and the treatment.

Each history follows the treatment protocol of the new medical paradigm, starting with surrender or intervention through detox, medical rehabilitation, and behavioral and lifestyle recovery. And each case is presented in the same way it would be approached in a medical school or teaching hospital.

A primary rule of good medical practice is to first observe and listen to the patient to establish the diagnosis ... and proper treatment depends on an accurate diagnosis. So go ahead—put on an imaginary white coat. Observe each of these "patients" and their personalized treatments. In each case, look for and follow the early clues that will lead to our diagnosis and successful treatment. Most of those clues are contained in the addiction intake form that each patient fills out. Don't just breeze by this form—study it. See if you can spot the clues; find out how good a diagnostician you are. (If you have taken Your Addiction Prediction on page 40—or applied it to someone you know—you will be surprised how easy it is to connect the dots and understand why specific drugs choose us and not the other way around.)

By following the Addiction Solution process step by step, you'll gain a better understanding of addiction and its new paradigm of medical treatment.

Cocaine/Dopamine Imbalance

ocaine is the world's most powerful natural stimulant. It is an alkaloid derived from the leaves of the coca plant (*Erythroxylon coca*) grown in South America, mostly in the Andean mountain climate. More than 90 percent of cocaine is originally "farmed" in Peru and Columbia.

Once processed for mass distribution, its chemical formula is $C_{17}H_{21}NO_4$ (cocaine hydrochloride)—a veritable recipe for addiction.

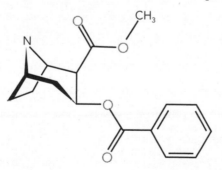

Also known as: *Blanca*, blow, Bolivian, C, caine, California cornflakes, coca, coke, cola, crack, fast white lady, flake, *flave*, freebase, girl, girlfriend, nose candy, *pariba*, *perico* (parrot), Peruvian, powder, product, shirt, snow, snow white, soda, stardust, sugar, toot, white boy, *yao*

Users known as: Baseball players, basers, coke fiends, cokeheads, coke whores, crackers, crackheads, snorters

How it's sold: On the street, powder cocaine is sold in grams, eight-tracks ($^1/_8$ ounce), quarters, halves, and full ounces. Dealers tend to buy single kilos (about 35 ounces) and then dilute or "cut" the powder (hopefully with a harmless substance like mannitol, a baby laxative) and sell it in smaller street quantities. Single grams have cost around $100 for the past 30 years. Crack cocaine is sold in smaller quantities, sometimes as single "rocks" or in transparent "vials" containing one to six rocks. Crack costs $10 to $15 per rock, depending on size. More experienced and affluent users usually buy powder grams, then use ether, baking soda and water, or ammonia and water to "cook" the powder into rock.

In South America, coca tea and *maté de coca* are regularly sold in bars, restaurants, coffeehouses, and grocery stores.

Brief history: Cocaine's recorded history dates from the pre-Columbian era, starting about 1200 BC. At first reserved for Incan royalty, who considered coca their gift from the gods, its use spread through the entire Inca empire from the lowliest worker to the Sun God himself. The Incas felt that chewing the leaves brought clarity of mind and vision and a content state of being. Coca was not only taken for social, mystical, and religious purposes, its effectiveness as a topical numbing agent made it useful as an all-purpose painkiller.

After the fall of the Inca empire to the Spanish in the 16th century, the returning conquistadors brought coca leaves to Europe, claiming they were "an elixir of life."

Two centuries later, around 1855, the active ingredient of the drug we know today was isolated and purified.

In 1885, the US pharmaceutical company Parke-Davis began selling cocaine in forms ranging from cigarettes, a powder, and a mixture to be injected. The following year brought the debut of a temperance drink brewed from coca leaves that was advertised as "offering the virtues of *coca* without the vices of alcohol." That beverage was Coca-Cola, which rapidly became the best-selling "refreshment" drink in the world.

For the next 60 years, cocaine was widely (and legally) used in health tonics, toothache remedies and patent medicines, cigarettes, and chocolates. Doctors, scientists, and prominent citizens the world over were both astonished and curious about this new "wonder" drug that so quickly lifted depression and enhanced a user's positive outlook on life. (In the late 1950s, Romanian physician Ana Aslan startled the world with Gerovital H3, an antiaging therapy comprised mostly of procaine— a close relative to cocaine—that had world leaders flocking to Bucharest for treatment.)

The Roaring Twenties brought the first widespread use of the powder form of illicit cocaine. And with its prolonged popularity came the emotional and physical carnage now associated with cocaine addiction.

The even more addictive crack ("freebase" cocaine) came to the forefront in the early 1980s, bringing with it a drug epidemic that became the scourge of Western society.

Usage today: After a decade of decline, cocaine use is once again on the upswing. In 2003, cocaine sold at street value exceeded $35 billion in the United States alone. Drug Enforcement Administration (DEA) officials estimate a roughly 10 percent increase per year since then, which translates conservatively to $60 billion in sales in 2009.

Such good business touches all demographics . . . and starts early. Roughly 2 percent of all eighth-graders have tried cocaine. By the time they graduate from high school, usage almost triples to nearly 6 percent. With college students, the number jumps to 7.7 percent. And 15.2 percent of young adults ages 21 to 35 have taken some form of cocaine. Statistics show the District of Columbia with 4.9 percent current usage among the general population. North Dakota ranks lowest at just under 2 percent. Average use across the national spectrum is about 3.5 percent.

And, too, a set of statistics drawn from prisons across the country clearly shows the bad choices made under the influence of cocaine. Thirty percent of all state prisoners admit to regular cocaine use in the month before their criminal offense; 46.8 percent of all state prisoners acknowledge cocaine use.

Altogether, present cocaine use is estimated at between 12 and 15 million Americans.

How it's taken: Cocaine is typically delivered in four different ways.

First and most benign is the coca leaf itself, most often chewed but also boiled as coca tea or made into drinks such as *maté de coca* or wine (*vin Mariani*).

The second and most common form is the powder, usually cut into "lines" on a mirror (or any flat, nonporous surface) and ingested nasally by snorting it through a makeshift straw straight into the nostril. Alternatively, users can sniff from miniature spoons dipped into tiny bottles (vials) that hold about a gram of powder. Lacking lines or spoons, some users pour a small pile of powder into the crook on the back of their hand, between the thumb and index finger (the "anatomic snuff box"), and snort it.

Powder is also sometimes rubbed into the gums to numb the mouth or rubbed onto genitalia to alter sexual sensation.

The third form, the "rock" (crack or freebase), is smoked, most often in a glass pipe but sometimes by burning it on aluminum foil and inhaling the smoke.

Finally, cocaine can be injected intravenously into the bloodstream. "Shooting the C" was popular in the early 20th century, but these days, largely due to the specter of AIDS and the inherent danger of sharing needles, shooting cocaine is socially unacceptable and rare, even among addicts.

Neurotransmitters involved: By releasing a large quantity of dopamine (the reward or pleasure neurotransmitter) and a splash of serotonin (a mood elevator) into the brain, cocaine triggers a state of exhilaration and well-being.

How it works: Cocaine creates an intense excitement of the senses, a "rush." It takes from 10 to 15 minutes to feel the full effects of a hit of powder cocaine, which usually comes on as a jolt of energy, followed by prolonged hyperactivity. Awareness and sexual arousal are heightened. Short-term performance is enhanced. The user may approach a state of euphoria.

Crack (freebase cocaine) is smoked and delivered in a vaporized form, and its effects are stronger and more immediate (about 10 seconds), resulting in both a heightened sense of consciousness and a sensual rapture. These effects are short-lived. The vapor acts rapidly on the nervous system but also withdraws quickly. Euphoria is quickly followed by anxiety, depression, irritability, fatigue, and paranoia—what is commonly referred to as the crash. From a biochemical perspective, crashing or "coming down" simply means the addict is running out of dopamine and must replenish the store to rebalance, hence the gnawing craving for another hit of cocaine.

The longer the period of use, the more physical health deteriorates. As recreation turns to addiction, compulsive behavior, hallucinations, severe depression, chronic delirium, and sometimes toxic paranoid psychosis settle in. Worse still for the addict, the chronically abused dopamine D-2 receptors eventually increase tolerance to their drug-induced overstimulation, so the brain's ability to experience pleasure is gradually diminished even as its craving for the drug increases. In short, the more you take cocaine—in any form—the more you need it and the less you enjoy it.

Risks: There have been instances of people dying from their first hit of cocaine, but most harmful effects are linked to long-term use. As a stimulant, cocaine is almost synonymous with adverse heart disturbance, most commonly cardiac abnormalities (an artificial speeding up of the heart's natural rhythm). This in turn can result in coronary occlusion, or spasm of a coronary artery, leading to heart attacks or strokes.

By their very nature, stimulants heighten behaviors, and cocaine often gives the user a feeling of invincibility. This leads to bad and reckless decisions, like driving while totally wasted or scoring more and more cocaine.

Associated behaviors: Powder cocaine is commonly used in public—at parties and clubs, etc.—while rock smokers tend to be private and isolated.

Powder irritates the nasal linings, so users experience constant sniffing, runny noses, and red, bloodshot eyes, as if they have colds; prolonged abuse can lead to destruction of the nasal septum, which can create serious sinus infections. Smoking irritates (burns) the palate and throat, leading to dryness (cotton mouth) and sore throats.

All cocaine addicts share a lack of appetite (with weight loss) and a drastic change in sleeping patterns (restlessness). These behaviors are followed by wild mood swings, from short-term hyperactivity (usually just following a good hit) to irritability and paranoia as they come down. The longer users are addicted, the more they can become withdrawn, depressed, tired, and careless about their appearance. Their grades or work begin to suffer. Then they start missing school or work. They change their group of friends and lose interest in just about everything except the drug and its "pleasure" cycle. Constantly in need of money to support their growing habits, they often begin lying and stealing from close friends or relatives.

Some positive effects: There are a few benefits from nonaddictive cocaine use. Many South Americans feel that chewing organic coca leaves can be therapeutic in relieving stress and tension. Taken orally in teas and *maté,* cocaine is a common home remedy for digestive problems and the easing of anxiety (and undeniably works as a mild mood elevator).

Like its cousin Novocain, cocaine hydrochloride can be an effective painkiller, mostly as a topical (or surface) anesthetic for numbing mucous membranes of the nose, eyes, and throat. Toothache sufferers often rub it into their gums to relieve pain (although oil of clove could be just as effective).

The medical detox: Since agitation is always the predominant symptom during withdrawal from stimulants like cocaine, antianxiety medications (anxiolytics) are prescribed to allow rebalancing of the dopamine and GABA neurotransmitters. These anxiolytics include benzodiazepines like Klonopin, Ativan, Valium, and Xanax; beta-blockers like Inderal; and GABAergic medications like Neurontin and Lyrica.

Seroquel, an atypical antipsychotic medication, is frequently advised to help soothe and sedate the patient.

Light exercise, like walking or swimming, is also recommended because it increases the body's natural endorphins, which also have a calming effect and are believed to increase levels of natural opioids in the brain.

Stabilizing medications: After detoxing from cocaine and restoring the natural dopamine balance, safer pharmaceutical options are available that create a new and improved baseline that stabilizes the equilibrium in the patient's brain chemistry.

When a patient's natural dopamine imbalance is mild, as in ADHD, stabilization can be accomplished through prescription solutions like Adderall, Ritalin, Dexedrine, Concerta, Metadate, Focalin, Strattera, Wellbutrin, Provigil, and Vyvanse.

The more serious natural imbalances associated with bipolar disorders are treated with medications like Zyprexa, Seroquel, lithium, Risperdal, Abilify, Lamictal, and Geodon.

CASE STUDY: KATE, ADDICTED TO COCAINE

Surrender

Everybody back in Nebraska thought fresh-faced and blonde Kate was as cute as a button. Even with a touch of the tomboy about her, she was the all-American Girl Next Door. That was her ticket out.

While she was glad she'd grown up with heartland values—church each Sunday and county fairs every summer—there was nothing there for her. She'd known that by her 10th birthday. At 18, she left to chase her dream in Hollywood.

She worked nights at a high-end restaurant earning huge tips. Her days were spent in acting class, at auditions, and on the occasional television job. Nights off meant networking at the right parties (and some wrong ones) and popular industry bars and clubs. Her life was a whirlwind, but she was young and ambitious. So what was wrong with a little pick-me-up now and then?

A year later, her efforts were starting to pay off: print ads, a national commercial, even a few good (if small) parts on prime time. Alex from class, a friend with benefits, introduced her to a hot young agent who liked her reel and her look. But he'd represent her only if she cleaned up her act. He wasn't in business to buy problems . . . and her addiction was definitely a problem.

Medical Evaluation

INTAKE FORM

Name: Kate   **Age:** 19   **SMDW:** S   **Sex:** F
Occupation: Actress/waitress   **Referred By:** My agent

Current Problems/Complaints:

I came here on my agent's "suggestion." He makes all his clients get clean from any drugs so he can get them work. I don't think I have a problem, but I'll do anything to make him happy. I admit I do coke socially, with friends or at a party, but I actually feel calmer on it. It focuses me a little. Sometimes I have a glass of wine when I'm with friends who are drinking—or a drink or two before bed, maybe even a Xanax, to calm me down and help me sleep. I don't see any harm in that! I mean, everyone out here drinks or does drugs and it's not so bad to try to fit in, is it? I smoke two packs a day. I know, I know, it's not good for me, but everybody in my family smokes and I've been smoking since I was 13.

Past Medical History:

❑ Childhood Illness   ❑ ADD   ❑ Trauma (Emotional/Physical)
☒ Anxiety   ❑ Depression
❑ Other Trouble paying attention in school

Medical Illnesses:

☒ Anxiety   ❑ Depression   ❑ Insomnia
❑ Chronic Pain   ☒ Hyperactivity/ADD   ❑ Bipolar
❑ OCD   ☒ Weight Changes   ❑ Stress
☒ Other I'm always watching my weight because I need to look good on camera!

Psychological History:

❏ Divorce in Family   ❏ Unexpected Death in Family
❏ Recent Change in Relationship
❏ Chronic Pain   ❏ Job Stress   ❏ Sexual Issues
☒ Recent Life Changes <u>I moved to LA from Nebraska last year, left my</u>
<u>family and boyfriend—and everything in my life is different now.</u>

Habits:

☒ Nicotine   ☒ Alcohol (beer)   ☒ Recreational Drugs
☒ Marijuana   ❏ Metabolic/Weight Problems
Exercise: ❏ Never   ❏ Occasionally   ❏ Often
❏ Other <u>Sometimes cocaine at a party</u>

Current Medications: <u>Xanax sometimes to go to sleep</u>

Surgeries: <u>Appendix taken out when I was 6</u>

Family History:

	Living	Deceased	Health Problems
Mother	✓		I think she's bipolar; she's been hospitalized twice for nervousness.
Father	✓		Smokes too much
Siblings	✓		One brother, 16, has ADD

Health Problems in Your Family:

❏ Irritable/Spastic Bowel   ❏ Depression   ❏ Suicide
☒ Hyperactive/ADD   ❏ Obesity   ☒ Bipolar
❏ Headaches   ❏ Back Pain   ☒ Anxiety
❏ Heart Disease   ❏ Cancers   ❏ Diabetes
☒ Nicotine   ☒ Caffeine   ❏ Alcohol
❏ Other Drug Abuse <u>Everyone in my family smokes—a lot—even my little</u>
<u>brother.</u>

Patient Interview (from Transcript)

"I came out here to be an actress. My parents think this whole Tinsel-town thing is crazy, but I know I have just as good a chance as anybody else. You know those girls in *Twilight*? I could be one of them.

"When I first got here, I met as many A-listers as I could—the industry's all about networking and hooking up with the right people. One night I was at a party where Judd Apatow was supposed to show up. I was really nervous, but a chick I'd met at an audition offered me a line of coke. It made me feel great—like wow! Suddenly, I wasn't inhibited at all, and I could talk to absolutely anyone and be funny and charming. Which you need to be. So whenever I knew I'd be at these parties or in situations with producers or directors or agents, I'd do some lines beforehand.

"Finally I met this really cute agent who wants to help me, but only if I stop doing drugs. He promised that if I got clean, he could get me a TV series. He doesn't know I only do drugs recreationally—well, maybe a little more than that—but if rehab jump-starts my career, I'll do it in a flash, even if I don't need it. Heck, lots of people who don't drink hang out at AA meetings just to network.

"This is a great opportunity—the best thing that's happened to me out here. I know he likes me, and I don't want to blow this chance.

"Plus which, I don't want to go back Nebraska. I want to show my family I can make it out here."

Physician Analysis

Kate shows signs of the classic stimulant addict. She calms down and focuses when she does cocaine, she has an associated smoking addiction, and she dabbles in other drugs like alcohol and marijuana but does not abuse either. She abuses caffeine for the same reason as cocaine—to actually calm herself.

She is very thin, partly from the stimulants, but mainly to meet her professional goals.

Her childhood history shows attention problems, and her genetics connects to her mom's bipolar history and her brother's ADD.

Her stressors include a sudden and dramatic change from a small-town ambience to her new life in the big city and a ferocious drive to succeed as an actor. "I'll do anything" is the mantra for those coming here to become famous.

She is further stressed by working long and hard hours as a waitress to support herself.

When she came to LA, she left her boyfriend of 3 years. While they still talk occasionally on the phone, this relationship is on life support as she struggles to integrate into a new social network that is a 180-degree turnabout from what she left behind.

In her interview, it eventually became clear that she is sleeping with her agent. While she sincerely likes him, it's mostly to get ahead in her career. This has created feelings of tremendous guilt.

She is in denial about the severity of her cocaine abuse and does not connect the dots of her substance issues, including her dependence on nicotine and caffeine.

Accepted for treatment.

Medical Rehabilitation

Stimulant abuse arises from an imbalance of dopamine, evidenced by the fact that cocaine, nicotine, and caffeine actually calm Kate's hyperactive behaviors by blocking the dopamine receptors.

Kate's medical rehabilitation will involve an initial detoxification from cocaine and then a stabilizing of her dopamine neurotransmitters with nonaddictive medications.

Medical Detox

The medical detoxification for cocaine, a stimulant, primarily involves the dopamine and glutamate receptors. When chronic cocaine use is interrupted (or stopped), the brain rebels—big time—with severe agitation. To counterbalance that physical reaction, the glutamate receptors must be soothed by either benzodiazepines (Klonopin, Xanax, Ativan) or antiseizure medications (Neurontin). Since benzos are associated with dependency problems, the latter is a safer option.

Sleep issues should be addressed with short-term use of nonaddicting choices like Ambien, Vistaril, or Seroquel. Kate will be taught sleep hygiene and how to maintain a regular daily schedule. Since sleep deprivation goes hand in hand with stimulant abuse, Kate's natural daily rhythms have been unstable for a long time. So rest is an important part of this initial recuperative period.

Kate's smoking addiction will be addressed with Chantix, a blocking agent that specifically targets nicotine receptors to remove the cravings for cigarettes. Once these receptors are coated (usually in a few weeks), they must remain covered for several months to prevent relapse. Since nicotine receptors also appear in the intestinal tract, side effects from Chantix may include nausea, cramps, and diarrhea. If any of these strike Kate, appropriate countermeasures will be taken.

Stabilizing the Brain Chemistry

Once the initial detoxification is complete, the real job begins—first restoring Kate's natural brain chemistry and then creating a new and better neurochemical balance that staves off any future biochemical wantings.

Several stabilizing medications like Wellbutrin, Concerta, Adderall, Ritalin, Dexedrine, Provigil, and other stimulant medications target the dopamine neurotransmitters. Newer dopamine receptor subtypes are being identified that will allow us to soon hit the bull's-eye with medications that improve the neurotransmitter rebalancing act.

Brain mapping and MRI scanning will reveal the extent of Kate's neurological damage in the cognitive and memory areas of the brain. Repeated imaging at periodic intervals will allow Kate to actually see the healing process as her recovery continues.

Regular aerobic exercise will produce endorphins that quiet the glutamate and opioid receptors and keep Kate less edgy and more comfortable, helping to ensure her long-term compliance. These same endorphins will also improve the quality of her sleep.

Behavioral Treatment and Lifestyle Adjustments

The goal is for Kate to be treated by a multifaceted team of caring professionals who will exchange their expertise for her compliance. Kate's recovery team will need a neuropharmacologist to help understand the imbalanced transmitters, a psychologist to help with life choices, a drug and alcohol counselor, a nutritionist to improve her metabolic status, and a primary doctor acting as the quarterback of her treatment team—coordinating her care, serving as her anchor, and ensuring she keeps her commitments by holding fast to the rules. The longer her relationships with each team member last, the more skills and knowledge Kate will accrue to deal with her disease.

Relationships

The people in Kate's life who are willing to provide support are her family (specifically, her brother, father, and one cousin) and her agent, whose draconian (and sensible) rule will help her stay on the straight and narrow. And as Kate repairs old relationships, she will learn how to build healthier new ones.

But the relationship that needs the most repair is Kate's with herself. She needs to get clean, set a life course, make changes that feel good, and deal with bad feelings with smart choices. With her self-esteem restored, she will become eligible for a happy, fulfilling, and even exciting life.

PERSONAL AND PROFESSIONAL GOALS

Kate will combine her sobriety with some options uncovered during her recovery. While acting opportunities become more accessible, Kate could benefit from vocational counseling that explores options (or fall-back positions) she may not have considered for her professional and personal journeys. Her passions can now be engaged with clarity and developed incrementally as each week and month passes. While she travels a bumpy road, Kate will eventually see and feel it as the most rewarding journey of her life—one of those rare good gifts that keeps on giving.

Starting Fresh/Reengaging with Life

Kate's treatment has been successful. Her life now looks like this:

1. She is not doing cocaine or any other drug.

2. She has stopped smoking.

3. She has significantly reduced her caffeine intake.

4. She continues taking medication to stabilize her dopamine balance. This has made her focus and stay on schedule while it wards off biochemical cravings.

5. She in touch with her family and is regaining a good relationship with her brother and cousin.

6. She exercises regularly.

7. She is eating a balanced diet and has gained 15 pounds . . . and looks great.

8. She is learning to recognize and cope more successfully with her stressors.

9. She is exploring career options that could ensure her happiness if "plan A" fails.

10. She now serves as a role model for *The Addiction Solution*.

Heroin/Serotonin Imbalance

Heroin is an opiate derived from a common poppy flower, *Papaver somniferum*. Raw opium, in the form of a juice or gummy paste, is found inside the seedpods. The main extract from opium is morphine, which is converted into heroin by a chemical process. Listed under the chemical formula $C_{21}H_{23}NO_5$, heroin is a hydrochloride salt, diamorphine hydrochloride, that can be up to two times stronger than its original morphine base.

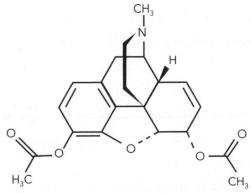

Uncut heroin is generally graded by color. The best processed and purest is called China white. Sold in fine white granules or powder, it's easy to dissolve and then inject and is considered the champagne of heroin.

Grade B heroin is simply called brown, although it can be either dark brown or tan. Its hue comes from the additives mixed in during processing. Like China white, brown heroin is sold in granules or powder, but because it is not as finely ground, it's the grade of choice for smoking or snorting.

Other shades of brown—and even red—indicate different ingredients used during processing. The off-browns get a C grade because they are usually of lesser quality or purity than brown.

At the bottom of the barrel, with a grade of D, comes "black tar," sometimes known in the United States as Mexican mud. As the name suggests, this product is black and sticky, like tar or thick, damp mud. While its purity has improved through the years, black tar is more toxic than other forms of heroin and retains some of its morphine base, which often allows its effects to last longer. Because of that, and due to its wide availability and lower price, it's the most widely used form in western and southwest US border communities.

Afghanistan is the main producer of heroin, but the Golden Triangle (Myanmar, Laos, and Thailand) in Southeast Asia is becoming a major player. Mexico and Columbia are the primary suppliers to the United States.

Also known as: Antifreeze, Aunt Hazel, the beast, big H, big Harry, black pearl, black tar, *blanco*, boy, brain, brother, brown sugar, *caballo*, caca, *carga, carne*, Charley, *chaw*, China white, *chiva*, crank, diesel, dirt, DOA, dope, downtown, H, hard candy, heavy stuff, *hombre*, horse, hot heroin, jive, juice, junk, Karachi, Mexican mud, the monkey, poison, poppy, shag, skag, smack

Users known as: Bedbugs, channel swimmers (injectors), cotton shooters, hypes, jolly pops (casual users), junkies, King Kongs (big users), schmeckers, skids, sleepwalkers, speedball artists (heroin and cocaine mixers), *tecatos*

How it's sold: The advent of cell phones ushered in a prosperous "call and delivery" business, but open-air markets (street corners, public parks, and arcades) are the common venue for heroin sales. The drug is often sold wrapped in balloons that the dealer holds in his mouth. In case of a bust, the dealer swallows the evidence (hoping the balloons do not burst in his stomach). Or the heroin is packaged in small glassine bags or paper bindles. Black tar is usually wrapped in aluminum foil.

Today, a gram of street heroin with purity ranging anywhere from 10 to 50 percent can be bought for $90 to $100, or 9 to 10 cents per milligram. A hit of 50 to 60 milligrams costs about 5 bucks. For longtime addicts needing dosages of 250 to 500 milligrams, the price per hit runs $20 to $30. Most frightening is that children can buy beginner hits (called tastes) of 5 to 10 milligrams for only 50 to 75 cents, less than the price of a comic book or soda pop.

Brief history: Opium use goes back more than 6,000 years, to the time of the ancient Egyptians. Its use was also widespread in ancient Greek and Roman cultures. The infamous opium dens took hold in 17th-century China. Travelers subsequently spread opium use across the globe; before long, opium was a common treatment in Europe for various health problems.

Early in the 19th century, morphine was extracted from opium, and in 1874, heroin was first produced from morphine. That, along with the 1853 invention of the hypodermic needle, opened the door to common, serious, and often lethal heroin addictions.

After successful use as a painkiller in hospitals, Bayer trademarked the name Heroin (from the German word *heroisch*, meaning "heroic") and brought it to market in 1898 as a legal, safe alternative to morphine.

On the upside, pharmaceutical-grade heroin resulted in few overdoses, mostly because of its consistent quality. On the downside, this pain-killer was rampantly addictive, causing more problems—both societal and medical—than it solved. In 1924, the US government outlawed the manufacture and sale of heroin, even in hospitals.

The ban left those already addicted without resources, so an illegal black-market industry began. From the mid-1920s through the mid-1970s, heroin was the kingpin of America's illicit drug culture. When anyone referred to an addict, they meant a heroin user. Other drugs were being consumed, but barely enough to garner attention.

That started to change in the 1950s, when pharmaceutical companies began marketing tranquilizers and antianxiety drugs ("tranks" and "dolls") primarily to women between ages 18 and 50. In the 1960s, psychedelics like LSD became part of the youth culture. Then, in the 1970s and '80s, first cocaine and then crack, methamphetamine, and prescription opiates swept through America like a hurricane. The aggregate use of these drugs surpassed heroin abuse. To compete in the crowded marketplace, heroin producers and dealers dropped prices. Once the most expensive narcotic, heroin now sells for about one-tenth of its 1975 price, making it the cheapest of the major drugs.

Usage today: Heroin abuse cuts across all age, race, gender, and economic demographics, although use and treatment statistics suggest that heroin abuse is more prevalent in large urban areas. In any given year over the past decade, between 550,000 and 600,000 Americans abused heroin. That includes just under 1 percent of children in grades 8 through 12.

Heroin addicts make up about 15 percent of total admissions to drug treatment facilities and 14 percent of all drug-related emergency room visits.

The average heroin addict spends $150 to $200 a day feeding the habit. Since most addicts cannot hold steady jobs, stealing from family and friends becomes commonplace and the first step in the long spiral downward.

How it's taken: Partly because of the HIV/AIDS connection to needles and partially because of increased purity, about a third of all heroin users now inhale the drug—that's up from about 5 percent 25 years ago. Heroin can be smoked or inhaled (sniffed or snorted) in its powder form. It can also be smoked in its "mud" mode, usually through a pipe, from the tip of a cigarette, or from aluminum foil heated from below ("chasing the dragon").

When mixed with water and heated—often in a spoon—it can be injected via a hypodermic needle straight into the bloodstream (called slamming), into a muscle (muscling), or under the skin (popping). It can also be taken orally. But before crossing the blood-brain barrier, it completely metabolizes, or converts, into morphine.

Heroin is the fastest acting of all the opiates. Slamming produces a rush in about 30 seconds. Smoking takes less time, around 10 seconds, but with a less powerful rush. Snorting, muscling, and popping produce the desired effects in 3 to 5 minutes.

Depending on the amount and quality taken, the effects wear off in 3 to 5 hours, so confirmed addicts must use up to four times a day to quell insatiable cravings. Tolerance rises rapidly, and ever-larger hits are needed to maintain the high: A beginner might take a 50-milligram dose, while a longtime addict might take perhaps 20 times as much. As dosage increases, the addict is caught in the vicious cycle of dependency, focused only on acquiring and taking the drug—the reason, perhaps, that heroin has been called the plague of the walking dead.

Neurotransmitters involved: Endorphins are composed of opioid polypeptides that are naturally manufactured by activities like a good physical workout, any thrill or excitement (like amusement park rides or winning the lottery), and orgasm. Along with causing a general feeling of well-being, endorphins produce analgesia, a natural painkiller.

By mimicking peptides and delivering to the same receptors, heroin and other opiates produce endorphins and analgesia. But since heroin actually binds to those receptors, it impedes the normal release of GABA neurotransmitters, creates a serotonin deficit, and increases the flow of dopamine to a veritable flood, bringing even greater pleasure and an almost total absence of pain . . . at first. As more heroin is artificially pumped in, the brain loses its ability to naturally produce endorphins and analgesia, so more heroin is needed to manufacture them.

How it works: Heroin is most often described as delivering an intense feeling of well-being—a brief but intense euphoria followed by a unique sense of security, reduced anxiety, sedation, and drowsiness. In this secondary stage, addicts feel as if they are "wrapped in God's blanket" and often "nod out" somewhere between sleep and consciousness.

With some users, addiction takes hold on the first hit, but most become physiologically dependent after perhaps half a dozen or so hits. But addiction always results sooner rather than later, usually in about 3 days.

Risks: Shooting heroin leads the pack of abused substances in fatalities. Even a small dose can lead to nausea, upper respiratory (breathing) problems, and hypothermia. Most addicts are recklessly unaware of the purity of the street-grade drug. For pushers, the profit is often in the "cut"—how much and what the heroin is mixed with . . . and dealers, generally not a savory lot, have been known to mix in such additives as procaine and lidocaine (local anesthetics), baking soda, powdered milk, sugar, laundry detergent, starch, curry powder, quinine, and cleaning powders. These additives are potentially lethal if injected into the bloodstream. Even flat-out poisons like strychnine are sometimes mixed into the pure heroin, resulting in a "hot shot" that kills the user in under a minute.

Because of its sedating quality, a heroin overdose (OD) can kill all by itself. Too much of it, especially high-quality heroin, depresses the respiratory drive to the point where the addict simply stops breathing.

The sharing of heroin needles by junkies often leads to HIV/AIDS. Long-term abuse increases the risk for hepatitis C and liver damage. Constipation is almost guaranteed. The circadian rhythm is interrupted. Bacterial and viral infections are common, as are skin and lung infections. Women on heroin often stop menstruating, a side effect of hormone suppression.

Associated behaviors: Heroin use is arguably the hardest to spot of all addictions. High-functioning heroin users blend in so easily that when their addiction is finally discovered, the most common reaction is "Who knew?"

Lesser-functioning heroin users can often be seen picking incessantly at their skin or, overcome by drowsiness, "nodding out" at inappropriate times and places.

Some positive effects: Heroin has no more positive effect in pain management than other, more reliable prescriptions. Interestingly, recent research has found that by killing certain types of T-lymphocytes, heroin may reduce the risk of some kinds of cancer.

The medical detox: Kicking heroin cold turkey is physically and mentally perilous. At the least, it can lead to agony and bone-shaking tremors; at worst, death. The new medical treatment withdraws patients from heroin (and all opiate-based substances, like morphine) safely and effectively by restoring and then stabilizing the patient's brain chemistry.

The short-term medical detox treatment has four separate but intertwined goals.

1. Transition: The addict tapers down from a lethal opiate (heroin) to a far less dangerous one that minimizes the risk of respiratory arrest. The patient is given buprenorphine (Subutex and/or Suboxone), an opiate so safe that it has been approved by the FDA for use during pregnancy and by children. Buprenorphine relieves pain and starkly diminishes cravings without creating the euphoria that accompanies opiate abuse.

2. Address sleep issues: To help patients sleep and restore their natural circadian rhythms, they are given antihistamines like Benadryl and Vistaril, hypnotics like Ambien, beta-blockers like Inderal, antipsychotic meds such as Seroquel, and antiseizure medications like Neurontin. None of these meds have addiction associations.

3. Relieve anxiety: To combat the anxiety that accompanies every withdrawal, the patient is given benzodiazepines such as Klonopin, Ativan, and Xanax. Since these medications do carry some dependency issues, they are prescribed only in the short term—for no more than a few weeks—and must be carefully monitored. GABAergic medications like Neurontin also promote an overall calming effect and are now the preferred frontline defense against the predictable anxiety of withdrawal.

4. Restore serotonin to its natural level: One or another of a variety of SSRIs is employed to repair the low serotonin level that is the primary instigator of opiate addiction. Simply put, it's a tapering up of serotonin at the same time as the opiate itself is tapering down.

All of these medications make up a full menu of available pharmaceuticals. Medical regimens must be tailored to the individual addict according to his or her need.

Stabilizing medications: In treating opiate addiction, the first goal is to rebalance the low serotonin that is the driving force of an opiate addiction. Once the patient's natural serotonin levels have been restored, a permanent improved balance is established via a prescriptive program of SSRIs like Prozac, Zoloft, Lexapro, Celexa, and Paxil. SNRI medications like Pristiq, Effexor, Cymbalta, and Savella not only raise serotonin levels but also help reduce noradrenalin, thereby easing anxiety. Cymbalta also has the potential to relieve pain. The treatment is customized to the individual addict by addressing his or her unique medical problems.

CASE STUDY: MICHELLE, ADDICTED TO HEROIN

Surrender

The essence of sleek and chic, Michelle would look great on the cover of *Vogue*. Black designer business suit, conservative with a pinch of daring. Pitch black hair, exquisitely styled.

She wasn't a model, but she used the same tools of style and perception in her work as an advertising executive in a large national firm. She had street savvy, a mind like a steel trap, and incredible discipline; Michelle was an unstoppable force. Except for her addiction. Work wasn't a problem—no one there knew or even suspected. Her habit didn't harm her performance, either. At least, not yet. But soon, maybe . . . and she needed to stay on top of, even ahead of, the game.

Like all addicts, Michelle had both a secret and a lie. But she had too much to lose, and she knew it was time to quit using. So, of her own volition, she surrendered to treatment.

Medical Evaluation

INTAKE FORM

Name: Michelle   **Age:** 33   **SMDW:** S   **Sex:** F
Occupation: Advertising executive   **Referred By:** Internet

Current Problems/Complaints:

I went to a few skin doctors because I had some ugly sores on my arms and face that were not healing. The last dermatologist I saw, who was Vietnamese like me, confided to me that he was a heroin addict during his early 20s and recognized these sores immediately. He was right. I have been using heroin for 7 years, and it was my little secret until now. I decided I should get this problem dealt with since my life is pretty good and I don't want it to come crashing down. My whole life has been a secret—from my gay lifestyle to my drug abuse. These secrets have created bad feelings that have made me feel depressed, and the heroin became my antidepressant. I couldn't tell my parents since they were already upset with me for my lesbian relationship. I could never tell my co-workers since I have a high position in my firm. I went online to search for help and I found you.

Past Medical History:

❑ Childhood Illness   ❑ ADD   ☒ Trauma (Emotional/Physical)
❑ Anxiety   ☒ Depression
❑ Other I knew I was different sexually since I was 11.

Medical Illnesses:

❑ Anxiety   ☒ Depression   ☒ Insomnia
❑ Chronic Pain   ❑ Hyperactivity/ADD   ❑ Bipolar
❑ OCD   ❑ Weight Changes   ☒ Stress Estranged
❑ Other Endometriosis   from my family

Psychological History:

❏ Divorce in Family   ❏ Unexpected Death in Family
❏ Recent Change in Relationship
❏ Chronic Pain   ☒ Job Stress   ☒ Sexual Issues
❏ Recent Life Changes _____

Habits:

❏ Nicotine   ☒ Alcohol <u>Social</u>   ❏ Recreational Drugs
❏ Marijuana   ❏ Metabolic/Weight Problems
Exercise: ❏ Never   ❏ Occasionally   ☒ Often <u>(Yoga)</u>
❏ Other _____

Current Medications: <u>Yasmin (birth control) for endometriosis</u>

Surgeries: <u>Laparoscopy 2004 for endometriosis</u>

Family History:

	Living	Deceased	Health Problems
Mother	✓		58
Father	✓		64
Siblings	✓		3 sisters, 2 brothers (I'm the second oldest)

Health Problems in Your Family:

❏ Irritable/Spastic Bowel   ☒ Depression   ❏ Suicide
❏ Hyperactive/ADD   ❏ Obesity   ❏ Bipolar
❏ Headaches   ❏ Back Pain   ❏ Anxiety
☒ Heart Disease   ❏ Cancers   ❏ Diabetes
❏ Nicotine   ❏ Caffeine   ☒ Alcohol
❏ Other Drug Abuse_____

Patient Interview (from Transcript)

"I'm the best example you can find of someone who's been really success-ful but is absolutely miserable. You have to understand that Asian fami-lies are very close-knit. Especially mine. My parents were boat people who left Vietnam 30 years ago. They settled in Little Saigon, worked hard, and made a good living. My brother was born a month after they arrived in America. I was next—the second eldest. I've got another brother and three sisters. While we were all born here, we're still regarded as outsiders, so we stick together, both within our communities and within our family.

"I love my family very much. They mean the world to me.

"By the time I was 18, I knew I was a lesbian, but I kept it hidden from them. I came out when I was 21. By then, I thought they'd accept it, but they shunned me instead. Almost totally. I reached out to them a couple of years later, but they couldn't forgive me. Of course, the thought that I needed to be forgiven merely for who I was got me very angry, so I never reached out again. Not really. I see them at Tet, our Vietnamese New Year, but it's very strained. I talk occasionally with my sisters and brothers, but in our culture, children must honor their parents. Espe-cially since I have brought shame on my parents, my siblings have to be more vigilant in displaying their respect.

"That's how I started shooting heroin. It took all my cares away and made me feel better. Those first few moments of the rush gave me an extreme sense of well-being. I got hooked pretty quickly. And, of course, the more I took, the harder it was to sustain that good feeling.

"I miss my family. I miss their love and support. I miss my commu-nity and the friends and relatives I grew up with. My addiction to heroin is removing me farther and farther from the life I want. I am depressed almost all the time, save for that minute or two after I shoot up.

"A couple of months ago, I started seeing this guy at work. I'm attracted to him and don't know what that's about. I still love my partner and I feel bad cheating on her. I am really confused and depressed all the time. I just want my life back."

Physician Analysis

In evaluating Michelle's intake, we find several clues that explain her addiction to heroin.

Heroin is an opiate that corresponds to a neurotransmitter imbalance of serotonin. Serotonin imbalances correlate with depression and obsessive thoughts and behaviors. Michelle discusses her depression in her initial statement, the interview, and the past medical history, medical illnesses, and psychological history sections of the intake form.

She mentions alcohol use under the habits section, and we know that serotonin imbalances are satisfied not only by opiates but also by alcohol. Both depression and alcohol abuse are listed under her family health problems section, giving credence to the genetic predisposition she has toward depression.

The stress of her life that aggravated her depression and accelerated her heroin use is clarified when she discusses her family's inability to accept her lifestyle choices and the stress she has been under at work.

What she failed to mention on this intake form, but did admit during her interview, was the real stress that tipped the scales in her worsening drug habit. She admitted that she has, over the past 2 months, been having a sexual relationship with a male co-worker outside of her long-standing lesbian relationship. This has created a devastating confusion, guilt, and anger that has translated into more heroin use and bad feelings.

Her laboratory evaluation revealed a positive result for hepatitis C, consistent with her use of intravenous drugs. Her HIV test was negative. Her liver enzymes were normal.

Michelle is intelligent, extremely disciplined, and highly motivated.

Accepted for treatment.

Medical Rehabilitation

Michelle's medical rehabilitation will involve a detoxification from heroin, treating the insomnia that typically accompanies any drug abuse, and maintaining her already established daily yoga classes to ensure the vital exercise component of her solution.

Since she has tested positive for hepatitis C, she will be referred to a herpetologist to assess the level of activity of the virus, and a genotyping of her blood will be sent to the lab to determine if she is a candidate for antiviral therapy. She will be scheduled for regular liver enzyme monitoring every 3 months, workups that will include checking her alpha-fetoprotein, a marker for liver cancer (hepatoma) that is also associated with hepatitis C.

Because of her injection history, she will need to have biannual HIV testing for 1 year to monitor for this disease.

Medical Detox

Michelle will undergo a buprenorphine-guided detoxification from her heroin. As an IV abuser, she will take Suboxone (buprenorphine combined with naltrexone), which is preferred over the pure form of buprenorphine (Subutex), since an IV drug user will get very sick if she attempts to inject this product. This is because naltrexone displaces all opiates immediately from their receptors, creating an immediate and dangerously uncomfortable withdrawal. (When someone overdoses on opiates and is brought into an emergency room, naltrexone—also called Narcan—is given to displace the opiate to bring someone out of the coma or respiratory arrest that accompanies any overdose.)

Michelle's Suboxone will be given as a sublingual tablet (under the tongue) in divided doses during the day. This medication may be given for up to 6 weeks, in tapering doses, to complete the detoxification.

During the detox, Michelle will also be given short-term medications to improve the sleep disorder created by the heroin abuse. These may include products like Ambien, Ativan, trazadone, Seroquel, Neurontin, and Vistaril. If sleep disorders persist, then one of the nonaddicting products will be offered for long-term management.

Michelle will experience severe anxiety during her detoxification, since withdrawal of any abused substance provokes a release of the neurotransmitters noradrenalin and glutamate, both of which create anxiety and agitation. There is a menu of receptor blocking agents that can be used, including the benzodiazepines (Valium, Xanax, Klonopin, and Ativan), which have dependency potential and are therefore used only for short-term treatment (2 to 6 weeks). We also have nonaddictive beta-blockers (like Inderal) and an antiseizure medication (Neurontin) that will block the same receptors and restore calm to the detoxing patient.

Stabilizing the Brain Chemistry

To address the serotonin imbalance that provoked Michelle's (and any opiate-dependent patient's) heroin abuse, we need to restore the

inadequate levels of this neurotransmitter. There are a number of serotonergic medications—commonly referred to as SSRIs and SNRIs—that
boost the body's natural levels of serotonin. SSRIs include Prozac, Zoloft,
Celexa, Paxil, and Lexapro. The SNRIs are Cymbalta, Effexor, Savella,
and Pristiq, among others.

There is some controversy as to when serotonergics should be started
during treatment, but we have learned that beginning these medications
as early as the initial detoxification period may be helpful. These drugs
take several weeks to take effect, and they all have potential side effects
that may test the limits of patients' compliance. For this reason, we now
give these medications as early as possible, starting with very small
doses and increasing them gradually over several weeks. Often one product does well with one person and another works better with someone
else, so this is a trial-and-error process.

The negative connotation to these medications from the general
public is another problem. A common reaction is: "If you're taking Prozac
you must be crazy." But by elevating Michelle's serotonin levels, her
underlying depression will gradually transition into better moods with
less anxiety and less vulnerability to the life stress that she will need to
better manage. Concomitantly, she will also be significantly less vulnerable to treating her bad feelings with heroin.

Michelle's anxiety and sleep disorders may resolve as she moves
further away from her heroin abuse, but if these problems persist
she will be prescribed nonaddicting medications to control these symptoms and placed on a more rigorous and regular exercise program in
order to produce natural endorphins that create a sense of calm and
well-being.

Behavioral Treatment and Lifestyle Adjustments

Combining the medications with counseling and therapy will give Michelle better insight and new tools to deal with the stress of her job, sexual issues, and family problems. Her week will now be scheduled to include a visit to a psychologist specializing in sexual and relationship problems, a family counseling session, and random weekly drug testing.

Couples counseling may also be incorporated to deal with the impact of her affair and the sexual confusion it has provoked on her long-term relationship.

She will see a liver specialist to deal with her hepatitis C.

Since Michelle has a good job and good medical insurance, she will choose her practitioners from the list she has been offered through her PPO.

Her primary doctor will coordinate these specialists with a weekly telephone conference to assess her progress and identify problems in her recovery.

Michelle will be required to exercise daily, get an adequate amount of sleep, and eat a balanced diet. She must also attend regular 12-step meetings.

Relationships

Michelle will need to strengthen her relationships with her family, her lovers, and her new sober community. Learning to have honest dialogues with these people will be her challenge and be guided by her therapists, her new sobriety, and her improved chemical rebalancing.

Personal and Professional Goals

Michelle is generally comfortable with her professional life, but she needs to clean up the relationships in that arena and set better professional boundaries with her co-workers. She now has the opportunity to clarify her sexual preferences and openly engage in those relationships without shame or secrets.

Starting Fresh/Reengaging with Life

Michelle now has the luxury of a support network of professionals and family that will allow her to live the life she wants.

Her mood disorder is being successfully managed with medications that address the chemical imbalance she inherited.

Her ability to live openly with her choices is a new beginning. Gaining validation from those close to her is welcome but no longer necessary for her to define and prosper on her own new journey.

Opiate–Based Painkillers

Two active ingredients form the foundation of a variety of today's most popular (and most abused) painkillers.

The first is oxycodone, an opiate analgesic with properties similar to both codeine and morphine. Its chemical formula is $C_{18}H_{21}NO_4$.

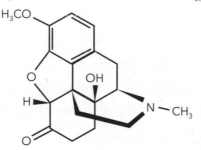

Oxycodone is the base, or foundation, of several commonly used pain medications, each of which combines it with a different substance. OxyContin and OxyIR is oxycodone mixed with an inert binder. Percocet is oxycodone combined with acetaminophen. Percodan is oxycodone and aspirin. And Combunox is oxycodone bonded with ibuprofen.

The active ingredient and basis of most other contemporary painkillers is hydrocodone, a semisynthetic opioid analgesic and cough suppressant derived from codeine and thebaine. Its chemical formula is $C_{18}H_{21}NO_3$, which differs from oxycodone only in a lesser molecular impact of its nitrogen-oxygen bond.

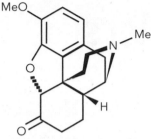

When mixed with other substances, hydrocodone is the base chemical of several pain medications. Vicodin is hydrocodone combined with paracetemol. Lortab ASA is hydrocodone bonded with aspirin. And Vicoprofen is a blend of hydrocodone and ibuprofen.

In general, oxycodone is about 30 to 50 percent stronger than hydrocodone. Largely because of that increased potency and its sustained-release mechanism (meaning it contains higher doses), OxyContin is currently the most abused pain reliever on the planet, with Vicodin and Vicoprofen vying for second place.

Also known as: For OxyContin: Cotton, 80, 40, 40-bar, hillbilly heroin, kicker, limbug, O.C., oceans, Oxy, Oxy coffin, Oxy cotton, poor man's heroin. For Vicodin and Vicoprofen: Vikes, Vikings, Watson, Watson 387. For Percodan and Percocet: Blue dynamite, Paulas, perks

Users known as: Pillheads. This moniker is applied by dealers (and some doctors); people who abuse opiate-based painkillers don't think of themselves as part of a drug community. After all, the drugs they're taking are aboveboard prescription medicines, right?

How they're sold: All the oxycodone-based and hydrocodone-based medications fall into the category of narcotic pain relievers; because they are controlled substances, they legally require a triplicate prescription from a doctor. Typically, narcotic pain relief pills are dispensed in 10-, 20-, 40-, 80-, and 160-milligram units. Given their addictive nature, they are dispensed sparingly, usually just 2 or 3 days' worth at a time.

Many addicts go from doctor to doctor complaining of extreme pain, gathering as many prescriptions as they can, often under aliases, and filling them at different pharmacies. To curb that flagrant abuse, watchdog groups like the federal Drug Enforcement Agency and state Departments of Justice have created real-time-access Internet databases (like CURES in California) that monitor narcotic prescriptions, allowing doctors, pharmacies, and law enforcement agencies to screen any patient's past and current prescriptions for controlled substances.

The illegal trade in prescription drugs is booming. Dealers often buy odd lots (from one pill to a whole bottle) from patients, off-loaders, and other insider sources. Burglaries of pharmacies directly target prescription drugs.

Knock-off pills manufactured in the black market pose a danger because they look like the real medications, down to the correct pharmaceutical brand stamped on each pill. But the knockoffs are made with no oversight or safeguards. They may be stronger or weaker than the originals. Or they could contain none of the active ingredients of the real McCoy. They may use toxic binders and fillers. In short, they're an unknown entity that can harm patients.

On the street, pain meds are sold individually or in bottles containing up to 500 pills and range from $10 to $100 per pill. Ironically, as the price of OxyContin soars, a growing number of addicts are forced into the more hard-core but more economical heroin to manage their "pain."

Brief history: Almost 6,000 years ago, opium was grown by the Egyptians, Sumerians, Babylonians, and Assyrians for its properties as a pain reliever. Then, in 1803, German chemist Friedrich Sertuemer discovered morphine. In 1843, Dr. Alexander Wood of Scotland first injected morphine into the bloodstream. In 1874, English chemist C. R. Wright synthesized heroin. Oxycodone was first synthesized in Germany in 1916. Hydrocodone was discovered in Germany 4 years later; it wasn't approved by the FDA for sale in the United States until 1943.

Vicodin was introduced to the US marketplace in 1978; the generic became available in 1983. OxyContin was released in 1996.

Usage today: In a 2006 national household survey, it was reported that 73 percent of all prescription drug abuse involved painkillers.

In 2005, 3.5 million Americans over the age of 12 admitted to nonmedical use of OxyContin, a twelvefold increase over just a single decade. Since then, it is estimated that OxyContin abuse has risen by at least 10 percent each year. In 2006, 9.7 percent of all high school seniors reported using Vicodin.

How they're taken: The prescription medications come in pill form to be taken with a glass of water: Addicts sometimes crush the pills and snort the powder nasally to get the drug absorbed into the body faster. Since these pills are also water soluble, they can be crushed into a fine grain, mixed with water, and injected. This leads to an almost instant relief of pain and also a pleasure high.

Neurotransmitters involved: Opiate-based painkillers produce endorphins and analgesics. But since they actually bind to serotonin receptors, they impede the normal release of GABA neurotransmitters, create a serotonin deficit, and increase the flow of dopamine. The result (at first) is great pleasure with an almost total absence of pain. As more painkillers flood in, the brain loses its ability to naturally produce endorphins and analgesics, so more painkillers are needed to "manufacture" them. Thus begins the cycle of addiction. Some users become addicted on the first hit; others take perhaps half a dozen doses before addiction grabs hold. But addiction always strikes sooner rather than later—usually in about 3 days.

How they work: These new opiate-based medications are medically prescribed to alleviate chronic and severe pain. They can also take the patient or addict beyond pain and into a land of inner peace and euphoria. Fear, paranoia, and hostilities drop away, leaving moods both exotic and sensual, followed by drowsiness and sleep. It's a nice feeling . . . until the crash.

Risks: An overdose of any of these painkillers can be fatal. Overdoses are usually preceded by respiratory depression, the skin turning cold and blue (from lack of oxygen), sleepiness, and widening of the pupils. Accidental death rates from prescription painkillers is now the second-leading cause of death among American teenagers. Sustained comas are also induced by overdoses.

Other potential side effects and health risks include various blood disorders, dizziness, nausea and vomiting, sweating, difficult urination, spasms and seizures, dryness of throat and mouth, hearing loss, constipation, fatigue, delirium, mood swings, rashes, depressed breathing, and allergic reactions.

Associated behaviors: Opiates deliver a laid-back high. Users exhibit calm, relaxed behavior while on the drug. But when coming down, users can experience wild mood swings (ranging from extreme agitation to almost somnambulist calm), intense sensitivity to sight and sound, delusions and/or hallucinations, heightened pain (real or imagined), and bursts of frenetic activity between long bouts of sleep.

Some positive effects: Modern painkillers pretty much accomplish their objective: They ease and erase even extreme pain, which aids the healing process in the treatment of serious diseases and surgeries. Beyond that, painkillers can take patients from pain to near euphoria, which is sometimes a good and humane use of the medication.

The medical detox: Since these painkillers are all opiate based, the medical treatment is similar in all respects to the protocol for heroin. Its goals are four-pronged.

1. Transitioning. To taper down from the potentially lethal opiate-based painkillers, the patient is given buprenorphine (Suboxone), an opiate so safe it has been approved by the FDA for use during pregnancy and by children. Buprenorphine alleviates pain and decreases cravings, but without the high that accompanies opiate abuse.

2. Addressing sleep issues. To reestablish the natural circadian rhythm, patients are given antihistamines like Vistaril and Benadryl, hypnotics like Ambien, beta-blockers like Inderal, antiseizure medications like Neurontin, and/or antipsychotic medications such as Seroquel. None of these prescriptions have addictive associations.

3. Relieving anxiety. Anxiolytics such as Librium, Klonopin, Ativan, and Xanax are given to relieve the anxiety of withdrawal. Since these benzodiazepines carry some risk of dependency, they are prescribed only for the short term—no more than a few weeks— and must be carefully monitored. Nonaddictive GABAergic meds like Neurontin also promote a calming effect by interacting with the same receptors as the benzos. Beta-blockers, originally intended to treat heart disease, produce the same soothing effect.

4. Restoring serotonin to natural level. SSRIs like Prozac, Zoloft, Lexapro, Celexa, and Paxil are prescribed to raise the low serotonin level that is the true cause of addiction to opiates. The serotonin level moves up as the opiate itself is moving down.

Stabilizing medications: The first priority in stabilizing any type of dependence on painkillers is to rebalance the low serotonin level that is the driving force of opiate addiction. Once the patient's natural sero-tonin baseline has been restored, a new and improved balance is estab-lished with a continuing program of SSRIs. SNRI medications like Pristiq, Effexor, and Cymbalta can also be prescribed when necessary, not only raising serotonin levels but also reducing noradrenalin, thereby further easing anxiety. As an added benefit, Cymbalta also relieves pain. The treatment is customized to the individual addict and whatever other medical problems he or she may have.

CASE STUDY: DANIEL, ADDICTED TO OXYCONTIN

Surrender

Daniel has a problem. His former mistress knows all about his habit—how much he uses and where he gets his stuff. Now she's threatened to go to his publisher, go public . . . do him some real damage. So between buckling under to her demands or cleaning himself up, there wasn't really any choice.

Being a high-powered newspaper exec didn't help Daniel's situation. He'd approved too many front-page scandal stories not to know he'd be a target himself. He would surrender to treatment, but only if he could keep it under wraps. Too many people would enjoy the tabloid headlines signaling his premature demise from power. He just couldn't let that happen. He'd heard about this doctor on the West Coast, sensitive to the confidentiality issue.

So a couple of thousand miles from home, he sat in the back of the limo, on his way to the doctor's office, hoping this so-called specialist wasn't just another idiot wasting his valuable time.

Medical Evaluation

INTAKE FORM

Name: <u>Daniel</u>   Age: <u>43</u>   SMDW: <u>S</u>   Sex: <u>M</u>
Occupation: <u>Newspaper executive</u>   Referred By: <u>My orthopedist</u>

Current Problems/Complaints:

I'm in a lot of pain, almost constantly, and it keeps me up at night and may even affect my work. My job is very stressful. I have more than 30 department heads reporting directly to me and scores more reporting to them. Most of them are morons or brain-dead, so the work is up to me. The pressure is enormous. I've taken Oxy for years and they helped me get through every day. But my doctor won't give me any more refills, and I've now got some personal problems with my former female co-worker, and I really need to be careful and protect myself.

Past Medical History:

❑ Childhood Illness   ❑ ADD   ❑ Trauma (Emotional/Physical)
❑ Anxiety   ❑ Depression
❑ Other _____

Medical Illnesses:

❑ Anxiety   ❑ Depression   ❑ Insomnia
❑ Chronic Pain   ❑ Hyperactivity/ADD   ☒ Bipolar
☒ OCD   ❑ Weight Changes   ❑ Stress
❑ Other <u>Back pain and migraine headaches</u>

Psychological History:

❏ Divorce in Family   ❏ Unexpected Death in Family
☒ Recent Chance in Relationship
☒ Chronic Pain   ☒ Job Stress   ❏ Sexual Issues
❏ Recent Life Changes _____

Habits:

❏ Nicotine   ☒ Alcohol <u>Socially</u> ❏ Recreational Drugs
❏ Marijuana   ❏ Metabolic/Weight Problems
Exercise: ❏ Never   ☒ Occasionally   ❏ Often
❏ Other _____

Current Medications: <u>Ambien</u> _____

Surgeries: <u>Back surgery in 2003 (a herniated disc)</u> _____

Family History:

	Living	Deceased	Health Problems
Mother	✓		Overweight, depressed, takes Prozac
Father		✓	Car accident; alcoholic
Siblings 2 sisters	✓		Both overweight; younger sister's an alcoholic

Health Problems in Your Family:

❏ Irritable/Spastic Bowel   ☒ Depression   ❏ Suicide
❏ Hyperactive/ADD   ☒ Obesity <u>Mom, sister</u>   ❏ Bipolar
☒ Headaches   ❏ Back Pain   ❏ Anxiety
❏ Heart Disease   ❏ Cancers   ❏ Diabetes
❏ Nicotine   ❏ Caffeine   ❏ Alcohol
❏ Other Drug Abuse _____

Patient Interview (from Transcript)

"I'm a top exec at a big-city newspaper, meaning there are a lot of people gunning for my job. I can't risk anyone thinking I have any sort of problem. I put in long hours and sit too much and eat irregularly—usually a sandwich at my desk. I know I don't exercise like I should. But it's a lot of pressure, especially with the morons I got working under me.

"But at least I can afford the best treatment.

"I had back surgery a few years ago, and this surgeon really butchered me. I went to physical therapy for a couple of months, but it was a waste of time. Oxy is the only thing that helps me make it through the day.

"I get migraines once in a while, and the Oxy is really good for those, too.

"My regular doctor gave me more and more pain meds for my back pain. I didn't want to write this on the intake form because, believe me, I know libel laws . . . but he's a quack—and now he's cutting me off.

"Then there's my ex-mistress. A real loose cannon, threatened to rat me out to my publisher. And she's just the type to do it. A woman scorned, eh, Doc?

"But since the bitch is making all sorts of noises and the quack won't help me with my pain anymore, I figured I might as well get off the meds.

"Sometimes when I get off work I stop at the Four Seasons bar for a couple of drinks. I fit in there—it's a better class of people. Or I go home and have a scotch or two before bed.

"I'm hoping there's maybe something else you can give me to keep me comfortable."

Physician Analysis

Daniel's intake statement and history is loaded with clues that define someone who is depressed and in serious denial.

His interview validates the denial by confessing that his ex-girlfriend was a loose cannon who would "rat him out to his boss at the newspaper" about his drug use. His narcissism is a cover for his inadequacy and his Napoleon complex fueled by his short stature and a bad toupee.

He refers to everyone around him as inferior and does not see the progressive abuse of opiates as an addiction, but merely as "necessary to control my pain."

Contrary to Daniel's comment, his doctor is not a quack but a professional with boundaries who sees an escalating problem of drug abuse. The doctor's advice to get help is viewed by Daniel as "cutting him off."

His intake form reveals a family history of depression (both parents and sister), which correlates to an imbalance of serotonin associated with alcohol abuse (father, sister, and Daniel, who admitted in his interview that he drinks almost daily) and opiate abuse (OxyContin). Daniel's genetics for this imbalance is clear: both parents and both sisters.

The stress that has aggravated his imbalance and provoked his addictive behaviors comes from his work and the recent and traumatic breakup with his girlfriend.

He is chronically stressed due to low self-esteem caused partially by his short stature and losing his hair in his late thirties. His chaotic relationship and breakup did not make him feel better about himself.

Accepted for treatment.

Medical Rehabilitation

Daniel's medical rehabilitation will initially involve his detoxification from OxyContin. He will also need to restore his sleep cycle and address the anxiety that accompanies all withdrawals. Engaging in daily exercise to generate endorphins will help soothe his glutamate imbalance, which provokes and exaggerates anxiety and agitation during withdrawal.

Medical Detox

Detoxification from OxyContin is a gradual process due to the long-acting properties of this opiate. (A long-acting opiate clings to the opiate receptor for 8 to 12 hours, which prolongs the detoxification.)

Daniel will first need to be transitioned to a shorter-acting opiate (Vicodin) for 5 to 7 days in order for the long-acting OxyContin to "unstick" from the receptors and clear out of his system. Once Daniel comes off the Vicodin, he will be transitioned to Suboxone (a form of buprenorphine), an opiate that creates neither euphoria nor cravings yet provides pain relief and offers some respite from the anxiety that will accompany detoxification. The Suboxone will be given for several weeks to a few months, with the dosage gradually tapering off, allowing Daniel to remain comfortable and compliant throughout.

Because serotonin is the underlying neurotransmitter imbalance in opiate abuses, Daniel will begin taking an SSRI to rebuild the levels of serotonin he will need to properly treat his depression (the primary disease) and thereby manage his addictive behaviors.

The sleep disorder that accompanies withdrawal will be managed with short-term, nonaddictive sleep aids, including Ambien (a hypnotic) and Vistaril (an antihistamine).

If Daniel is anxious, he will be given Neurontin (a nonaddictive medication).

Daily exercise (producing natural endorphins) will also help mute his anxiety. A balanced diet will restore the metabolic damage caused by his prolonged drug abuse.

Stabilizing the Brain Chemistry

Serotonin is the primary neurotransmitter associated with opiate abuse. Rebalancing this transmitter was initiated during Daniel's detoxification and will continue to be fine-tuned. This stabilization of his serotonin levels may take months, and he will perhaps require an SSRI (Prozac, Zoloft, Lexapro) or SNRI (Effexor, Cymbalta, Pristiq) throughout his lifetime. As he develops new tools to deal with his anxiety and back pain and gains insight into his behavioral problems, he may be able to eliminate these medications from his treatment.

Once Daniel's serotonin levels are balanced, his anxiety is likely to diminish significantly or even disappear, especially if he maintains a daily aerobic exercise program. If not, and he does experience continuing anxiety, several nonaddicting medications can solve the problem. These include the beta-blockers (Inderal) and certain antiseizure medications (Neurontin).

Restoring Daniel's sleep disorder may be as simple as rebalancing his neurotransmitters and maintaining his exercise program, but if he needs pharmacological help, there are nonaddictive alternatives like Ambien and Vistaril that can restore his circadian rhythm.

Behavioral Treatment and Lifestyle Adjustments

Once Daniel has rebalanced his brain chemistry, he will be able to address his lifestyle and behavioral issues.

Daniel's treatment team will include his supervising physician, a therapist to deal with his depression and self-esteem issues, a 12-step counselor, a nutritionist, and a trainer to coordinate his exercise program. His primary physician will oversee these specialists, and a monthly review will involve all members of the team to assess his progress and plan his continued recovery.

He will attend regular 12-step programs and submit to random drug testing by his primary doctor.

Daniel's back pain will be managed by an orthopedist and, if necessary, a pain management program to provide nonnarcotic options like epidurals, acupuncture, nonaddictive analgesics to control his symptoms, and anti-inflammatories. A physical therapy program should ease his lower back issues by strengthening his core and lumbar muscle groups to protect him from future pain problems.

He will develop a structure to his daily activities, including morning exercise, three healthy meals, and a calendar for his weekly doctor appointments.

Relationships

Daniel has few relationships left to salvage, but he will start by rebuilding his professional ties. He will be guided, through cognitive therapy, to take responsibility for his abusive behaviors and begin to make amends with those he has alienated. Through his 12-step program, he will nurture new friendships within his sober community. The members of his treatment team will also provide a nest of support for him to practice his new relationship-building tools.

Personal and Professional Goals

Daniel will see a change in his professional life through his sobriety and general health and will be able to set new career goals.

He will be assessed in his therapy for hobbies and interests that he has always fantasized about and be guided toward them.

With his new sobriety, balanced brain chemistry, and healthy life-style, Daniel will finally be in a position to develop and pursue a healthy and intimate relationship.

Starting Fresh/Reengaging with Life

The once abusive and caustic Daniel can now transform into a socially engaging man with friendships, interests, and clarity. He will still be short and bald, but his new reality-based self-esteem will enable him to set attainable goals that will define his new and satis-fying life.

CASE STUDY: HOWARD, ADDICTED TO VICODIN

Spousal Intervention

Marion drove, her eyes frozen on the road ahead. Howard sat in the passenger seat, his head consciously turned away from her, sight-lessly gazing through the window, with nothing but an arctic chill between them.

Almost by reflex, he reached into his jacket pocket, took out a vial, plucked out a pill, and popped it in his mouth.

Her eyes darted to him, then fled quickly back to the road. Her hands tightened on the steering wheel. She had to let this one go. It just wasn't worth it. He'd finally agreed to see the doctor, and she wasn't going to give him even the smallest excuse to back out. Not now, not when they were already on the way to the clinic.

Medical Evaluation

INTAKE FORM

Name: <u>Howard</u>   **Age:** <u>52</u>   **SMDW:** <u>M</u>   **Sex:** <u>M</u>
Occupation: <u>Stockbroker</u>   **Referred By:** <u>Friend (Frank)</u>

Current Problems/Complaints:

I get a lot of headaches and take prescription medications. My doctor has no problem with this so I don't know why someone *who does not have a medical license*—like my wife—should question that. If my Vicodin is taken away, I'll be in constant pain and I can't do my job. Then my wife will be the one with the headaches—no new designer clothes or new convertible. I'm here so the doctor can convince my wife that I really do need these medications. I don't feel good most of the time anyway, and taking them away would make my life a living hell.

Past Medical History:

❑ Childhood Illness   ❑ ADD   ❑ Trauma (Emotional/Physical)
❑ Anxiety   ❑ Depression
☒ Other <u>Bad acne as a teenager</u>

Medical Illnesses:

❑ Anxiety   ❑ Depression   ❑ Insomnia
☒ Chronic Pain   ❑ Hyperactivity/ADD   ❑ Bipolar
❑ OCD   ❑ Weight Changes   ☒ Stress
❑ Other _____

Psychological History:

❑ Divorce in Family   ❑ Unexpected Death in Family
❑ Recent Change in Relationship
☒ Chronic Pain   ☒ Job Stress   ❑ Sexual Issues
❑ Recent Life Changes _____

Habits:

❏ Nicotine   ☒ Alcohol <u>One or two</u>   ❏ Recreational Drugs

<u>martini when I get home</u>

☒ Marijuana   ☒ Metabolic/Weight Problems

Exercise: ☒ Never   ❏ Occasionally   ❏ Often

❏ Other _____

Current Medications: <u>Vicodin for headaches; Ambien when I can't</u>

<u>sleep</u>

Surgeries: <u>Surgery for broken wrist, age 8</u>

Family History:

	Living	Deceased	Health Problems
Mother	✓		Alcoholic
Father		✓	Alzheimer's
Siblings	✓		<u>One brother, one sister; my brother is an alcoholic</u>

Health Problems in Your Family:

❏ Irritable/Spastic Bowel   ☒ Depression <u>Grandmother</u>   ❏ Suicide

❏ Hyperactive/ADD   ❏ Obesity   ❏ Bipolar

☒ Headaches   ❏ Back Pain   ❏ Anxiety

❏ Heart Disease   ❏ Cancers   ❏ Diabetes

❏ Nicotine   ❏ Caffeine   ❏ Alcohol

❏ Other Drug Abuse_____

Patient Interview (from Transcript)

"My wife has no idea what I go through to maintain our standard of living. I'm telling you, she's constantly on my back about this. Not a moment's peace—bitch, bitch, harp, harp. I am so tired of it.

"I just need someone to straighten her out and tell her I need these prescriptions for my pain. And to stop all this stupid talk about addictions. That's all.

"It's not like I've got much time left anyway. My father died of Alzheimer's—I watched him fade away over 5 or 6 years. Saw him become just . . . I don't know . . . nothing. If memories make us who we are, then who are you—what are you—if you don't have any memories? Nothing, that's what. And that's what I saw him slowly become. I know the same thing is going to happen to me. It's an inherited disease. I've told my wife that when it happens, I don't want our kids to see me that way, remember me that way, like I do my old man. It truly scares the hell out of me . . . but there's nothing I can do.

"I'm trying to make enough to leave my wife and kids something after I'm gone. But if it were even whispered that I had any sort of problem with drugs, who would invest with me? The financial business is built around trust, especially these days. The big hitters on Wall Street, Madoff—they made it a whole lot tougher for the rest of us. Or am I supposed to start over in a new profession at my age? Maybe I should work at Starbucks just for the health insurance. God knows I'm going to need it."

Physician Analysis

Howard's is a sad story. He has myriad medical problems: He smokes, is obese and prediabetic, has sleep apnea, and has a family history of early coronary death and Alzheimer's disease. He is scared to death and feels doomed no matter what he does, so he numbs his bad feelings with opiates.

Howard feels no incentive to stop taking drugs. In fact, all he really wants me to do is talk to his wife and validate his imagined medical need for Vicodin. His own internist won't do that, and he knows it.

Rejected for treatment.

Howard is too depressed and frightened to make any life changes. However, we will offer him referrals to a pain specialist and a psychologist to deal with his headaches and depression, respectively. And he will be referred to a doctor to treat his sleep apnea and be given the name of a nutritionist to begin a weight-loss program. If he accepts treatment for all of these conditions, he will begin to feel better.

Family counseling is also recommended to help his wife understand the fears that are driving Howard's depression and bad behaviors. Hopefully, this will help her abandon the counterproductive and adversarial role she is playing and transition her into becoming his advocate.

Howard will also be encouraged to undergo a dementia PET scan, which can indicate the onset of Alzheimer's at its earliest stage. Those scans should be done every few years to identify his actual disease, if any. It will also empower him by giving him some control over managing what is now only fear of something that has not been proven.

At some point, Howard will need to be detoxified from opiates and treated with serotonergic medications (Prozac, Zoloft, Lexapro, Paxil, Celexa) for his depression. While he certainly is not ready for treatment at this time, if he accepts our recommendations, we will open our arms to help him in the future.

10

Methamphetamines

While cocaine and heroin derive from natural sources—the coca leaf and the poppy, respectively—methamphetamine, or meth, in any form is an entirely manmade formula of chemicals described as $C_{10}H_{15}N$.

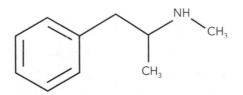

The two common types of methamphetamine are L-meth and D-meth.

L-meth is a mostly benign chemical mixture found primarily in over-the-counter products like Vick's inhalers. If used as directed, it's safe and nonaddictive, presenting few if any health risks.

D-meth is a pharmaceutical-grade prescription drug named Desoxyn used to treat ADD, narcolepsy, and obesity. A controlled substance, it is available only by prescription from a doctor.

Since it gains easy access to the brain and stimulates the central ner-

vous system, D-meth is the model for all illicit and addictive meth variations. Pharmaceutical-grade methamphetamines are manufactured in
antiseptic conditions and following safe and strict government regulations. Illicit meth is manufactured in homemade labs with an array of
toxic and explosive substances such as drain cleaner, paint thinner, anhy-
drous ammonia, muriatic acid, Freon, lithium batteries, iodine, starter
fluid, red phosphorus, ephedrine, cold medications, and a host of other
ingredients sold in hardware stores, farm supply depots, and pharmacies.

Three types of meth are available on the street.

The first and most common is white powder, manufactured by what
are called superlabs. Because of highly sophisticated equipment and
refined "cooking" methods, powder is extremely potent, with up to
90 percent purity.

Second is homemade meth cooked in trailers, motel rooms, abandoned houses, and/or any number of run-and-gun, makeshift mom-
and-pop "labs" using coffee tins or pots, empty liter-size pop bottles,
portable stove tops, and other unsanitary "equipment" to make what is
often a highly toxic product. Homemade meth is more granular and
often appears (due to additives) in brown, pink, and red hues.

The third, and most sought-after, form is crystal meth, which looks
like crystalline shards of glass that glisten like its street moniker: "ice."
Crystal is smoked and produces a faster and longer-lasting effect than
powder. It's also more addictive.

Also known as: Amps, bathtub crank, bling, chrome, cinnamon,
clear, CR, crank, Cris, Cristina, crypto, crystal, geep, get-go, glass, go-
fast, ice, jet fuel, meth, orange, P, pink, po' coke, scootie, sketch, spackle,
speed, spoosh, stove top, tick tick, Tina, twek or tweak, wash, white
cross, work, workin' man's cocaine, yellow barn.

Users known as: Battery benders, cluckers, chicken-headed clucks, cranksters or crankmeisters or crankers, doorknobbers (Nova Scotia), *fienda*, fiends, fiendz, gacked, geek(er)s, geekins, geeters, go go losers, jibbheads, jibby bears, jubbies, Kristas, lokers, neck creatures, shadow people, sketchpads or sketchers, skitzers, sketch monsters, speed freaks, spin doctors, spinsters, tweakers, wiggers.

How it's sold: Street meth is usually sold in sizes from small quarter-gram packets to larger eight-balls (3½ grams, or ⅛ ounce). Beginners buy a ¼- or ½-gram packet, while longtime addicts go for whole grams or eight-balls. Street dealers usually buy ounces in bulk directly from distributors.

Generally speaking, ¼ gram costs about $20, ½ gram about $40, a full gram from $60 to $80, and an eight-ball from $160 to $200. Long-term addicts normally need an eight-ball every couple of days.

Brief history: In 1885, Japanese organic chemist and pharmacologist Nagai Nagayoshi isolated the chemical ephedrine from the plant *Ephedra vulgaris*. Eight years later, he synthesized methamphetamine from ephedrine. In 1919, Akira Ogata created the first crystallized form of meth.

In 1938, pharmaceutical giant Smith, Kline and French marketed an inhalant for congestion under the name Benzedrine. That same year, the German drug company Temmler patented meth in a tablet form called Pervitin. A huge public success, it soon came to the attention of Nazi leaders as a means of keeping soldiers and pilots alert and at attention, able to fight their enemies for days on end. One internal report even claimed that Pervitin was "a power drug that diminishes human empathy."

At first, Pervitin was distributed liberally to SS storm troopers, pilots, and regular army. In one 3-month period in mid-1940, over 35 million tablets of Pervitin were shipped to Nazi soldiers. Later, Pervitin was laced in chocolate bars for soldiers. And from 1942, Adolf Hitler was given daily injections of meth as a treatment for depression and fatigue. EvenJapan handed out meth to soldiers during World War II.

The US military has used meth in every war since WWII. American soldiers took more meth during the Vietnam War than did all military personnel on all sides of WWII.

In the 1950s and '60s, over-the-counter Dexedrine and Methedrine became popular with truckers, college students, and people seeking increased athletic or sexual performance.

After the US government criminalized meth in 1970 for all but a few medical purposes, the illicit manufacture and use of meth gained steam throughout the 1980s as blue-collar meth use exploded. In the late '80s, Mexico became the leading source of US meth. While federal drug agents focused on coke and heroin in the government's heralded War on Drugs, meth arguably became the most abused drug in the country.

Meth abuse increased every year in the 1990s. In this new century, meth use has reached epidemic proportions. Many law enforcement and medical experts consider it the most dangerous and lethal drug on the street.

Usage today: According to 2005 federal estimates, more than 12 million Americans had used methamphetamines at least once. In 2006, the National Survey on Drug Use and Health upped the figure to 5.7 percent of all Americans over age 12 (or about 14 million). At any given time, about 1.5 million Americans are abusing meth.

How it's taken: Meth powder is the all-purpose form of the drug: It can be smoked from foil or a pipe, snorted (inhaled), or injected (in a solution of water) via a hypodermic needle. It can be ingested mixed into a liquid (or something like salad dressing) or scooped into gelatin tablets (obtained at drugstores).

Most meth addicts start by snorting a BB-size amount. If it takes hold in under 5 minutes, it's good stuff and should be handled with care. If 5 minutes passes and the high is not sufficient, the tweakers dole out good-size lines. The high lasts from 4 to 15 hours.

From many addicts' perspectives, smoking from a pipe delivers the most bang for the buck. The high comes on in 10 to 15 seconds but lasts only 4 to 8 hours.

Intravenous injection delivers the most dangerous, fastest-acting, and shortest high, usually lasting only 1 to 4 hours. The crash from an IV injection can be hell on earth, leading addicts to "slam" more meth before a crash can occur. The high from muscling an injection can last from 10 to 30 hours.

Crystal meth shards can be smoked whole or cut into smaller pieces. Crystal can also be ground and taken just like powder, albeit a lot stronger, with rushes coming faster and lasting longer . . . and crashes that are more devastating.

Homemade meth is the choice of smokers, but it can also be ground to powder for snorting, injecting, or ingesting. Any form of meth can be liquefied and absorbed through the anus, resulting in a localized rush similar to snorting.

Neurotransmitters involved: Meth is a stimulant that acts on the reward center in the brain by releasing dopamine, creating sensations of euphoria and excitement.

Meth also releases noradrenalin, the neurotransmitter that regulates alertness and sleep cycles. At the same time, it blocks the reabsorption of epinephrine, causing the brain to race full speed ahead. To complicate matters further, meth suppresses serotonin, triggering anxiety, depression, paranoia, aggressive or violent behavior, bad judgment, and more chemical abuse.

How it works: Meth can make anyone feel like Superman or Wonder Woman. It's a brief chemical illusion, but one so powerful that it easily passes for reality in the diminished mind-set of the user. Euphoria, excitement, increased attention and energy, the ability to stay awake, loss of appetite, and heightened sexual drive—these are the attractions of a meth high.

Risks: There are perhaps more serious downsides to meth than any other abused substance. High blood pressure and damage to the heart and vascular system often result in heart attacks and strokes. When meth is smoked, its toxic ingredients can cause emphysema and lung cancer. The same toxic ingredients can bring about irreparable liver damage. The systematic breakdown of muscles brings on life-threatening kidney damage. Addictive use of meth increases the body's normal temperature, which can lead to death from hyperthermia. Snorting meth wreaks havoc with the nasal passages and can erode the septum (the partition between the nasal passages).

People who inject meth may develop collapsed veins and pneumonia and increase their exposure to HIV/AIDS, tuberculosis, and hepatitis C.

Meth is flammable. It's estimated that anywhere from a quarter to a third of all critical burn center cases across the country are meth-related injuries caused by cooking or smoking explosions.

Other meth risks include: constant diarrhea and nausea that almost always strike within a week of steady meth use; unhealthy weight loss;

rampant insomnia (users often stay awake for days at a time); open sores from picking at imaginary crawling insects (Morgellons disease or syndrome); excessive sweating; and facial tremors or tics.

Dental hygiene suffers to the point of rotting and missing teeth. Dentists are often the first to spot and diagnose what's called meth mouth. Meth dries out the salivary gland, resulting in a limited ability to resist bacteria . . . and tooth decay sets in. Lack of saliva equates to dryness, so users drink an overabundance of sugary sodas. Meth also causes jaw clenching and grinding of teeth so severe that the teeth break. And as meth decreases blood flow to the mouth, the gums eventually erode and teeth fall out.

Ironically, even as meth is often used for supercharged sex, it eventually renders many users impotent.

Meth can literally drive you crazy, starting with all-around poor judgment and leading to anxiety, extreme paranoia, aggression or violence, and finally to toxic psychosis. After long-term exposure to meth, the brain loses its ability to produce serotonin, and lifelong clinical depression often occurs. Of all the abused substances, meth is the most toxic to the prefrontal cortex of the brain. This can cause irreversible, sometimes catastrophic damage to judgment, memory, cognition, intelligence, creativity, skills, and performance.

Once their reward centers are activated to a certain threshold, meth addicts as a group also have a significantly impaired ability to control their cravings . . . and so the cycle of addiction deepens.

Associated behaviors: Appetites vanish, as do fatigue and sleep. A feeling of near invincibility sets in. Meth is the drug of choice for staying alert and awake, from driving eighteen-wheelers coast-to-coast to cramming for an exam to dancing at an all-night rave. Initial usage usually occurs from the simple desire to stay up all night in a highly energized or attentive state.

Some take meth to lose weight after all diets have failed, arguing that such use is acceptable or at least safer than obesity. (Skeptics refer to this no-nutrition plan as the Jenny Crank diet.)

Some positive effects: Medically supervised pharmaceutical meth can help in the treatment of narcolepsy, ADHD, and obesity. For these purposes it is sold in the United States as Desoxyn, in 5- and 10-milligram tablets, taken orally.

Some members of the military have been known to use meth to combat "cockpit fatigue" (from flying long missions or flying at night). Yet military-issue "go pills" come with the same side effects as all-meth products, including bad judgment. (The military also issues "no-go pills," usually a form of Flexiril, a muscle relaxer, to bring pilots down gently.)

The medical detox: Meth is a stimulant, so the protocol for its medical detox mirrors that of cocaine. Anxiolytics like Klonopin, Ativan, Valium, and other antianxiety benzos are used to reduce agitation and promote calm while the natural dopamine and GABA balances are restored. Specific drugs, like Neurontin and Lyrica, stimulate GABA to help restore calm and, unlike the benzos, don't produce dependency.

Seroquel, a nonaddictive atypical antipsychotic medication, is frequently administered to help soothe the withdrawal in extreme cases.

Moderate exercise, which produces endorphins, also helps by creating and improving dopamine balances in the brain.

Stabilizing medications: To create a new baseline balance for meth patients with a naturally mild dopamine imbalance, like ADD, medications such as Adderall, Ritalin, Dexedrine, Concerta, Metadate, Focalin, Strattera, Provigil, and Vyvanse similarly reduce both anxiety and agitation by reducing excess dopamine levels in the brain.

More extreme dopamine imbalances like bipolar disorders are treated with prescriptions like Zyprexa, Seroquel, lithium, Risperdal, Abilify, Lamictal, and Geodon.

CASE STUDY: DIEGO, ADDICTED TO METHAMPHETAMINES

Intervention

By gathering information on the Internet and conferring with the family doctor, Diego's older sister Angelica arranged a family intervention. After discussing and agreeing to the rules of engagement with her parents, Angelica asked her mother to invite Diego to the house for a family dinner. Diego was half an hour late. During their meal, Diego was sullen and uncommunicative. After dinner, they convened to the small living room. Almost immediately, the parish priest and family doctor arrived and the intervention began.

Within half an hour, Diego agreed to begin treatment the next morning. The doctor gave him an addiction intake form to fill out and hand in on arrival the next morning at his office.

Medical Evaluation

Diego was driven by his mother and arrived on time at the doctor's clinic. After submitting his intake papers, he was given a full physical exam, including laboratory tests.

INTAKE FORM

Name: <u>Diego</u>　　　　Age: <u>24</u>　　　　SMDW: <u>S</u>　　　　Sex: <u>M</u>
Occupation: <u>Mechanic</u>　　Referred By: <u>Family intervention</u>

Current Problems/Complaints:

<u>I have been back from Iraq for 8 months and working in my dad's shop. In Iraq,</u>
<u>the Army said I had PTSD because of my nightmares. I don't do a good job in my</u>
<u>dad's shop because I have a hard time concentrating. In Iraq I had the respect of</u>
<u>my CO and felt good about myself, but everything changed when I got home. I</u>
<u>had trouble sleeping, more flashbacks, and didn't fit in anywhere. A friend from</u>
<u>high school gave me some crystal and it made me feel better. My dad cut me some</u>
<u>slack for a while but then got so fed up with me coming in late all the time and not</u>
<u>getting much done. I kept using meth because it was the only thing that made me</u>
<u>feel okay. But I was never hungry and started losing weight and didn't want to see</u>
<u>anyone, especially my family. My flashbacks got worse and I felt screwed and</u>
<u>angry all the time. The only thing that helped was the meth.</u>

Past Medical History:

❑ Childhood Illness　☒ ADD　　❑ Trauma (Emotional/Physical)
❑ Anxiety　　❑ Depression
☒ Other　<u>Had trouble paying attention in school</u>

Medical Illnesses:

☒ Anxiety　　　　☒ Depression　　　　❑ Insomnia
❑ Chronic Pain　　❑ Hyperactivity/ADD　❑ Bipolar
❑ OCD　　　　　☒ Weight Changes <u>Lost 30 pounds</u>　❑ Stress
☒ Other　<u>Racing heartbeat, sweating, headaches, memory loss, PTSD</u>

Psychological History:

❏ Divorce in Family   ❏ Unexpected Death in Family
☒ Recent Change in Relationship
❏ Chronic Pain   ☒ Job Stress   ❏ Sexual Issues
☒ Recent Life Changes <u>I just finished a tour in Iraq. My family is mad at me</u>
<u>and each other. I went from being a soldier to being a nobody.</u>

Habits:

☒ Nicotine   ☒ Alcohol   ☒ Recreational Drugs
❏ Marijuana   ❏ Metabolic/Weight Problems
Exercise: ❏ Never   ☒ Occasionally   ❏ Often
☒ Other <u>Meth and a few beers to take the edge off</u>

Current Medications: <u>I tried sleeping pills but they didn't work. The Army</u>
<u>doctor gave me Xanax for my PTSD. It helped a little.</u>

Surgeries: <u>Tonsils when I was a kid</u>

Family History:

	Living	Deceased	Health Problems
Mother	✓		
Father	✓		Smokes too much
Siblings sister	✓		One brother, 16, has ADD
Uncle			My mom's brother is crazy·and has been in and out of jail.

Health Problems in Your Family:

❏ Irritable/Spastic Bowel   ❏ Depression   ❏ Suicide
❏ Hyperactive/ADD   ❏ Obesity   ☒ Bipolar <u>My uncle maybe</u>
❏ Headaches   ❏ Back Pain   ❏ Anxiety
❏ Heart Disease   ❏ Cancers   ❏ Diabetes
❏ Nicotine   ❏ Caffeine   ❏ Alcohol
☒ Other Drug Abuse<u> My uncle had a cocaine problem.</u>

Patient Interview (from Transcript)

"When I went to Iraq, I thought it was the right thing to do. You know, noble and patriotic. I volunteered with a couple of friends of mine. One of them was killed by an IED—I saw him explode, man. All his body parts flying around. The other got hit in the head real bad. He'll never be himself again.

"It pissed me off, my friends and others getting killed and injured. I couldn't see no reason for it. After 9/11, I'm in all the way. But the Iraqis didn't attack us. Hell, far as I know, they never even threatened to attack us. We were lied to . . . and me and my friends bought their bill of goods. So I went there and saw these innocent people dying horrible deaths all around me and I said to myself: *What for?*

"But you had to do what you had to do to stay alive, you know what I mean? It was, like, totally FUBAR. I'm still here, I'm alive . . . but what I had to do—sometimes I wonder if it was worth it.

"My parents—they're very religious. Catholics. I used to be, but not no more. Anyway, my folks said it seemed like I left my soul in Baghdad. They're probably right. I try not to feel nothing no more.

"Everybody over there was doing something—smack, the white lady, something. I started snorting meth. Whenever I got pissed off or scared—and that was a lot—the meth made me feel better.

"When I came back home, I kept using meth whenever I got stressed, you know. A week, a month later, I kept getting more and more stressed and I couldn't figure why. I shot the meth and it made everything okay. Well, not okay, but you know how it is.

"Eventually, I stopped going to work, stopped hanging out with friends, even stopped combing my hair and brushing my teeth. I mean, what's the use?

"I stopped everything except the meth.

"My mom and dad and my sister finally did an intervention. I couldn't come here on my own. I know I'm breaking their hearts, and I want to get well, be the person they want me to be, the person I was before I left. But I just can't get myself to care about anything anymore."

Physician Analysis

Several clues in Diego's intake explain his addiction to methamphetamines. By his own admission, Diego has a history of problems concentrating in school, indicating a probable ADD diagnosis in addition to his post-traumatic stress disorder (PTSD) from his military experience. His use of methamphetamines is consistent with these diagnoses, as these stimulants tend to calm the agitated brain created by a surplus of the neurotransmitter dopamine. His sleep disorder, weight loss, and severe anxiety are also characteristic of his neurotransmitter imbalance. His examination and blood testing failed to demonstrate a hormonal (hyperthyroid) or metabolic basis (sugar imbalance) for his symptoms, giving more weight to the diagnosis of an imbalanced brain chemistry (excess dopamine).

Diego's lab evaluation did produce one surprise, however: a positive HIV testing. On further questioning, Diego admitted that he had unprotected sex on several occasions when he was "high" but did not admit this initially because he was embarrassed to discuss his sexual behaviors.

Although Diego had been given sleeping pills and Xanax, they were not effective in controlling all of his behaviors because these medications address only the noradrenalin neurotransmitter system, which is not Diego's primary chemical imbalance. The genetic basis of his problem is alluded to by his uncle's history of cocaine abuse and possible bipolar disorder. ("He's crazy and has been in and out of jail.") The stress that provoked his downfall and aggravated the dopamine imbalance was due to his PTSD from the military experience and his inability to assimilate back into life at home.

It was clear that Diego had not only a willingness to change but also a supportive and loving family to ensure his success.

Accepted for treatment.

Medical Rehabilitation

Diego's medical rehabilitation will initially involve detoxification from methamphetamines, establishing a normal circadian rhythm by ensuring adequate sleep and daily exercise, creating a balanced nutritional program to restore his normal weight, and allowing him to break the cycle of his bad behavior chasing his bad feelings.

Medical Detox

Detoxification from methamphetamines (and other stimulants like cocaine) involves treating the neurotransmitter imbalances of dopamine.

The acute change in the dopamine levels caused by withdrawal sparks a sudden release of glutamate that creates discomfort and unpleasant feelings, most often characterized by agitation and sleep deprivation. Medications that block the glutamate receptor and will make Diego more comfortable include the benzodiazepines (Xanax, Klonopin, and Ativan) and the GABAergics (Neurontin and Lyrica). Since benzos can create dependency and withdrawal problems, they must be considered only for short-term use. The GABAergics, on the other hand, have no dangerous side effects or potential addictive predispositions and can be safely prescribed beyond the detoxification to treat anxiety.

Restoring sleep deprivation that accompanies stimulant detoxification can be accomplished by the use of Ambien (a nonaddictive hypnotic), Vistaril (an antihistamine like Benadryl), or short-term benzodiazepines (Ativan). The safe and effective GABAergics (like Neurontin and Lyrica) can also be prescribed. These medications may be needed for a few weeks or several months, depending on the underlying (and inherited) sleep problems.

Stabilizing the Brain Chemistry

Once the methamphetamine detoxification is complete and the circadian rhythm is reestablished, we can move toward stabilizing the imbalanced brain chemistry.

Dopamine imbalances are the driving force for stimulant addiction, and longer-term stabilizing treatment involves addressing these neurotranmitters with medications like Ritalin, Adderall, Dexedrine, Focalin, Concerta, Provigil, and Wellbutrin. Selecting the appropriate medication will depend upon the severity of the dopamine imbalance, individual compliance, and the side effects and efficiency of the specific drugs (some simply work better than others in different patients).

If his sleep issues do not resolve after his return to a scheduled lifestyle that incorporates daily exercise, a balanced diet, and cognitive therapy, we will consider adding a nonaddicting sleep product like melatonin, Benadryl, or one of the homeopathics (valerian or kava-kava).

In view of his HIV, Diego will simultaneously be referred to an infectious disease doctor to consider antiviral treatment.

Behavioral Treatment and Lifestyle Adjustments

Diego will now need to address his behavioral and lifestyle issues.

Diego's treatment team will include a nutritionist, a personal and family counselor, a vocational counselor, a consultation from a neuro-pharmacologist, and an infectious disease specialist—all supervised by his coordinating doctor. He will be introduced to a 12-step program, assigned a sponsor, and receive random weekly drug testing. The latter validates his compliance to the treatment team and allows him an objective way to feel good about his progress.

Because Diego is a veteran, he will access the Veterans Health Administration for most of these support services. If he cannot get the appropriate help from the VA, he will be given a list of state and local programs that can fill in the blanks.

He will need to develop a structured pattern to his day—exercising in the morning, eating three balanced meals, submitting to daily drug testing, and participating in a 12-step program. He will be required to incorporate follow-up visits with his psychologist, supervising doctor, family therapist, and infectious disease specialist into his regular schedule.

His PTSD must be addressed if Diego is to succeed in his recovery. Cognitive behavior therapy, a technique developed in the past several years, has shown great promise in treating this complicated disorder.

A monthly team meeting will assess his progress and redefine his treatment goals. (The frequency of these assessments will change according to his compliance.) He will be given vocational counseling during this period.

Relationships

Rebuilding Diego's fractured relationships will require family therapy. He will be encouraged to seek out his childhood relationships and military friendships that were a source of support, and he will be counseled on avoiding people who could drive him back into his addictive behaviors.

In view of his underlying HIV, he will be counseled by his doctors on safe and healthy sexual relationships.

Diego will be encouraged to look for support from the new relationships with veterans who can share his unique experience from serving in Iraq.

Personal and Professional Goals

Diego wants to get out of his dad's garage, where he is living both literally and figuratively. To accomplish that, he needs to redefine his life goals by meeting with his vocational counselor to explore his options. During his initial interview, he said that he always liked to draw and constantly read comic books during his childhood and in Iraq. He will be encouraged to take art classes, visit modern and folk art museums, and visit comic book conventions, all with an eye to finding an avenue to pursue his love of art and cartoons.

Starting Fresh/Reengaging with Life

Diego now emerges as a new and better version of himself. He begins a life of sobriety and clarity.

- He will continue to be treated with medications that will allow him to focus and function better in his life and family.

- He will be given the opportunity to mend the broken relationships with his mom, dad, and his sister.
- He will become responsible for his health and get treatment for his HIV, which is now considered a treatable illness.
- He will aim for a more satisfying professional life that could involve something to do with his art and love of comics.
- He will learn to understand the impact of his PTSD and develop tools to intervene with the trauma it has imposed on his life.
- He will develop a very comforting and loving nest of support from professionals and family members to cushion him if he falls back into bad behaviors.

Diego is no longer a victim of his neurochemical dopamine imbalance. His prognosis for a healthy and productive life is excellent.

The Benzos/ 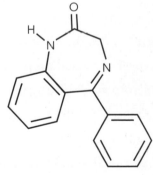 Noradrenalin Imbalance

11

Valium, Ativan, Xanax, and Librium are just four of more than 15 brand-name medications derived from one substance—benzodiazepine. Commonly called benzos, these drugs serve mainly as tranquilizers to relieve anxiety, but they are also widely used as muscle relaxers and sedatives.

The chemical composition of benzodiazepine is $C_{15}H_{12}N_2O$.

Valium is the gold standard of benzos and is listed as a core medicine by the World Health Organization.

Also known as: For Valium: V, valleys, vitamin V. For Rohypnol: Date-rape drug, forget-me pill, La Roche, Mexican Valium, rib, roach, roofenol, roofies, rope, rophies, R2, ruffies. For all benzos: Blue heavens, Blues, candy, diazepams, dolls (as in *The Valley of the Dolls*), downers, downies, drowsy highs, drunk pills, idiot pills, nerve pills, no worries, sleeping pills, stoppers, stumblers, tranks, tranquilizers, yellows, z-bars

Users known as: Bashed, blitzed, bobs (from *discombobulated*), hammered, loaded, skunked, stiffs, trashed, toasted, totaled, tuned-out, wasted, wiped out

How it's sold: In pharmacies and on the street, benzos are sold almost exclusively in pill form.

In pharmacies, most benzos are relatively inexpensive: a dime to a quarter per pill. On the street, they start at about a dollar a pill and are often sold in bottles of 50 to 100 that have been stolen from legitimate sources.

Like most other drugs with a profitable street value, counterfeit benzos that look nearly identical to the real medications are manufactured in large quantities and distributed throughout the world. Sometimes these bogus pills contain the same ingredients as the real ones. Sometimes not.

Brief history: Throughout the first half of the 20th century, barbiturates were the most widely used sedatives, even as their sometimes harsh side effects motivated researchers to find a safer class of tranquilizers.

In the 1930s, while working for Hoffman-LaRoche, Leo Sternback discovered benzodiazepine. It took 20 more years for the company to produce a viable pharmaceutical from the compound. That was Librium, introduced in 1957. Another version of benzodiazepine, this one called Valium, was marketed in 1963.

During the 1950s, three versions of meprobamate—Miltown, Equanil, and Meprospan—were the most widely prescribed tranquilizers. But benzos were so effective that by the mid-60s, Librium and Valium were the two best-selling drugs in the entire world.

As barbiturate usage declined steadily year after year, the future belonged to benzos. In the next decades, more than a dozen varieties of benzodiazepines—medications such as Ativan, Xanax, Dalmane, Doral,

Klonopin, Halcion, and Serax—were developed and found wide global acceptance.

Usage today: According to the American Psychiatric Association, up to 15 percent of adults (32 million people) take a benzo one or more times a year. Up to 2 percent (5 million adult Americans) take benzos daily. It is estimated that 6 to 8 percent of all high school seniors take some form of benzos.

How it's taken: As pills ranging from 2.5 to 30 milligrams, benzos are swallowed orally and their effects felt within 30 minutes. They should be taken with water—not with citrus juice and absolutely never with alcohol.

To induce a good night's rest, the most common dosages are 5 mg and 10 mg. For chronic sleep disorders, up to 30 mg at bedtime could be indicated, but their use should then be carefully monitored because of drug dependency issues. For recurring anxiety, 2 to 10 milligrams two to four times a day is commonly prescribed.

Benzos can also be dissolved under the tongue for faster and, some say, stronger relief.

As a seizure medication, benzos are normally injected. This liquid form takes effect in about 5 minutes.

To reduce preoperative surgical anxiety, a benzo can be administrated through an IV drip.

Neurotransmitters involved: An excessive level of the neurotransmitter glutamate causes anxiety and agitation. To counterbalance that distress, benzos increase activity in GABA, the neurotransmitter responsible for calming.

How it works: Benzos are one class in a category of medications called central nervous system depressants. By raising GABA levels, they slow (or depress) the central nervous system, which in turn decelerates brain activity. A tranquilizing effect—drowsiness and/or calm—results.

Certain benzos like Valium also impact the limbic system, which affects behavior, memory, and emotions.

Risks: Partly because they work so well and partly because they are relatively easy to obtain, the most common risk associated with benzos is addiction. It's a simple equation: Long-term use of benzos leads to higher tolerance and the need for increased dosage.

Some testing has shown a higher chance of birth defects if benzos, particularly Librium and Valium, are taken during pregnancy.

Overdoses on benzos are rare when they are taken alone. But add to them any other substance, especially another central nervous system depressant like alcohol, and the results can be deadly.

Associated behaviors: If taken as prescribed, benzos lead to calmer, more relaxed states. But if abused or taken with other medications, benzos can trigger uncharacteristic behavior, dizziness, memory loss and confusion, slurred speech, shaking hands, depression, drowsiness, and/or hallucinations.

In rare instances, irritability, aggression, hostility, and impulsive actions may stem from long-term use, causing unjustified or severe rage, violence, and other antisocial behaviors. These side effects are more likely to occur in children and in adults over age 50.

Some positive effects: Benzos are effective in treating general anxiety, agitation, and panic attacks. Dentists often prescribe one or another benzo (usually Xanax) to relax patients before oral surgery. Indeed, benzos are appropriate for initiating colonoscopies and other invasive medical procedures that would otherwise set the patient on edge.

Used as sedatives, benzos are helpful in treating myriad sleep disorders.

Benzos are effective in treating seizures, spastic disorders, and acute types of muscle spasm associated with cerebral palsy and multiple scle-rosis. Their antispasmodic properties also guarantee their success as simple muscle relaxers.

Benzos are frequently used in treating PTSD (post-traumatic stress disorder), social phobias, and obsessive disorders.

They are employed to successfully calm withdrawal symptoms in addiction treatment, allowing for safer and more comfortable detoxes.

The medical detox: Benzos pose a special problem for detoxifica-tion. If they are abruptly withdrawn after long-term use, the conse-quences can be especially harsh—the most common problem being seizures. Ironically, the symptoms of anxiety and agitation that sparked the need for benzos are the same hallmarks of their withdrawal, only more so. This is due to a rebound effect that involves an exaggerated release of noradrenalin and glutamate into the brain. One of two approaches is necessary to keep patients compliant.

1. The simplest and most frequently used method is to gradually reduce, or taper down, the dosage of these medications. Depending on the level of dependency, this can take months to accomplish. (The withdrawal reduces the daily benzo dosage by 25 percent every 2 weeks.)

2. The second method protects the brain from the profound rebound of glutamate and noradrenlin that occurs as soon as these meds are abruptly withdrawn by introducing a long-acting benzo called phenobarbital. Large doses are initially administered and then tapered down over a shorter period of time—a few weeks—to ensure the patient's comfort and safety during withdrawal. It is critical to carefully monitor vital signs during this treatment.

Daily exercise and restoration of the patient's normal sleep cycle are also essential during the initial detoxification from benzos.

Stabilizing medications: Once the benzos are distilled out of the system, the patient's intrinsic anxiety disorder must be identified. The specific anxiety disorders that provoke the use of benzos can be broken into three types: primary anxiety, situational anxiety, and anxiety associated with depression and/or obsessive/compulsive disorders. The treatment varies with all three.

1. Primary anxiety disorders respond to anxiolytics like Neurontin, Buspar, and beta-blockers, all of them nonaddicting.

2. Instead of depending upon long-term medication, patients with situational anxiety respond best by proactively dealing with the situational issues at hand. In this instance, professional counseling is vital. So is getting endorphin-producing exercise, normalizing sleep patterns, and restoring general wellness to ensure a clear head and the ability to negotiate the choppy waters of everyday life.

3. In the depressed or obsessive benzo addict, serotonin replacement is the bull's-eye of treatment and can be accomplished through a prescriptive regimen of SSRIs or SNRIs.

All anxiety treatments need to incorporate daily cardiovascular exercise, which releases endorphins that neutralize those noradrenalin and glutamate receptors that would otherwise create or exacerbate anxiety.

Restoring the patient's circadian rhythm and REM sleep eliminates another cause of anxiety. This can be accomplished by a variety of nonaddicting medications like melatonin, tryptophan, Ambien, trazodone, Seroquel, Neurontin, or Vistaril.

Stress management counseling is beneficial, as it teaches anxiety-prone patients how to identify and prepare for stressors by creating new behavioral tools and techniques. Since stress is inevitable, learning how to cope with minimum anxiety is essential for all of us. Especially as stress is the catalyst for all addictive behaviors, managing it is fundamental to any recovery program.

CASE STUDY: SANDRA, ADDICTED TO BENZOS

Intervention

Easing down the canyon road, Sandra was in a foul mood. Court-ordered rehab was a condition before sentencing. She still couldn't believe it. It wasn't like she'd been falling down drunk. It was all a silly mistake—just like the first time. And they were treating her like a common criminal.

Now she'd miss the Rothman party and the opening night of Placido's new opera. What would her friends think? "Did you hear about poor Sandra?" Stubbing her cigarette out and lighting another, she wondered if any of them would defend her. Probably not.

That selfish bastard of a husband wouldn't even drive her here. Something about an early morning client conference. Who did he think he was kidding? She knew what he was up to.

She'd show that two-timing lowlife. When she got out, she'd remake herself. Get a little work done here and there, nip and tuck. Maybe find a young stud—two could play that game.

And she'd do it, too. If only she were up to it. Right now, she just felt so . . . overwhelmed. By everything. All she really wanted was to cry.

Medical Evaluation

INTAKE FORM

Name: <u>Sandra</u>　　　Age: <u>38</u>　　SMDW: <u>M</u>　　Sex: <u>F</u>
Occupation: <u>Fund-raiser</u>　Referred By: <u>Court</u>

Current Problems/Complaints:

I'm being forced into rehab because I got a second DUI, and I only had two
drinks. Really! I thought the cop pulled me over just to check out my new breasts.
Or maybe my new Bentley—it's a convertible. You never know with cops. My
husband is a successful lawyer and even he couldn't get me out of this. As if he
even tried.

　I swear I don't have a drinking problem. Maybe I take more Valium than I
should, but my doctor gives that to me so I can calm down. I'm so stressed.
The pills probably made my blood alcohol level go up. I'm going to Paris in 2
weeks, so we'll have to work the rehab around that.

Past Medical History:

❑ Childhood Illness　❑ ADD　　☒ Trauma (Emotional/Physical)
☒ Anxiety <u>nervous</u>　❑ Depression
☒ Other　<u>Mother very nervous and never available—always on Valium</u>　and
<u>Librium</u>

Medical Illnesses:

☒ Anxiety　　　　❑ Depression　　　　☒ Insomnia
❑ Chronic Pain　　❑ Hyperactivity/ADD　❑ Bipolar
❑ OCD　　　　　❑ Weight Changes　　☒ Stress
❑ Other <u>Spastic bowel—mostly constipated; migraines</u>

Psychological History:

❏ Divorce in Family   ❏ Unexpected Death in Family
☒ Recent Change in Relationship
❏ Chronic Pain   ❏ Job Stress   ❏ Sexual Issues
☒ Recent Life Changes My husband is a cheater and comes home very late, leaving me to take care of the house and kids.

Habits:

☒ Nicotine   ☒ Alcohol Wine with dinner   ❏ Recreational Drugs
❏ Marijuana   ☒ Metabolic/Weight Problems I have trouble keeping my weight down.

Exercise: ❏ Never   ❏ Occasionally   ❏ Often
❏ Other Coffee in the morning and Diet Coke during the day (about six a day)

Current Medications: Xanax, Ativan, Ambien

Surgeries: Nose job at age 16, breast implants after my second child; liposuction in 2007

Family History:

	Living	Deceased	Health Problems
Mother	✓		Nervous condition, smoker
Father	✓		Overweight
Siblings	✓		Two sisters, both smokers; one is anorexic

Health Problems in Your Family:

☒ Irritable/Spastic Bowel   ❏ Depression   ❏ Suicide
❏ Hyperactive/ADD   ☒ Obesity   ❏ Bipolar
☒ Headaches   ❏ Back Pain   ☒ Anxiety
❏ Heart Disease   ❏ Cancers   ❏ Diabetes
☒ Nicotine   ❏ Caffeine   ❏ Alcohol
❏ Other Drug Abuse

Patient Interview (from Transcript)

"You want to hear something funny? My husband—he's the alcoholic . . . and I'm the one who gets sent here. Can you believe it? And he's never home—he's either working or with some bimbo. A younger model.

"It's not like I don't try. I'm 38, but everybody thinks I'm 5 or 6 years younger. I got the mandatory boob job. What's wrong with getting a little help?

"If it weren't for Helena, our nanny, I couldn't manage. She cooks, cleans, and watches the kids—takes them to and picks them up from school and helps with their homework. I always try to be home to tuck them in at night, but when I can't, Helena's there. Both my kids, they really love Helena . . . and, frankly, she's better with them than I am.

"My kids are always on me about smoking or whatever. I do chain-smoke, I admit it, but they don't understand the constant stress of my life. What do kids know about pressure?

"But getting back to my husband. He's the one who should be here getting treatment, not me—the rotten scumbag."

Physician Analysis

Sandra is a difficult woman to analyze, even for the trained addiction specialist. Her story is filled with lies and partial truths, and her sense of entitlement makes you dislike her from the instant you meet her. (In dealing with addicts, it is often difficult to warm up to them initially, especially those whose lifestyles and morality seem to come out of left field and without boundaries.)

When confronted with a difficult case history (and historian), it's important for the doctor to integrate the information from both the intake form and the patient interview. The former is often missing vital details that body language and targeted questioning cannot hide. At a certain point in the interview, most people will unconsciously reveal their truths without wanting to or even knowing it.

Sandra is a 38-year-old woman who spends her days popping pills (benzos) and smoking two packs of cigarettes to get through her life.

She is married to a philandering husband (a wealthy but disreputable lawyer) and has two children, ages 5 and 7, who were never mentioned in her initial statement. Her parenting reflects this lack of involvement. She relies on a nanny to raise her kids and spends most of her day shopping, lunching with friends, and trying to "keep up with the Joneses."

She has had numerous cosmetic surgeries—collagen lips, liposuction, and breast enhancement—while only admitting to the latter.

Sandra is very thin and appears to have an eating disorder.

Since anything and everything "overwhelms" her, she takes 30 to 40 milligrams of Valium a day to relieve her anxiety, with the occasional Xanax to combat panic attacks. (It is guaranteed that in the first encounter, every addict will understate drug intake by at least a third.)

She is furious about her husband's infidelity but won't or can't leave because he brings home a nice paycheck, which she transforms into material things as fast as she can. She wears designer clothes, mentions her Bentley several times during the interview, and complains that the first-class cabin in United has "shitty" champagne.

Sandra comes from a working-class family. Her parents and older sister are struggling financially, and she does nothing to help them.

The anxiety disorder that drives her bad behavior is rooted in an imbalance in noradrenalin. The genetic basis for this is uncovered in her mother's nicotine addiction and extreme controlling behavior. Her sister's panic attacks give further evidence of the inherited basis for Sandra's chemical imbalance.

The headline of this interview is that Sandra is unable to cope with the stressors that provoke her anxiety and drive her addiction.

Court-referred addiction treatment has an inherently low yield of success. Even as the justice system "orders" addicts to change, many are not ready to do so. Still, Sandra is extremely unhappy and knows her life cannot continue like this. She's even cancelled, albeit reluctantly, her trip to Paris.

Accepted for treatment.

Medical Rehabilitation

Sandra will need to be detoxified from her benzodiazepines and nicotine addictions. The underlying anxiety disorder will become exaggerated as she withdraws from these abused substances.

A healthy dietary program needs to be established, and Sandra must address her sleep disturbance with something other than a martini and a handful of cigarettes.

Medical Detox

The medical detoxification from benzodiazepines can be accomplished in two ways. The first and most common method is to gradually taper off the Valium and Xanax, cutting the intake by 20 to 25 percent every 2 weeks. A rapid taper or abrupt withdrawal from benzos is dangerous and can result in seizures.

The anxiety that bubbles up when these drugs are removed from the receptors can be paralyzing, and Sandra will need some replacement product to quiet these irritable noradrenalin and glutamate receptors that are being uncovered. Several nonaddicting medications are available to smooth this transition. The most targeted include the beta-blockers (Inderal) and the antiseizure medications (Neurontin, Depakote). The former act immediately; the latter can take days to weeks to produce their calming effect. Sometimes adding an SNRI (Effexor, Cymbalta, Pristiq, or Savella) helps soothe anxiety by raising serotonin levels while blocking the noradrenalin receptors.

The second approach to detoxification from benzodiazepines is using a stronger and older form of benzo (phenobarbital), with its dose calculated from Sandra's honest level of intake and rapidly tapered to zero (usually in about 1 to 4 weeks).

This approach requires careful 24/7 monitoring because of the risk of cardiovascular problems. The advantage here is speed, but rebalancing irritable neurotransmitters before behavioral therapies begin renders this approach dangerous and fraught with possible failure.

Since sleep disorders from substance abuse typically take weeks to months to treat successfully, Sandra will require nonaddictive sleep aids (Ambien, Neurontin, melatonin, or Vistaril) and time.

Regular exercise that creates endorphins will be essential to restore calm to Sandra's agitated brain.

Nicotine addiction has its own receptor issues that need to be addressed. Nicotine receptor blocking agents (Chantix is the prototype) work well and in a relatively short period—7 to 10 days—to block the receptors and eliminate the cravings for cigarettes. Once covered with this medication, the receptors must remain coated for several months for them to sufficiently "go underground" and remain silent. Side effects from these blocking agents are infrequent and are primarily gastrointestinal (nausea, cramps, and diarrhea are the most common), and they result from the interaction of the blocking agent with nicotine receptors in the intestinal tract. While reports of suicidal and agitated behaviors have also been cited, this appears more likely related to the underlying anxiety disorder that reoccurs when nicotine is suddenly discontinued.

Smoking is the nation's number one health risk and perhaps the most difficult addiction to battle. (Obesity is a very close second and is predicted to take the lead during the next decade.)

Stabilizing the Brain Chemistry

Stabilizing Sandra's noradrenalin and glutamate receptors requires non-addicting anxiolytics. This menu includes beta-blockers (Inderal), which can adversely affect blood pressure and must be carefully monitored, and atypical antiseizure medications (Neurontin, Lyrica, Depakote), which must be diligently supervised due to their side effect profile and relatively slow clinical response. If uncomfortable anxieties are not quickly suppressed—or if side effects from the stabilizing medications interfere and slow progress—patients can get discouraged, abandon their treatments, and revert to their old habits.

Endorphin release from an exercise program will help Sandra in combating her immediate bad feelings and improve her sleep disorder.

Long-term anxiolytic therapies may include the SNRIs that work as mood stabilizers by enhancing serotonin levels and reducing the exaggerated noradrenalin response to stress.

Sandra will also need to remain on nicotine blockers (Chantix) for several months after her initial detoxification.

Behavioral Treatment and Lifestyle Adjustments

Sandra's life can only get better. If she engages in cognitive and family therapy, she will redirect her nervous energy into reestablishing meaningful relationships with her children, her biological family, and perhaps even her husband.

The treatment team that Sandra needs to successfully help her with her addiction must involve a therapist who can transform her anger into action—specifically, confronting her husband's destructive behavior.

She will also need a neuropharmacologist who can treat her chemical imbalance with nonaddictive medications.

She will attend parenting classes to connect her to the responsibilities that are most important in her life. Family counseling—with both her own family and her biological family—is essential. A 12-step program must be included in this formula.

A nutritionist specializing in eating disorders will also be mandatory to restoring a healthy metabolism.

Incorporating an exercise program into her daily routine will likewise help ease her stress, ensure a better night's sleep, and perhaps expose her to a social network committed to a healthy lifestyle.

To achieve success, a general contractor (her primary care physician) must bring this team together and keep Sandra focused on her recovery. The relationships she establishes and nurtures with her treatment team will give Sandra a support network essential to maintaining her recovery. Dealing with the difficult stressors in her life will take patience and expertise, but a sober, functional, and even contented life can be hers.

Relationships

With any luck, this step will be the backbone of Sandra's recovery and beginning of her new life. Sandra will have the opportunity to redirect her choices in relationships to those who share parenting, not shopping, as a primary focus. She has the opportunity to become involved with her children's school, after-school activities, and other healthy and engaging tools to manage her stress.

Becoming a functional mom, sister, and daughter will give Sandra a new, positive identity . . . and the self-confidence to deal honestly with her marriage. It may be too late for her to regain trust and intimacy with her husband, but the opportunity for fresh starts and respectful relationships in every arena changes from fantasy to reality. The friendships she cultivated based on materialism and status can now be replaced by ones with the values necessary to integrate as a good parent. Her life on the roller coaster can be transformed to a life as a role model for her children.

Most important, her relationship with Valium and cigarettes will be discarded for a healthy, functional, and happier life.

Personal and Professional Goals

Sandra's image as a lawyer's wife and social butterfly can be redefined based on her own personal journey. She has the opportunity to pursue a professional career of her own, indulge in hobbies or causes that have been only fantasies, and become the best parent on the block. In doing so, she will evolve her own life and send her children the message that anyone can overcome their problems and re-create themselves based on good choices. Her options have heretofore been clouded by her severe anxiety disorder and her need to compete with false values and restricted by her addictive behaviors. This all changes . . . starting now.

Starting Fresh/Reengaging with Life

Sandra will always have the reflex to be anxious. The difference now is she will have a new and improved toolbox for dealing with life's inevitable stressors. She will be discover the joy of parenting, the freedom of living without a philandering husband, and the pursuit of friendships based on common values and healthy life choices.

The world awaits her, and she can cancel her reservation at the state correctional facility.

12

Alcohol

A popular novelty T-shirt proclaims: "A bartender is just a pharmacist with a limited inventory." Yes, it's mildly funny, but it rings true. Alcohol is a drug, and it always has been the most commonly abused substance in the world. The alcoholic concoction may vary, but the alcohol in every drink is the same ingredient the world over—ethanol (also called ethyl alcohol, grain alcohol, or pure alcohol). Its chemical formula is CH_3CH_2OH.

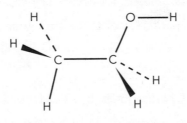

Given alcohol's well-recognized potential for destroying lives, families, and careers, perhaps the most remarkable aspect of this drug—and what most sets it apart from all other addictive substances—is its universal acceptance as a common bond. Bars, pubs, and saloons prosper and serve as social hubs in almost every society. Happy hours and cocktail parties flourish across all demographics. Lovers court, friends relax, and entrepreneurs do business over drinks. Wine is used symbolically and to consecrate blessings in world religions. Good news is celebrated with an alcoholic toast; bad news is cause to drown sorrows.

There's no doubt about it: Alcohol is here to stay. Fortunately, the new addiction paradigm shows how its abuse can be almost eradicated even as its social intake can be more responsibly managed.

Also known as: Belt, black death, booze, brew, bug juice, cocktail, corn, cough medicine, do-it fluid, firewater, gargle, giggle juice, giggle water, grog, home brew, hooch, jack, juice, Kentucky dew, liquid panty remover, liquor, medicine, moonshine, mouthwash, old tennis shoe, paint, panther sweat, pop skull, red eye, rotgut, sauce, sheep dip, short on, skee, stump juice, suds, swill, swish, tarantula juice, tiger milk, train miser, vino, white lightning

Users known as: Atkoholics (low-carb drinkers), boozers, chimney fish (smoking and drinking), drunks, five sheets to the wind (or six or seven . . .), goofs, hammered, juiced, lit, loaded, pint patriots, pissed, porch climbers, rap packers, riding the turkey, sauced, shelf shufflers, shit-faced, 13-steppers (after completing the 12 steps, the 13th is forgetting them), tipsy, toasted

How it's sold: Alcohol is sold in sizes from a shot glass of liquor ($1\frac{1}{2}$ ounces) and a miniature 50-milliliter bottle to a keg of beer holding 31 gallons. Whether served at bars and restaurants or sold by volume in retail settings, beer, liquor, and wine are marketed in consumer-friendly sizes.

Although prices range widely—from a buck or two for a shot of rotgut to as much as $160,000 for a 1787 bottle of Château Lafite—

alcohol is the most affordable of all abused substances.

Brief history: Alcohol consumption dates from 10,000 or 12,000 BC, as evidenced by Stone Age beer jugs found in West Africa. Wine appears to have originated in the Middle East around 4000 BC. Through the next 2,000 years, wine spread throughout the Western world. In ancient Greece, Plato praised both its social and medicinal properties.

The first written record of wine in the East dates from China in 1116 BC, when an imperial edict declared wine as a drink "prescribed by heaven."

It fell to the Roman Empire, circa 783 to 3 BC, to invent the concept of world-class drinking. All the excesses of Rome are well chronicled, and none more than its voracious appetite for alcoholic refreshments. As the empire expanded, so did the popularity of beer and wine.

After the collapse of Rome, the Western world fell into the Dark Ages. For centuries, only monasteries maintained the knowledge and skills to brew quality beer and tend to vineyards.

In the 13th century, Albertus Magnus distilled spirits and called his miraculous concoction _aqua vitae_—the water of life. We know it today as brandy. Some 400 years later, the Irish distilled alcoholic spirits from grain and created whiskey. Rum made from molasses was developed in the Caribbean as early as the mid-1600s and was soon exported to the colonies on the eastern seaboard of America. Dom Pérignon, a wine-maker in a French abbey, invented champagne in the 17th century and pioneered the use of strong bottles and corks.

Since that time, brewing (beer), fermenting (wine), and distilling (liquor) have remained the triad of alcohol production. In the past few hundred years, advances in alcohol production have been in the areas of mass production, improved flavoring, wider variety, and better marketing.

Usage today: Sixty-one percent of American adults age 21 or older (or about 180 million people) drank alcohol in the past year. In early 2009, the percentage of adults who had five or more drinks in 1 day was 23.4 percent (or 40 million people), according to the Centers for Disease Control and Prevention. Ninety-two percent of heavy drinkers have binged in the last 30 days, and the rate of binge drinking among men is three times higher than in women. One in 10 American adults (or about 25 million people) has a "drinking problem."

How it's taken: Alcohol is consumed as a liquid drink. Any other methods of intake—like injection—are rare and impractical. Baking or cooking with alcohol burns off most of the alcoholic content; what remains is some flavoring.

Neurotransmitters involved: By releasing serotonin and GABA into the brain, alcohol triggers disinhibition followed by drowsiness and sleep. A dab of dopamine sends news of these good feelings via the reward pathways to the memory and behavior regions of the brain and thus reinforces the behavior.

How it works: Alcohol works cumulatively: The more you drink, the higher you get—until you hit the tipping point and your high turns to sluggishness, fatigue, disorientation, or worse.

The first drink usually relaxes the muscles and the mind and starts to erode inhibitions and fears. Depending on a person's level of tolerance, body weight, and percentages of muscle and fat (and also influenced by the alcohol content of the drink), a second drink will probably heighten the feel-good experience. By the fourth drink, most adults hit or start to reach the 0.08 percent blood alcohol level—the tipping point—that seriously impairs physical, mental, and emotional functioning.

Progressive Effects of Alcohol

Blood Alcohol Concentration	Changes in Feelings and Personality	Physical and Mental Impairments
0.01–0.06	Relaxation Sense of well-being Loss of inhibition Lowered alertness Joyousness	Thought Judgment Coordination Concentration
0.06–0.10	Blunted feelings Disinhibition Extroversion Impaired sexual pleasure	Reflexes Reasoning Depth perception Distance acuity Peripheral vision Glare recovery
0.11–0.20	Over-expression Emotional swings Anger or sadness Boisterousness	Reaction time Gross motor control Staggering Slurred Speech
0.21–0.29	Stupor Loss of understanding Impaired sensations	Severe motor impairment Loss of consciousness Memory blackout
0.30–0.39	Severe depression Unconsciousness Death possible	Bladder function Breathing Heart rate
>0.40	Unconsciousness Death	Breathing Heart rate

Source: Virginia Tech, Campus Alcohol Abuse Prevention Center

When the party's over, the crash arrives, and the severity of the crash depends on how much alcohol was consumed. Headaches, nausea, vomiting, oversensitivity to sound and light, and lack of REM sleep leading to physical and mental sluggishness are common parts of the hangover.

Like all the other potentially addictive substances, alcohol rides on an ebb of good feelings diminishing to a flow of really bad feelings. And for those with a low serotonin imbalance, the quickest way back to feeling good is having another drink as soon as possible.

Risks: Alcohol impairs good judgment and motor skills. It's a dangerous combination. More than 100,000 deaths per year in America are attributed to alcohol abuse. Alcohol abuse also leads to cardiovascular disease and illnesses like hypertension, kidney and liver dysfunctions, swelling of the ankles, high blood urea, muscle cramps, chronic sleeplessness, sexual impotence, diabetes mellitus, and hemochromatosis. The incidence of alcohol poisoning is rising parallel with the popularity of binge drinking.

Associated behaviors: Emotional responses to alcohol are unpredictable and vary from person to person. Some people will feel more elated as their drinking continues, others will feel progressively more depressed, and still others will become angry and violent. A few will simply pass out before reaching an extreme emotional state. Alcohol has a built-in disinhibition factor in which personal, social, and moral restraints are momentarily thrown to the wayside and the inebriated tend to act out previously constrained dreams and grievances.

Certain behaviors are considered warning signs of alcoholism, including failing to care for physical appearance; drinking alone; drinking daily in order to function; drinking secretly; making excuses at work, home, or school; manufacturing reasons to drink; inability to reduce or stop drinking; uncharacteristically erratic, sometimes violent, behavior; becoming angry when confronted about drinking; unhealthy diet and eating habits; experiencing morning tremors; and experiencing short-term memory loss.

Generally speaking, three or more of these signs indicate a drinking problem, but certain signals alone—like morning tremors—are telling.

Some positive effects: There seems little doubt in the medical community that *moderate* alcohol intake can be good for many people. Taken in moderation, drinking is a socially acceptable way of dealing with stress, and for those who are shy or intimidated in gatherings, it's a useful social lubricant. Many scientists believe that certain properties in wine, beer, and hard liquor (such as antioxidants like resveratrol) are actually good for cardiovascular function and long life.

The medical detox: During alcohol detox, the goal is twofold: to prevent serious anxiety and/or agitation and to restore a normal sleep cycle.

To relieve anxiety, benzodiazepines are prescribed short term to counteract the release of glutamate that always causes agitation during withdrawal. Librium is the gold standard in this regard, but other benzos such as Klonopin, Xanax, and Ativan are effective.

At the same time, GABAergic drugs like Neurontin increase GABA concentration in the brain to provide a calm and safe rest. These medications are essential when prescribing benzodiazepines to help calm the glutamate reaction and reduce the need for long-term benzo therapy (which can be habit forming).

Sleep is induced and the circadian rhythm restored through the use of simple antihistamines (Benadryl and Vistaril) and nonaddictive hypnotics like Ambien, Lunesta, and Sonata. With highly anxious or agitated states, a short-acting benzo like Xanax or Ativan is occasionally given for a limited time to help reset the patient's internal clock. Seroquel, an atypical antipsychotic, is given in extreme cases of agitation and insomnia.

Stabilizing medications: Because chronic alcoholism is associated with low levels of serotonin, the aim of medically stabilizing the alcoholic brain is to first restore serotonin to its natural level and then to create a new and stronger serotonin concentration that will withstand the stresses of life and prevent relapse.

Low serotonin levels create mood disorders and obsessive thinking and behaviors. To counteract bad feelings and raise serotonin concentration, medicines called SSRIs and SRNIs are prescribed. (Prozac was the prototype, followed by drugs like Zoloft, Lexapro, Pristiq, Effexor, Cymbalta, Celexa, Savella, and Paxil.) Since these medications can have serious side effects that may interfere with compliance, doctors have learned to initiate treatment with low dosages that are raised slowly over several weeks.

Behavioral therapies accompany the medical management and include therapies such as individual and family counseling, daily exercise, nutritional guidance, support groups, and 12-step programs.

Sleep disorders and pain must be managed throughout the process with both pharmacological and behavioral therapies.

CASE STUDY: GLORIA, ADDICTED TO ALCOHOL

Employer Intervention/Surrender

A few years ago, Gloria earned well over half a million dollars a year, but it didn't come easily. She busted her hump 6 days a week, showing houses and condos to a mixed bag of prospective buyers, always running from one property to the next. But it was worth it—she had it all: a great house, a great car, great clothes. A great life.

So why did she feel so bad?

After the jolting crash of the housing market, her sales were down significantly, but that didn't give her boss the right to order her to rehab. Everybody's numbers were down. He had absolutely no call to single her out. She worked hard and partied hard, the same as everybody else in the office.

But it was his company. If she moved to another shop, she'd lose her seniority and her choice of high-end properties.

Okay, she'd surrender herself to treatment. She could do this rehab thing on a dime. It didn't mean she had to quit drinking completely. Just cut down a bit. Maybe just a couple every now then to help her relax.

Medical Evaluation

INTAKE FORM

Name: <u>Gloria</u>   Age: <u>47</u>   SMDW: <u>D</u>   Sex: <u>F</u>
Occupation: <u>Realtor</u>   Referred By: <u>n/a</u>

Current Problems/Complaints:

<u>I lost a $3 million sale and my boss (and lover) blamed this on my drinking.</u>
<u>I don't agree that I have a drinking problem—the problem was that these clients</u>
<u>could never make up their minds! I only drink at night when my boss is with his</u>
<u>family, or when I think about how bad the economy is, which makes me a little</u>
<u>nervous. The houses I used to sell for $5 million are now going for half of that, so</u>
<u>my commission is a lot less. I think my boss is overreacting, but I still don't want</u>
<u>to lose my job. I also wonder if my boss isn't trying to get rid of me because his</u>
<u>wife found a note I gave him in his wallet!</u>

Past Medical History:

❏ Childhood Illness   ❏ ADD   ❏ Trauma (Emotional/Physical)
❏ Anxiety   ❏ Depression
☒ Other <u>Colitis</u>

Medical Illnesses:

❏ Anxiety   ❏ Depression   ❏ Insomnia
❏ Chronic Pain   ❏ Hyperactivity/ADD   ❏ Bipolar
❏ OCD   ❏ Weight Changes   ❏ Stress
☒ Other <u>Herpes</u>

Psychological History:

☒ Divorce in Family   ❏ Unexpected Death in Family
❏ Recent Change in Relationship
❏ Chronic Pain   ☒ Job Stress   ❏ Sexual Issues
❏ Recent Life Changes

Habits:

☒ Nicotine <u>Only when I drink</u>   ☒ Alcohol <u>Only at night</u>   ❑ Recreational Drugs
☒ Marijuana <u>Every now and then</u>   ❑ Metabolic/Weight Problems
Exercise: ❑ Never   ❑ Occasionally   ❑ Often
❑ Other _____

Current Medications: <u>Zoloft, acyclovir, Advil, Xanax</u>

Surgeries: <u>Botox every 3 months</u>

Family History:

	Living	Deceased	Health Problems
Mother	✓		Alcoholic; on Prozac
Father		✓	Committed suicide at 52
Siblings	✓ 2		Two older sisters—both alcoholics

Health Problems in Your Family:

❑ Irritable/Spastic Bowel   ☒ Depression   ☒ Suicide
❑ Hyperactive/ADD   ❑ Obesity   ❑ Bipolar
❑ Headaches   ❑ Back Pain   ❑ Anxiety
❑ Heart Disease   ❑ Cancers   ❑ Diabetes
☒ Nicotine   ☒ Caffeine   ☒ Alcohol
❑ Other Drug Abuse_____

Patient Interview (from Transcript)

"I've sold real estate for the last twenty-some years, and I've made the 1 percent club—the top 1 percent of realtors nationwide—14 times. The last time was a few years ago. But my boss, the man who owns the company, thinks I've been slacking off the last couple of years because of my drinking.

"I do drink, but only after work and never enough to lose control. The real estate business is very dog-eat-dog. When houses are routinely going for seven or eight figures, agents will offer up their firstborn to make a sale. An occasional martini hits the spot, relaxes me. I deserve that, don't I?

"Believe me, my mother was an alcoholic—my sisters probably are, too—so I know one when I see one . . . and I'm not an alky.

"I think this is all because I lost a big sale last week. My boss got angry. He accused me of cutting corners because of my drinking. He said I could sell a lot of houses if I were sober and he doesn't want to lose me, but if I didn't dry up—that's the expression he used—I was of no use to him.

"He's not Mr. Perfect himself. He's married, but he sleeps with me whenever he can. Maybe he's sleeping with one or two other agents as well. Who knows? But he's the piper I have to pay, so here I am."

Physician Analysis

Gloria is not ready for treatment. She is in denial of her alcoholism and blames external issues (her boss, the economy, and her job stress) for her "occasional" drinking at night. Treatment can only succeed if the addict recognizes his or her addiction and agrees to get help.

Clues to the addictive behaviors in Gloria's intake form include her lying about her problem ("I don't agree that I have a drinking problem"); her strong family history of depression, suicide, and addiction (alcohol); her current stressors (her job and extramarital affair) provoking her addictive behavior; and the antidepressant and anxiolytic medications supporting her imbalanced brain chemistry (serotonin and noradrenalin, respectively).

Rejected for treatment.

Postscript

Gloria does not see her rejection from treatment as a problem but rather as validation that she has no problem.

In the beginning of my practice, I would have tried to help Gloria and would have failed because she was not ready. I would have believed her sad story, felt sorry for her, and tried to rescue her from her difficult life situation. I now realize that despite these issues, her denial would only serve to waste everyone's time and resources.

Instead, I referred Gloria to a psychologist to sort out her problems and gain enough insight to seek treatment for her addiction, hopefully in the near future.

CASE STUDY: JAMES, ADDICTED TO ALCOHOL

Surrender

James pulled over to the side of the road and stopped. Taking a bottle from the glove compartment with trembling hands, he shook out half a dozen aspirin, popped them in his mouth, then reached for a bottle and took a long, urgent drink of cool water. A whiskey would stop the tremors, but he was determined not to do that. Not anymore.

He was getting too old for this. The mornings were getting harder, the headaches getting worse. He had to give it up—all of it.

Time to surrender.

Medical Evaluation

INTAKE FORM

Name: <u>James</u>   Age: <u>60</u>   SMDW: <u>D</u>   Sex: M
Occupation: <u>Civil service</u>   Referred By: <u>City medical office</u>

Current Problems/Complaints:

I've been coming in to work late too often. I can't seem to get up on time. I don't sleep well and have been getting god-awful headaches every morning. At work I'm always tired and my hands shake. Sometimes I put vodka in a water bottle and sip it throughout the day, but it's just to keep my hands still. It affects my work—I get it done, but it takes longer than it should. I think my co-workers, maybe even my boss, suspect my little secret. I chew cinnamon gum and pop breath mints all day long, so I didn't think anyone noticed.

Since my liver tests were a bit off, my doctor asked if I was drinking. I told him no, but it was stupid to lie. Now he has me on blood pressure pills. I take them most of the time but sometimes I forget. There's a lot of depression in my family— mother, father, sister—and I'm afraid I'm headed that way myself. I've been really down lately and can't seem to get myself up.

Past Medical History:

❑ Childhood Illness   ❑ ADD   ❑ Trauma (Emotional/Physical)
❑ Anxiety   ☒ Depression
☒ Other <u>Pneumonia (age 10); hospitalized in 1997 for chest pains—</u>
<u>I thought I had a heart attack, but it was indigestion</u>

Medical Illnesses:

❑ Anxiety   ❑ Depression   ❑ Insomnia
❑ Chronic Pain   ❑ Hyperactivity/ADD   ❑ Bipolar
❑ OCD   ❑ Weight Changes   ❑ Stress
☒ Other <u>Headaches, fatigue, high blood pressure, indigestion</u>

Psychological History:

☒ Divorce in Family   ☐ Unexpected Death in Family
☐ Recent Change in Relationship
☐ Chronic Pain   ☒ Job Stress   ☐ Sexual Issues
☒ Recent Life Changes I think I might be in trouble at work.

Habits:

☒ Nicotine Only when I drink   ☒ Alcohol   ☐ Recreational Drugs Never!
☐ Marijuana   ☐ Metabolic/Weight Problems
Exercise: ☒ Never   ☐ Occasionally   ☐ Often
☒ Other I drink a lot of coffee in the morning to help me wake up.

Current Medications: Maalox (for indigestion), aspirin (for headaches), blood pressure pills (can't remember name)

Surgeries: Set broken arm (high school), appendectomy (30 years ago), hernia (about 15 years ago)

Family History:

	Living	Deceased	Health Problems
Mother		✓ Died at 66	Alcoholic, chain-smoker, sugar diabetes
Father		✓ Died at 58	sickle cell anemia, obese, depression
Siblings Sister—Lena; She'd be 68 now	I don't know		Depression as a young woman
Son—Wesley, 29; grand-son—about 8 years old			Estranged

Health Problems in Your Family:

☐ Irritable/Spastic Bowel   ☒ Depression   ☐ Suicide
☐ Hyperactive/ADD   ☐ Obesity   ☐ Bipolar
☒ Headaches   ☐ Back Pain   ☐ Anxiety
☒ Heart Disease   ☐ Cancers   ☒ Diabetes
☒ Nicotine   ☐ Caffeine   ☒ Alcohol
☐ Other Drug Abuse

Patient Interview (from Transcript)

"I just turned 60, and that milestone made me take a good look at my life, what little there is to see, I'm sad to say.

"I've worked in the mayor's planning office over 25 years. Served six mayors in that time. Back in the day, I was good at my job. Very conscientious. I did a lot of good for a lot of people. But lately, my work hasn't been so good. Not bad, just not what it should be, you know?

"I've only got a few years until my full pension, so I've got to hang in there . . . somehow.

"For years I drank socially. Maybe a bit too social, you know? Now I don't have any friends to speak of. No social engagements.

"My wife and I divorced—oh, about 15 years ago—and I haven't met anyone in a long time who I wanted to, you know, go out with. I haven't seen my son in over 10 years. He's all grown now. About a year ago, I heard he and his wife had a baby boy. I guess he doesn't want him to meet his grandpa.

"So work is all I have, you know? Nothing else. Nobody.

"When I leave the office, I usually stop at a bar for a little pick-me-up. Not all the time, but usually. Maybe I drink to feel connected to something, even if it's just to my pal Johnny Walker. I don't know—it's just that life doesn't seem so bleak when I drink.

"When I get home, sometimes I check out one of the—uh, you know—sex sites on the Internet. I still got the urges, you know. I just don't have the spirit for it anymore.

"I need to quit all this before I lose the little bit I spent my life working for. I just want to keep my job, you know. I don't want any trouble. I just want to keep my job. That's why I'm here."

Physician Analysis

James isn't on his way to depression—he has been there a long time. His family tree produces this bruised fruit, and he deals with these uncomfortable feelings by drinking.

Depression comes in two forms. One is intrinsic and part of imbalanced brain chemistry (the inherited part of your hard wiring); the other is provoked by situational events. The relative lack or imbalance of serotonin is associated with inherited depressions, while situational depressions (a death in the family, loss of a job, a change in a relationship) are normal life events but exaggerated in those who already have a serotonin imbalance. When stress is added to the endogenous (inherent) form, depression is inescapable.

An important factor consistent with James's depression is the life transition he is beginning to experience. Having reached a milestone birthday—one on which people often begin to feel their mortality—he is transitioning from a working life to retirement. He is also transitioning further away from his only anchor, his growing family.

This stress, added to his medical conditions (hypertension and a sleep disorder), stack the deck of depression against James. Now his only way out (alcohol) no longer gives him the relief or solace he seeks. Quite the opposite: Keeping his "little secret" from his co-workers has added more stress to his otherwise empty life.

He is tired all the time, especially in the late afternoon, because he isn't getting adequate sleep. He may fall asleep with the help of his friend Johnny Walker, but his sleep cycle is upset due to the alcohol's impact on stage 3 and 4 and REM cycle sleep, causing him to get insufficient deep (or restorative) sleep.

This is a sad and lonely man, but one who desperately wants to change the circumstances of his life.

Accepted for treatment.

Medical Rehabilitation

James's medical rehabilitation will require a detoxification from alcohol, a rebalancing of his serotonin levels, and establishment of a better sleep cycle.

Careful monitoring of his blood pressure and liver enzymes will be an important part of his program.

Daily exercise to boost endorphins will also help James deal with his stress. Given his age and hypertension, this should start with a light, low-impact program and inch forward as he's able to handle more.

Medical Detox

Detoxification from alcohol involves initial rebalancing of the glutamate neurotransmitters, restoring normal sleep patterns, and initiating healthy nutrition and exercise regimens. The glutamate neurotransmitter is released in high quantities as the alcohol levels in the brain begin to recede, creating a physical sense of anxiety and agitation. This usually drives the addict toward alcohol to counteract these bad feelings. But by blocking these glutamate receptors with short-acting benzodiazepines (Librium, Xanax, Valium, or Klonopin), calm is restored and the body's craving for the abused substance is satisfied, at least temporarily. Librium is the most commonly used benzo for this process and is delivered throughout the day to diminish agitation and drug seeking. This treatment may take a few days to a few weeks, depending upon the duration and intensity of the alcohol addiction.

Neurontin, a nonaddictive antiseizure medication, is another good choice during detox since it also interacts with the glutamate/GABA neurotransmitters to calm the chemical storm in the brain. Neurontin has the added advantage over the benzos of not creating dependency or abuse.

The sleep disorder that accompanies withdrawal is managed by a combination of antihistamines (Vistaril, Benadryl) and longer-acting benzodiazepines like Klonopin or Ativan. Ambien, a nonaddicting hypnotic sleep aid, is also a good choice during the initial weeks of detoxification.

Adding into this equation morning exercise for 30 minutes (a simple uninterrupted walk is adequate) will produce endorphins in the brain, which will be an important nonprescription additive for relieving anxiety during detox and throughout his recovery.

As soon as detoxification begins, it is important to administer vitamin B_{12} and thiamine (vitamin B_6) to prevent the development of an organic brain syndrome (Wernicke-Korsakoff syndrome) that can occur when the alcoholic brain begins its recovery. The syndrome is characterized by acute changes in cognition and memory and by profound irritability.

Stabilizing the Brain Chemistry

Stabilizing the alcoholic brain involves a different neurotransmitter, serotonin. When genetics hands us inherently low levels of serotonin, it creates the bad feelings of depression or obsessive thinking and behaviors that drive the addict toward alcohol. Restoring this neurotransmitter to normal levels will cause depressive feelings to fade and allow for greater functioning, thereby eliminating the drive toward an unhealthy relationship with alcohol.

The stabilizing process can take several months, and the choice of serotonergic medications—the SSRIs and the SNRIs—will depend on several factors, most importantly on James's ability to tolerate their side effects, which include dizziness, nausea, agitation, and sexual dysfunction.

(The SSRIs include Prozac, Zoloft, Lexapro, and Celexa. The SNRIs include Cymbalta, Effexor, Savella, and Pristiq and differ from the SSRIs because of their combined ability to relieve anxiety.)

Selecting the appropriate medication and the dosing is an art that should be directed by a physician who is experienced in the use of these specific drugs.

Since these medications are metabolized in the liver, and as James's liver is already compromised by alcohol abuse, careful monitoring of the liver enzymes and functioning is vital.

During alcohol recovery, anxiety is exaggerated by the obsessive thinking and behaviors normally associated with serotonin imbalances. This anxiety is caused by a surplus of noradrenalin that occurs in response to the serotonin imbalance, and it must be addressed during both the detoxification and rebalancing of serotonin levels. The best antidote for all anxiety disorders is endorphins, which are created by exercise. The endorphins actually block the noradrenalin response and create a sense of calm. But endorphins are fickle: Since they last in the brain only up to 18 hours, they must be regenerated daily to help with the anxious feelings the recovering alcoholic experiences.

Other solutions to blocking the noradrenalin receptors include the benzodiazepines and the newer antiseizure medications (Neurontin and Lyrica). The former have a strong tendency toward dependency and are less desirable than the latter. As the serotonin levels normalize (a process that could take months), these anxiolytic medications can often be eliminated.

Behavioral Treatment and Lifestyle Adjustments

Behavioral and lifestyle changes must accompany James's medical therapy. A successful treatment plan for James will involve the participation of a neuropharmacologist to help guide his antidepressant medications. A nutritionist will offer healthy meal planning designed for someone who does not cook and who often eats fast food or bar fare.

James will need to engage in "talk therapy" or cognitive therapy to understand the issues in his life that contribute to his alcoholism and to gain some tools to deal with these problems. A 12-step program with a compassionate sponsor will be added in to his treatment formula, and he will be regularly drug tested by the doctor who will assume his primary care and coordinate with all the other members of his treatment team.

He will need a structured daily regimen, beginning with a 30-minute exercise program, a regular and well-balanced eating plan, and a new habit of sleep hygiene to ensure good sleep. This means no computers, books, television, phone conversations, or snacks in the bedroom. The bedroom should be for only two things: sleep and sex. All other activities interfere with the brain's ability to initiate the sleep cycle. Drug addiction, no matter what the abused substance, impairs this cycle, and it must be restored. Sleep patterns are genetically determined, and more than half of us don't sleep well. It may be difficult to ensure 8 hours of sleep without some sleep aid. There are several nonaddicting choices to assist in restoring the sleep cycle if long-term therapy is required.

Relationships

James now has an opportunity to rebuild his life with the important people who have become estranged. He will need guidance from his counselors, but it is never too late for redemption, forgiveness, and understanding. He will need to reconnect with his son and meet his new grandson. And he must make his co-workers secure in his new sobriety.

As friendships are rare for James, his counselors can help by giving him new tools to meet people and establish a relationship. And his 12-step program should help in this area, especially since many in these programs have worked hard for their sobriety and will understand his issues. Making sober friendships is the first step toward staying clean.

The potential for James to become a caring and involved grandfather is a gift that only some are ever given, and he needs to embrace this opportunity.

Personal and Professional Goals

James's personal goals begin with regaining his sobriety and his general health.

Since his professional life is coming to an end with his impending retirement, he must transition into some hobby or activity to keep his mind active and stimulated. Studies show that workers facing retirement have a significantly higher vulnerability toward depression, so James needs to involve himself in something he enjoys. He will be referred to a counselor who specializes in this area.

Starting Fresh/Reengaging with Life

The new and improved James should look like this: sober, on antidepressant medication for at least 6 months, engaged in counseling and a 12-step program, and surrounded by professionals who care for him. He will gracefully transition into his retirement with an exit plan that includes hobbies and new relationships with his son and grandson. He will be exercising, eating well, monitoring his liver, and sleeping much better. He will look back on his breakup with Johnny Walker with pride and a new view of the world.

13

Marijuana

The most popular illegal drug in America, marijuana consists of the buds and flowers from either of two plants: *Cannabis sativa* and *Cannabis indica*. The tall, gangly, sweet-smelling *C. sativa* is the most common in the United States, while the short, stout *C. indica* that emits what is described as a "skunky" smell is abundant in the Middle East, India, and Central Asia. Marijuana is "all natural" in the sense that no synthetic chemicals are added. Just grow it, dry it, and smoke it.

That's not to say these plants lack powerful chemicals. Indeed, traces of about 400 naturally occurring chemicals are found in any given batch of cannabis. The most potent chemical in marijuana—and the

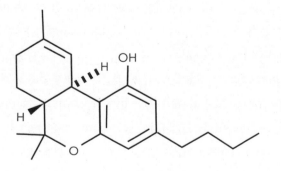

psychoactive drug that makes it work—is delta-9-tetrahydrocannabinol, commonly known as THC.

The higher the content of THC, the stronger the effect. The average joint or bowl of marijuana today contains about 10 percent THC, double or triple the potency of the drug in the 1970s.

Also known as: Ace, Afghan, bammy, blow a stick, blunt, boom, brick, bud, Buddha grass, cannabis, chronic, ditch weed, doobie, fingers, gangster, ganja, giggle weed, grass, hash, hashish, hay, hemp, herb, J, Jane, Jay, jive, joint, kief, kif, Mary Jane, pot, reefer, resin, roach, sativa, schwag, shit, skunk, smoke, splif, sticks, stuff, tea, temple balls, Texas tea, Thai sticks, weed, whacky-backy, whacky tobaccy

Users known as: Annies, apple-pied, baked, blanking, blazed, blot-toed, bowlers, bowling, boxed, caked, faded, geeked, half-baked, keished, potheads, ripped, Sachs, smitten, smoke eaters, stoned, stoners, trans-moglephides, twitted, xooted

How it's sold: In small quantities, marijuana sells from a few dollars for a single joint or for a gram with sufficient leaves to make two or three joints. Especially in the larger quantities, purity influences price. The lowest quality sells for $800 to $1,500 per pound; the best costs $3,000 to $6,000 per pound. Most customers buy quarter ounces or half ounces for $100 to $200. Marijuana sold legally through medical dispensaries generally costs 20 percent more than the street variety, but that's because it is of higher quality.

Brief history: Cannabis can be traced back to 5,000 years ago, when it was used for medicinal purposes by the Chinese. In Western civilization, it appears around 500 BC in the Middle East, northern Africa, and southern Europe, apparently used for medicinal and ritual purposes. Around the 5th century AD, the Talmud cited the properties of marijuana as they related to the human mind. Early in the 12th century, hashish (a by-product of cannabis) became a tool by which to recruit and train mercenaries and hired killers. Active trading of hashish began in northern Africa at the turn of the 13th century. The drug trade was officially born.

By the 17th century, hashish was a major trade item between central and southern Asia. Returning from fierce battles in Egypt in 1798, Napoleon and his army brought hash to France and all of Europe.

In 1840, the United States legalized marijuana for medicinal use. In 1936, the antimarijuana propaganda film *Reefer Madness* depicted marijuana as "the devil's weed" (hence the sobriquet *weed*) and scared upright Americans half to death. The following year, the United States banned marijuana, a federal prohibition that stands to this day.

During World War II, the US Office of Strategic Services (OSS), the forerunner of the Central Intelligence Agency, found marijuana to be the "most effective truth serum" developed at their research labs in Washington, DC. OSS interrogators found subjects who smoked pot to be "loquacious and free" in the surrender of information vital to the war effort.

In the past few years, more than a dozen states have legalized the use of marijuana for medical purposes. The Obama administration has made it clear that arrests for simple possession of marijuana will be neither vigorously sought nor prosecuted. Some media pundits view this policy as the first step toward the legalization (and taxation) of the multibillion-dollar-a-year cannabis trade.

As the medical marijuana movement spreads, some colleges and universities have expanded their curriculum to include courses and majors in marijuana.

Usage today: Next to alcohol, marijuana is the single most popular recreational drug in America . . . and the world. According to a recent United Nations survey, 4 percent of the world population uses marijuana, which roughly translates to 162,000,000 people. Of those, around 22 million use it daily. Just in the United States, 83 million people admit to having tried marijuana. The 2007 National Survey on Drug Use and Health reported that 14.4 million Americans age 12 and older used marijuana at least once in the month prior to being interviewed. Every day, almost 6,000 Americans use marijuana for the first time, or roughly 2.1 million every year. Of this number, 62 percent are under age 18.

How it's taken: The most common method is to roll loose marijuana in cigarette paper to fashion a "joint," then light it and inhale the smoke. Or the marijuana can be placed in a hollowed-out cigar and smoked as a "blunt." Another popular method is to smoke it through a water pipe, called a bong, or a smaller, screened pipe without water, called a bowl.

A lot of users like to ingest marijuana. But you can't just eat the leaves; the marijuana cannot release the all-important THC unless it is heated. A common method is to bake the leaves in something fatty, such as cookies and brownies. Baking marijuana decreases its potency but skirts the negative health issues involved with smoking.

Another method is to mix marijuana leaves with tea leaves and brew it into a beverage.

Neurotransmitters involved: THC, the psychoactive ingredient in cannabis, interacts with a group of receptors called cannabinoids found in various parts of the brain. Not coincidentally, the highest volume of cannabinoids is found in the regions impacting pleasure, memory, sensory perception, and motor control. The resulting neurocellular reactions lead to the distinctive marijuana high.

Dopamine is the major neurotransmitter to play a part in the cannabis experience. It carries the message of pleasure from the reward center to the memory and behavior areas of the brain.

Marijuana also reduces anxiety through its effect on noradrenalin and GABA receptors.

How it works: Generally speaking, most drugs are either stimulants, depressants, or hallucinogens. Cannabis, however, is a potpourri of all three, with a slightly stronger emphasis on psychedelic effects. It is this impact on perception that gives marijuana its reputation for enhancing "creativity."

When marijuana is inhaled, THC passes from the lungs to the bloodstream and then to the brain. Within half a minute, the user begins to relax. Another minute and he or she begins to feel *really* good. Euphoria can set in, as can playfulness or serenity. A marijuana high is, for the most part, pleasant and peaceful.

Risks: Over the years, marijuana has garnered more fearmongering mythology than perhaps any other illegal substance. The often cited "gateway theory" claims that smoking pot increases the likelihood of later use of "hard" drugs. In truth, no scientific report has ever shown a cause-and-effect relationship between marijuana and hard drugs. Controlled medical studies indicate that smoking tobacco is a better indicator of subsequent cocaine and heroin use than any cannabis-based product.

Still, there are real health issues connected to marijuana. First are risks related to smoking. While marijuana has no nicotine, it does contain more carcinogens than tobacco. Pot smokers tend to inhale more deeply than tobacco smokers and hold the smoke in their lungs longer, which irritates the lungs and leads to several kinds of respiratory problems. The jury is still out on the correlation between smoking marijuana and lung cancer. A recent New Zealand study reported that those who smoke marijuana daily have an approximately five times higher risk of lung cancer than those who do not. But a report in Los Angeles showed no connection between smoking pot and lung, head, or neck cancers, and some medical analyses have shown that smoking pot can lessen the frequency of those forms of cancer.

Marijuana increases the heart rate from 20 to 100 percent in the first couple of hours after use. While this temporarily increases the risk of heart attacks, palpitations, and arrhythmias, no causal link to chronic heart disease has come to light.

Marijuana negatively effects motor coordination, so physical accidents can befall users. And, as with alcohol, cannabis impairs judgment, often leading to risky behaviors like getting behind the wheel of a car or having unsafe sex. By causing short-term memory loss and altering perception, marijuana can also impede learning and weaken the ability to solve problems.

Associated behaviors: The most apparent behavioral effects of marijuana are laughing for no apparent reason, clumsiness, loss of balance, grogginess, bloodshot eyes, the inability to measure time, short-term memory loss, vastly increased appetite, and a relentless craving for sweets.

Most people who smoke grass do so moderately, without many associated problems. But, as with alcohol, there are a few warnings that signal overuse: frequent absences, tardiness, too many workman's comp claims, the inability to hold a job or stay in school, loss of motivation and/or professional drive, and an increased unwillingness to engage in family and/or social activities.

Some positive effects: Benefits of marijuana have been recorded throughout history by almost every culture. Some swear it enhances creativity, while others praise its mind-altering qualities as a key to finding true spirituality. Most people use marijuana as a way to relax and mediate the stresses of a hard day or week. It's been suggested, but not proven, that marijuana helps relieve clinical depression. Some major medical institutions are presently studying the impact of marijuana on depression and other emotional illnesses.

Patients in pain find relief with marijuana, especially those suffering from arthritis, multiple sclerosis, muscular dystrophy, and cancer. For them, smoking marijuana can mean the difference between a peaceful sleep and suffering in pain all night long. Chemotherapy patients experience a huge reduction of nausea and vomiting after smoking pot. Other studies have discovered antitumor properties in cannabis that have some researchers examining its effectiveness in reducing types of tumors, especially breast cancer.

Medical marijuana stimulates appetites in AIDS patients at a cost of $500 to $600 a year—much less expensive than the legal alternative, human growth hormone, which costs around $36,000 annually.

By lowering intraocular eye pressure, marijuana has helped countless victims of glaucoma over the last decades.

The medical treatment: An extremely low number of marijuana users ever seek recovery treatment. Those who eventually quit appear to do so on their own.

Since marijuana use is not linked to any sustained neurotransmitter imbalances in brain chemistry, medical detox and stabilization is unnecessary.

Still, anxiety and agitation are common during cannabis withdrawal. Medications like Neurontin, Inderal, and selected benzodiazepines can be prescribed to raise GABA levels (increasing calm) and decrease glutamate (reducing agitation), thus soothing the user and the transition to nonuse.

14

Designer Drugs

At first glance, designer drugs appear to be all over the place. Some, like LSD, are largely hallucinogenic (with stimulant effects); others, like Ecstasy, are mostly stimulants (with hallucinogenic effects); still more, like ketamine (originally developed as a veterinary anesthetic) are classically viewed as depressants (with both hallucinogenic and stimulant effects). In truth, most of these drugs are deliberately "designed" as mixtures of various substances to produce multiple and different effects—like "combination plates" at a chemical cafeteria . . . with a little of this, a little of that, and a side course of something completely different.

Precisely because these psychoactive drugs are combinations of different substances, they do not follow a single cause-and-effect line from specific neurotransmitter to specific substances. Rather, designer drugs temporarily flood multiple neurotransmitter-receptor interactions, spark an intense high, and then roll back like an ebbing tide, often leaving nothing but a hard crash in their wake.

For this reason, the predisposition for chronic abuse of designer drugs is different and their addictive potential is less problematic. Ecstasy, for instance, causes a tremendous serotonin and dopamine rush. While the comedown is tough, it has no *specific* addiction potential, so its dependency issues are more psychological than physiological.

Since these drugs don't relate to specific biochemical imbalances or wantings, they are less likely to create a biological dependency that results in addictive behavior. Instead, use of designer drugs is more often linked to availability, peer influence, and socioeconomic class and tends to be recreational: at clubs, raves, concerts, and group getaways . . . Friday through Sunday drugs for weekend party warriors.

A second and more dangerous class of so-called designer drugs is created largely to get around existing drug laws. Starting with the precisely defined chemical formula of an illegal substance, a chemist alters the basic formula just enough to skirt the illegal status but not so much as to negatively impact the desired effect of the drug. Since law enforcement agencies move quickly to place each altered formula on the list of banned substances, these often hastily manufactured designs are temporary, constantly changing, and extremely dangerous. The consumer cannot know the quality or quantity of the drug's ingredients nor even which chemicals were used in its making. There is no production oversight and no quality control. Using these mystery substances is like playing Russian roulette with drugs instead of bullets . . . and no one should play that game.

Also known as: Club drugs. For Ecstasy: Adam, beans, clarity, E, hug, love drug, lover's speed, X, XTC. For LSD: Acid, back breaker, doses, dot, Elvis, Looney Tunes, Lucy, pane, Superman, tab, windowpane, zen. For ketamine: Blind squid, breakfast cereal, cat Valium, green, K, Keller, Keller's day, ket, ketaject, ketalar, Kit Kat, new ecstasy, psychedelic heroin, purple, Special K, special la coke, superacid, super C, super K, vitamin K, vit K

Usage today: Because they so often slip through legal loopholes, designer drugs are considered the most underreported of all drugs.

After widespread use from the mid-1960s to the mid-1970s, they fell from favor for about 2 decades, then sparked again in the mid-1990s. While a consensus of drug agencies believes that use of designer drugs has declined since 2002, it is estimated that today about 15 percent of Americans between age 16 and 35 take at least one designer drug every year.

The medical treatment: If dependency on a designer drug develops, it most often implies a general state of unhappiness. For that reason, short-term therapy should target counseling, peer influence, stress management, and, in severe cases, short-term use of serotonergics (medications that raise serotonin levels).

15

Cross-Addiction

CASE STUDY: GREG, CROSS-ADDICTED TO ALCOHOL AND COCAINE

Intervention

The manager was sweating. Another 3:00 a.m. phone call. Another load of trouble. Would it never end?

First things first. Post bond, have Greg released. Get a groupie to sit on him, make sure he stays put. Then call the lawyer, offer him 50K to cut a deal—all cash. Hell, the legal fees, fines, penalties, even the treatment facility—they were all expensed from the artist's end anyway. And one lousy gig would pay for it all. Well worth it. Anything that would keep Greg out of jail so he could finish one more tour. Scalp a few tickets at each venue, maybe 4,000 overall. A quarter mil, tax free, in his own pocket.

But all this was getting to be too much, too often. The last time was . . . where? Chicago, New York? And when . . . 5 months ago?

Time to roll the dice and hope for another year, then take his percentage and walk. The Bahamas, Hawaii, wherever. Laze in the sun with a young beauty who wanted to break into the business. That was the ticket—one more year, then say good-bye and let that sick, arrogant jerk fend for himself.

Medical Evaluation

INTAKE FORM

Name: Greg_____ **Age:** 34_____ **SMDW:**_____ **Sex:** M
Occupation: Rock and roll **Referred By:** Manager

Current Problems/Complaints:

I was partying with friends and was playing around with my gun and the cops got
involved. Made a deal to come here.

Past Medical History

❑ Childhood Illness   ❑ ADD   ❑ Trauma (Emotional/Physical)
❑ Anxiety   ❑ Depression
❑ Other _____

Medical Illnesses

❑ Anxiety   ❑ Depression   ❑ Insomnia
❑ Chronic Pain   ❑ Hyperactivity/ADD   ❑ Bipolar
❑ OCD   ❑ Weight Changes   ❑ Stress
❑ Other _____

Psychological History

❑ Divorce in Family   ❑ Unexpected Death in Family
❑ Recent Change in Relationship
❑ Chronic Pain   ❑ Job Stress   ❑ Sexual Issues
❑ Recent Life Changes _____

Habits

- ❏ Nicotine ❏ Alcohol ❏ Recreational Drugs
- ❏ Marijuana ❏ Metabolic/Weight Problems
- Exercise: ❏ Never ❏ Occasionally ❏ Often
- ❏ Other _____

Current Medications _____

Surgeries _____

Family History

	Living	Deceased	Health Problems
Mother			
Father			
Siblings			

Health Problems in Your Family

- ❏ Irritable/Spastic Bowel ❏ Depression ❏ Suicide
- ❏ Hyperactive/ADD ❏ Obesity ❏ Bipolar
- ❏ Headaches ❏ Back Pain ❏ Anxiety
- ❏ Heart Disease ❏ Cancers ❏ Diabetes
- ❏ Nicotine ❏ Caffeine ❏ Alcohol
- ❏ Other Drug Abuse_____

Patient Interview (from Transcript)

"Everybody's making a big deal about nothing, man. I was playing a stadium concert here and we had an afterparty in my hotel suite. You know—sex, drugs, and rock 'n' roll. One of the roadies got some Peruvian flake, primo stuff. I got wired and started drinking some Chivas to chill the high. Liquid gold, man.

"Anyway, my big sister said something to me and I must have grabbed my gun and threatened her. She got scared and called hotel security. They came in when the party was full blast and called the cops. It was all a mistake. I mean, my sister can be a huge pain in the ass, but I'd never hurt her.

"So I was arrested on both a gun and possession charge. The drug beef was shaky from the get-go. They really couldn't prove they were my drugs or anything. My lawyer made a sweet deal: I'd go to rehab if they'd settle the weapons charge for just a fine. What the hell, we got a tour coming up; we'll make back the cost of the fine in about 2 minutes. So instead of jail, I'm here.

"The shows, the music—they're a rush. The drugs help me come down afterward. I have all the money and women I'll ever want or need and hundreds of so-called friends to get me whatever I want. It's not what you'd call exciting or a challenge anymore, but it's cool. I just say the word and it's there.

"Drugs get me high and ready to party . . . and I deserve a little fun."

Physician Analysis

Greg couldn't be bothered to fill out the intake form, so he's probably not taking the idea of rehab seriously. Or he thinks he can slide through it with no commitment and a minimum of effort.

Greg is a good example of the common occurrence of cross-addiction, which is defined as the abuse of more than one substance. While it can imply multiple imbalances (or primary diseases), cross-addiction is more often the result of an addict's self-medicated response to the effects of his primary addiction. In Greg's case, cocaine is most likely his primary addiction, and he abuses it to such an extent that his "high" is extremely intense, so he lessens (or "cuts") its impact by self-medicating with a similarly abusive amount of alcohol.

Mired in his addictions and sense of entitlement, with seemingly unlimited financial resources and a host of enablers and codependents, Greg is myopic to his level of danger. He can have anything he wants—any girl, any car, any house, and any drug. Anything that money can buy or celebrity can seduce. And no bad feelings, ever. Nobody says no to him.

He has the ego development of a 2-year-old, and no one parents his bad behaviors. He is in denial of his abuse and the seriousness of its consequences; pointing a loaded gun at his sister is an interesting metaphor for his own life. He has always managed to avoid the rules and has no respect for boundaries.

Greg is neither willing to change nor ready for treatment.

Rejected for treatment.

Postscript

After Greg was dismissed from our outpatient treatment, he was redirected—through the efforts of his manager and lawyers—to a posh 28-day beachfront inpatient program. He lasted less than 2 weeks. While going through the motions, he was supplied drugs by an employee of the facility who was a big fan of his.

Greg will need to hit bottom financially to shed the parasites from his life who enable him and prevent him from getting his disease under control. Or, more likely, he will continue to act recklessly until he eventually trades his beachfront treatment center for a court-ordered cell at a correctional unit. Or worse.

Preventive Care

CASE STUDY: ALICIA

Alicia is one of my favorite people . . . and her experience became one of my most illuminating cases. At age 16, she was far wiser than her years. We can all learn from her.

I met Alicia at an intervention for her cousin. At the time, she was secretly going through her own issues with substance abuse. She wasn't addicted or even using—not yet. In fact, she seemed to be the only one in her crowd and immediate environment who didn't use any substance. If her teenage friends weren't already abusing drugs, they were starting to dabble (called chipping). But I didn't know any of this when Alicia took me aside and asked if she could talk to me about "something important." Figuring it was related to her cousin's treatment, I made an appointment to meet her in my office the next day.

At our meeting, Alicia told me the whole story about her vulnerability to drug abuse. She had done her homework well and was justifiably concerned about the red flags she had found in her history that pointed to a life of addiction.

She was genetically predisposed: Her mother was an alcoholic, and her cousin and her father abused opiate-based painkillers. She was imprinted by growing up in an alcoholic family clouded by depression and by living in a neighborhood rife with drugs and crime. Alicia herself had frequent bouts of depression and sadness. And she had stressors that had begun to weigh heavily on her: a recent and painful breakup with a boyfriend, difficulty keeping up in school, and a body that had changed dramatically over the past year, further confusing and complicating her sense of self.

Alicia felt an almost impending doom, trapped by indicators over which she seemingly had no control and yet were leading her down what she feared was an inevitable path to addiction. But she was determined not to become yet another helpless victim of circumstance, so she came in to explore proactive options that might keep her from falling into the dark pit of substance abuse.

There is a critical moment when every teenager reaches a fork in the road. They can make a right turn or a left. The choice they make will impact the rest of their lives.

Alicia had reached her moment of truth and wanted more than anything to know how to find her way, to travel the road not taken by her addicted family and friends.

Here's what I told her . . . and it became the outline of a program she started that very day. (Did I mention that Alicia was very smart?)

"You can't change your genetics, but you can choose the way you cope when you're dealt a bad hand. Do you stand pat, helpless against onrushing disaster, or do you acquire new cards that change the bad hand to one of infinite possibility? Let's be clear—genetic predisposition is an indicator, *not a certainty*. Predisposition is *not* predetermination. Especially when smart choices are made that put you on the right path instead of a wrong one."

Smart choices are often not easy for teenagers. The brain begins to develop its prefrontal cortex and inferior cortex—the areas that supervise judgment and self-control—only in the late teens, a process that completes itself sometime in the mid-twenties. Until then, teenagers and young adults are vulnerable to bad judgment, a lack of inhibitory control, and a higher likelihood of addictive behaviors. But even this susceptibility can be mitigated to some extent by preventive action.

In Alicia's case, serotonin is the imbalanced neurotransmitter responsible for her family's strands of depression and alcoholism and their use (and abuse) of prescription opiates (painkillers). If Alicia pharmaceutically rebalances and stabilizes her serotonin, her moods and functioning will improve. She will be in a better place to understand her stressors and gain insight into healthy options that don't involve drug abuse. Bad balance risks bad judgments . . . and good balance more often results in good decisions.

In addition to receiving proactive medical treatment, Alicia will be introduced to a team of professionals who will evaluate and then supervise the behavioral changes she needs to employ. Initially, these will include regular exercise, a good night's sleep, and a balanced diet as part of her routine. As she integrates more fully into her program, Alicia will receive counseling to help deal with her parents. She will be given options for career planning and assistance with her schoolwork. Her team of professionals will protect and guide her by establishing one-on-one, long-term relationships built on mutual respect and trust—something she has missed and wanted all her life.

Ultimately, Alicia will be empowered, educated, supported, and encouraged to stay on the path of sobriety.

Alicia is a special but all-too-rare case of preventing potential addiction before it happens. As our global understanding of addiction becomes clearer, we will no doubt see more successes like hers. The sooner that happens, the better we'll be able to prevent at-risk individuals of any age from falling prey to the disease of addiction before it needlessly destroys more lives.

Why 10 Percent Fail

In a perfect world, there would be no failures. Especially in medicine—a field in which failure so often spells tragedy—and most particularly in addiction, a shadow world populated by tortured souls and heartbroken friends and family.

But in the real world, even the best, safest, and most foolproof methods sometimes fail. Even though the new medical treatment of addiction carries a success rate of over 90 percent, failures occur in nearly one in 10 patients. Discovering the reason behind each failure and addressing it can lead to better practices and a higher success rate in the future—a win-win scenario for everyone.

In the new medical paradigm, failures can occur when:

1. Patients are not sincerely motivated or willing to change.
2. Patients are given the wrong stabilizing medications, are inappropriately medicated, or are not medicated when necessary. Doctors prescribe drugs according to guidelines set by pharmaceutical companies, but those are merely target doses. In the case of psychotropic medications, the target

must be achieved slowly. This requires careful medical supervision to ensure the patient's safety and to minimize uncomfortable side effects brought on by the sudden rush of neurotransmitter changes caused by those drugs. When unpleasant side effects persist, patients often discontinue the meds and lose trust in the treatment.

3. Doctors don't work in a team.

4. Associated problems like sleep disorders, pain syndromes, and metabolic disorders are not treated concomitantly with a patient's addictions.

5. When the new paradigm takes months to show real progress— and sometimes it does—patients get impatient or frustrated and return to bad habits.

6. Patients are inadequately monitored, and bad behaviors take over.

7. Addicts possess a long-ingrained sense of entitlement that renders rules and consequences unenforceable.

8. Codependents or enablers sabotage the therapy.

9. A huge life stress hits too early in treatment.

10. Nonoperable pain syndromes worsen, particularly in cases of opiate addiction.

11. Long-term substance abuse has wreaked irreversible damage to the prefrontal cortex to the brain, negatively and severely impacting the memory and behavior centers, making it almost impossible for patients to restructure their lives.

12. Other medical problems like cancer, diabetes, Alzheimer's, or heart disease render patients less functional.

Note: In circumstances like those described in points 11 and 12, the medical treatment can still promote limited success, but relapses are more common and unpredictable than desired.

It must be emphasized that just because one or another of the previous 12 situations occurs during treatment, it does not necessarily mean the treatment will fail. Patients with entitlements can and do succeed, patients with brain damage can and do succeed, improperly monitored patients can and do succeed, and so on. But when treatment does fail, which is less than 10 percent of the time, it's most often a result of one of these 12 reasons.

But remember, "stuff happens" to everybody . . . and there's always another opportunity for success.

Postmortem

U nlike our composites, the person in this case history was real, and his story is true. While he is no longer alive, his story reveals what it was like to be trapped in a multifaceted disease without benefit of science or modern medicine.

CASE STUDY: WILLIAM

William's genetic background was a veritable breeding ground for addiction. His grandfather, father, and countless other relatives suffered from severe alcoholism, chronic depression, and/or obsessive and compulsive behaviors.

When William was a child, his father abandoned the family, leaving William with a mother so physically abusive he eventually had to be raised by his grandmother.

By his early teens, William was plagued by depression, obsessive behavior, and mood swings. He started smoking heavily—up to two packs a day.

While in the military, William had his first drink, a glass of beer that didn't do much for him. But later on, at a dinner party, he drank a few

Bronx cocktails—gin, vermouth, and a splash of orange juice—and found what he later described to friends as "the elixir of life." Alcohol had relieved his social anxiety and replaced it with a confidence, personal ease, and disinhibition William had never felt before. After a lifetime of feeling bad, William finally felt good. He was hooked. Even drinking to the point of passing out (something he did with increasing frequency) could not deter him from his miracle elixir.

While everyone acknowledged his high intelligence, William's behaviors grew increasingly destructive. He failed at university, in law school, and as a stockbroker. His relationships with family, friends, and co-workers became abusive, driven by his depression, frightening mood swings, personal obsessions, and alcohol.

These disappointments subtracted from his already low self-esteem and exacerbated his stress. But like so many other addicts, William's self-medicating "solution" was to drink even more, because alcohol was the only thing that made him feel better.

His health began to deteriorate. He contracted emphysema, a severe lung disease associated with cigarettes and nicotine addiction.

William was soon a regular patient at a hospital for drug and alcohol addictions, in and out the revolving door at least four times. During his stays, he met a doctor who theorized that alcoholism was akin to "a physical allergy with an obsessive aspect"—in other words, *a medical condition*.

William was thrilled to learn that his addiction was an illness and not something due to a lack of good character or a moral failure on his part. *(Does that sound familiar?)*

At the hospital, William was given various medications to little effect. Then he tried a prescribed dose of belladonna, a homeopathic remedy containing toxins that can cause delirium and hallucinations.

Under the drug's influence, William had "a hot flash spiritual conver-
sion" and finally quit drinking.

Feeling isolated in his recovery, William white-knuckled his sobriety,
holding on 1 day, 1 hour, 1 minute at a time—fueled by cigarettes (reaching four packs a day) and prodigious amounts of coffee and sweets. He
remained sober, but he still felt bad.

Then he had an idea. There had to be other alcoholics just like him,
hanging by a thread, toughing out their far-from-easy sobrieties alone,
with no real help from any quarter.

With a friend, William organized a group of alcoholics who met regularly to support each other in their quest for sobriety. The idea caught on
and the circle grew and grew . . . until it became the most important
lifestyle approach to addiction treatment of the 20th century.

It should be clear by now that William was Bill W., cofounder of Alcoholics
Anonymous. His achievements, by any standard, were remarkable.

Seventy-five years ago, AA was the new paradigm on which almost
all subsequent and conventional treatment was eventually based. In the
intervening years, AA provided comfort and solace to millions. But for
Bill W., the AA model was incomplete.

Bill thought of AA as a three-legged stool. One leg was the mental,
another was the spiritual. The third was physical or medical. In Bill's
mind, the three legs were equal; each had an identical amount of responsibility for supporting the stool. Without any one leg, the stool would be
imbalanced and incomplete.

Now sober but still chronically depressed, compulsive, and unhappy, Bill
realized that the important medical leg of the stool was missing. To that

end, he shared in meetings and with anyone he could the story of the "medical" belladonna treatment that sparked his sobriety. He brought aboard Dr. William Silkworth—the physician who theorized addiction as "a physical allergy with an obsessive aspect"—to serve as medical director of AA.

Most telling of all, Bill spent the rest of his life searching for the missing link that would complete his sobriety—the medical component that would erase his constant and obsessive urges (or wantings) and eradicate his depression and mood swings and bring his life into balance.

At one point, Bill believed that niacin (a B vitamin) stabilized his mood swings—he even sold it to other alcoholics to help their transition into sobriety. When that didn't pan out, he tried LSD and myriad other experimental drugs with little or no success. Until the end of his life, he never abandoned his quest to find the medical leg of his metaphorical stool.

In the days before his death from emphysema and pneumonia, Bill still suffered from depression and mood swings, still smoked heavily (despite the need for an oxygen tank to help him breathe), and struggled daily with his decades-long sobriety.

Sadly, while Bill had the foresight to see that medicine was the essential aspect to any lasting solution of the addiction puzzle, the missing piece wouldn't be found for more than 3 decades after his death.

Bill W. lived in an era vastly different from the world we live in today. Modern imaging techniques giving visual access to the mysteries buried in the mind were the stuff of science fiction. The sciences of brain chemistry, genetics, and heredity were in their infancy. Even the concept of stress as it related to medicine was years away from full realization.

But what Bill believed would eventually occur has finally happened. Science has found the missing medical link in treating addiction—the

recognition that addiction originates in specific imbalanced neurotransmitters in the brain, is determined by genetics, and is triggered by
stress.

In hindsight, we can see that in most ways Bill's alcohol addiction was
predictable. With everything that modern science has discovered about
brain chemistry, we can now medically connect the dots from his depression to low serotonin to alcohol abuse. Today, we can spot the genetic red
flags that point to Bill's depression and alcoholism. And with a runaway
father, an abusive mother, and his constant failures in early adulthood,
Bill was a veritable poster boy for cumulative and major stress.

Bill was correct in his belief in a relationship between addiction and
disease, and he was typical of those caught in an era when only behavioral
therapies that failed at a rate of more than 90 percent were available.

If Bill were alive today, the new medical paradigm would improve his
chances not only for a vastly more comfortable sobriety but also for the
happiness that eluded him. He would be safely and medically detoxed.
During his medical stabilization, a new and improved baseline balance
would be created to successfully manage his serotonin deficit. Smart-targeting pharmaceuticals would eliminate his biochemical wanting for alcohol and treat the major issues of his depression, mood swings, and
obsessive behaviors. Bill's four-packs-a-day dependency on nicotine
typifies cross-addiction. Of course, we now know that smoking is a self-
medicating reaction to elevated glutamate and noradrenalin levels created
by a serotonin deficit. Today, we can successfully treat this specific anxiety
response with Chantix, a pharmaceutical that targets nicotine receptors.

Co-occurring problems related to addiction, like sleep disorders and
pain management, would be treated. Modern behavioral therapies and
lifestyle counseling, importantly including sophisticated stress management techniques, would contribute to a better quality of life.

Bill W.'s case history shows just how far addiction treatment has evolved over the last half century and illustrates how the new medical paradigm could have benefited not only Bill himself but every person of his and succeeding generations who struggled courageously against a disease that was once so tragically misdiagnosed and misunderstood.

Let's be clear—the new medical paradigm *does not* invalidate AA. Rather, it takes AA's most effective features and adds to them the medical aspect that completes Bill W.'s ideal model. For instance, Bill not only recognized the benefits of treating this disease medically, he also created a team approach by focusing on the sharing of his mental and spiritual aspects in AA meetings.

The new paradigm incorporates Bill's group concept even as it expands the team approach to include patient partnerships with specialists in all fields necessary to each addict's *personalized* recovery program. Whether it's family and/or vocational counseling, private therapy, nutritional guidance, neuropharmacology, exercise and training, stress management programs, or anything else the patient needs to augment his or her recovery, the new paradigm provides it.

As Bill believed, attaching the medical treatment gives patients a model that treats *all* aspects of the disease, paving the way to a complete and comprehensive addiction solution.

POWERLESS . . . OR EMPOWERED?

Before the advent of modern medicine, addicts were largely powerless over their illnesses. Back then, medical professionals had barely an inkling of how or why addiction manifested. In the absence of any real knowledge based on proven scientific facts, diagnosis and treatment were haphazard guesswork based on behavioral observation and not on medicine.

But times—and things—change.

Technology has opened a wide window of scientific discovery, shining a light of hope and possibility where before there was only darkness. Today, people with diabetes effectively manage their disease with insulin throughout long and healthy lives. Every passing day sees more cancer victims become cancer survivors, thanks to treatment options made available by modern medical technology. Heart patients are the welcome recipients of advanced diagnostic tools and treatments that extend their lives for decades.

The same kind of technological progress has imbued the world of addiction with proven science on which it has built successful treatment options. We now know that addiction originates in brain chemistry, is determined by genetics, and is triggered by stress. Medicine has pinpointed the specific neurotransmitter imbalances responsible for specific addictions and offers numerous medical options to alleviate its destructive impact.

The practice of medicine has similarly evolved. Physicians in every field now encourage patients to actively participate in a productive doctor-patient partnership, empowering them toward wellness.

Why shouldn't they?

Has any chronic but treatable disease ever been solved by powerlessness? Especially when successful treatment options are available?

Should people with diabetes, cancer, or heart disease remain powerless over their diseases . . . or should they empower themselves to engage in effective treatment?

And what about addicts? Back in the days when nothing substantial was known about the disease of addiction, there were good reasons to seek serenity by powerlessly accepting the things they could not change. But now we live in a world that would have seemed miraculous just 75 years ago. Change is not only possible, it is here.

So should addicts remain powerless—or should they empower themselves to change their lives by seeking wellness (and serenity) in the new and successful treatment options supported by science and medicine?

What would Bill W. do?

Powerlessness implies inactivity, like an appliance that is not plugged into its electrical current. Empowerment is about plugging into responsible choices and then acting upon them to your fullest capacity.

Bill W. was a man who sought choices even when there were no choices . . . and then made them happen. He cofounded AA and built it into one of the largest networks in human history. But he didn't stop there. He spent the rest of his life searching for the medical component that would complete his tripartite vision. Until the end of his days, he actively sought positive change that would restore and improve the lives of addicts everywhere.

If truth be told, there wasn't a powerless bone in Bill's body.

So, given his firm belief in science and his empowered, proactive, and lifelong search for a medical solution to the addiction puzzle, what would Bill do today?

Would he empower himself to choose a safe, comfortable, and medically managed sobriety, one that would successfully treat his severe depressions, obsessive behaviors, erratic mood swings, and nicotine addiction as well as his alcoholism?

Or would he powerlessly bear a torturous sobriety—just as unhappy as it was in his real life—filled with depression, obsessive behaviors, mood swings, and four packs of cigarettes a day, white-knuckling it through 1 day, 1 hour, and 1 miserable moment at a time?

If you were Bill W., which one would you choose? And which one would you choose for yourself?

ACKNOWLEDGMENTS

The writing of any book is a journey on which many people help in many different ways. The following people made this journey a rewarding one for us both.

Barry Krost, Steve Troha, and Shannon Welch—our manager, agent, and editor, respectively—for expertly guiding us through the publishing maze.

Our families—Michael Kipper, Stuart Kipper, and Gretchen Ochsenschlager—for always being there.

Our legal eagles—John Harwell and Amy Lawrence.

In the office—Valentina Ikan, Greg Hausmann, Connie Wilson, and David's amazing nursing staff.

Jessi Quinlan for research, commentary, drafting, and filling in all the various holes.

Allan Taylor and James Robert Parish for wise and experienced counsel on all aspects of the project.

Those who provided both encouragement and support at various stops along the way: Candy Finnigan, James L. Brooks, Albert Brooks, Danny DeVito and Rhea Pearlman, Florence Henderson, Peter Tilden,

Stuart Birnbaum, Steven Cole, Dr. Harland Winter, Danny Kopels, Alan Blaustein, Marc Block, Brenda Friend Brandt, Efren Saldivar, Steven Chapman, Steve Feke, John Kalodner, Dr. Alexander Tovar, Terry Thompson, Nicole Powers, Dr. Maurice Jay Smith, Ken Giurandella, Thomas Erie Haste III, Martin Levitt, Tim Mertz, Andre Morgan, Dr. Michael E. Scott, Bob Timmons, Will and Susan Utay, Barbara Ann Quinlan, and the Bakers of Camberwell.

And all the addicts and caregivers who shared so openly with us during the research and writing of this book.

Our deepest and most profound thanks to them all.

APPENDIX 1

PRIMARY DISEASES

Although the human brain can work wonders, the slightest neuro-chemical imbalance can wreak havoc on your mind, body, and (as a result) your life. Problematic behaviors and mood disorders—often characterized as primary diseases—can manifest as a result of these imbalances, leaving you at risk for addiction. In fact, when the roots of addiction are examined, a connection can be found between specific neurotransmitter imbalances that cause specific primary diseases and result in specific types of addiction.

Because addiction is a secondary disease, it's vital to take a brief look at the primary diseases that precede it. These often ignored disorders are not only good indicators of potential addiction, they also identify the type of substance (stimulants, depressants, and so on) to which the addict will be predisposed.

Since abused substances are linked to specific imbalanced neu-rotransmitters, the primary diseases are listed here by their direct rela-tionships to imbalanced neurotransmitters.

FROM DOPAMINE IMBALANCES

ADD/ADHD

Attention deficit disorder (ADD) and attention deficit hyperactive disorder (ADHD) are conditions characterized by an inability to focus and/or a surplus of activity due to a dopamine imbalance. Those who suffer from ADD or ADHD (the more intense disorder) struggle to concentrate and often feel distracted, scattered, and irritable.

In the past decade, diagnoses of ADD have skyrocketed. This may be a sign of doctors and parents pinning a convenient (and treatable) label on annoying behavior, or it could be a chemical trend—it's too early to tell. In truth, every individual has nuanced brain chemistry that shows at least slight tendencies toward one or another primary disease. Like many other disorders or syndromes, ADD is a continuum of gradations and distinctions. If someone seeks (or wants) an ADD diagnosis, usually some evidence can be found to support it.

True ADD/ADHD is medically treated with prescriptive stimulants such as Ritalin, Adderall, and Dexedrine that target the brain's excess dopamine that is the root cause of this primary disease. Absent these medications, the dopamine imbalance responsible for ADD/ADHD can, under stressful conditions, create biochemical wantings for stimulants such as cocaine, meth, nicotine, and caffeine.

Bipolar Disorder

This multifaceted personality disorder differs from person to person. Indeed, the disorder comes in so many different shapes and colors that it's difficult to quickly define, and it's nearly impossible to compare one bipolar experience to another. Yet every bipolar expression originates from the same neurochemical imbalances of dopamine.

Generally, bipolar disorders are characterized by sudden and severe mood swings—ranging from extreme mania and elation on one end of the scale to fatigue, depression, and resignation on the other. The duration and intensity of these mood swings, or "cycles," are differentiated by the degree of dopamine imbalance in each individual.

The most effective treatments for bipolar disorder are drawn from mood stabilizers (like lithium and Lamictal), atypical antipsychotic meds (like Zyprexa, Abilify, and Risperdal), and antidepressants (like Wellbutrin), all of which target and restore dopamine imbalances. Careful monitoring of these medications is mandatory because side effects are common.

Since excess levels of dopamine can create a sensation of pleasure, bipolar patients presenting with mania often reject treatment because they already feel great. They often view their behavior as acceptable and normal and are unaware of its impact on those around them. Many also mistakenly fear that treatment will dull both their creativity and their emotions, which is not the case.

CAUSE →	PRIMARY DISEASE →	SECONDARY DISEASE
EXCESS DOPAMINE→	ADD/ADHD →	
	BIPOLAR DISORDERS	ABUSE OF STIMULANTS

FROM SEROTONIN IMBALANCES

Depression

This emotional condition—characterized by feelings of sadness, loss of energy, short-term memory loss, and overall resignation from life—is caused by a chemical imbalance in the serotonin neurotransmitter. Other common symptoms include depression, insomnia, social anxiety, obsessive thoughts and behavior, significant changes in weight, impaired concentration, feelings of worthlessness, and, in severe cases, recurring thoughts of death and/or suicide.

Victims of depression often assume their bad feelings are caused by sad events and don't realize that their feelings are triggered by imbalanced brain chemistry, so they don't seek treatment until family and/or close friends intervene. These inherited serotonin imbalances are chronic, and those affected often adapt to their bad feelings and accept them as normal.

When correctly diagnosed, depression can be effectively treated with antidepressant medications such as Prozac, Zoloft, Paxil, and Lexapro or other SSRIs (selective serotonin reuptake inhibitors) that increase serotonin in the brain, creating a true physiologic "normal." A newer class of these medications, the SNRIs (serotonin and noradrenalin reuptake inhibitors), modulate both the depressed serotonin levels as well as the increased noradrenalin levels that often accompany this imbalance. Examples of SNRIs include Effexor, Cymbalta, and Pristiq.

Alcohol and opiates temporarily increase low serotonin levels, making the depressed and obsessive feel better and less anxious and thus paving the way to substance abuse.

Compulsions

This component of addiction is generally displayed through repetitive or even ritualistic thoughts that drive addicts into self-destructive behavior. Compulsions create the need for constant reinforcement and drive behavior and actions to unnatural rhythms.

Compulsions stem from a serotonin deficit or imbalance that, in turn, provokes an urgent and unreasonable need to gain emotional and/or physical equilibrium.

Those with compulsive disorders who are under stress cannot achieve any sort of balance or harmony unless their serotonin levels are augmented with SSRI and SNRI medications.

Obsessions

A behavior commonly associated with addiction, obsessions are characterized by an unwanted drive toward a specific object, person, or idea that behaviorally manifests as a fixation.

But an obsession is not an ordinary road trip. People with obsessive disorders drive as fast as they can toward the objects of their fixation, seemingly unaware of any roadblocks, as if their survival depends on reaching their always unreachable destination. It's a very real and perilous mental journey fraught with anxiety and frustration.

Since those suffering from obsessive disorders can never satisfy their need to achieve their goals, they are constantly anxious and often experience depression and insomnia.

OCD

Obsessive compulsive disorder (OCD) is characterized by unwanted thoughts and/or repetitive and often ritualistic behavior, both clear signals of a serotonin deficiency.

OCD can be described as a toxic blend of obsessive and compulsive behaviors, incorporating the worst of both. Those with OCD may incessantly wash their hands, constantly check to see that the doors are locked, or endlessly ruminate over issues they cannot control. Whatever relief they get from their behaviors is always short-lived, leaving them in a constant state of anxiety.

OCD is now almost completely manageable with medications that address the imbalance in the serotonin neurotransmitter.

In the movie *As Good as It Gets*, the character played by Jack Nicholson is the poster boy for OCD. He had to lock his door six times, could not step on the cracks in the sidewalk, had to sit at the same table in the same restaurant at the same time each day, and washed his hands repetitively with soap lined up in neat and orderly stacks on his spotless bathroom sink. When he finally submitted to taking medication (SSRIs), his behavior changed, his anxiety was relieved, and his ability to function and enjoy life dramatically improved.

CAUSE →	PRIMARY DISEASE →	SECONDARY DISEASE
LOW SEROTONIN →	DEPRESSION; OCD; →	ABUSE OF DEPRESSANTS
	COMPULSIONS;	(ALCOHOL AND OPIATES)
	OBSESSIONS	

FROM NORADRENALIN IMBALANCE

Anxiety Disorders

This constellation of the aforementioned nervous behaviors results from an inability to gain control over life events and is caused by an increase in the brain's noradrenalin levels. There are four main disorders in this category.

- **Generalized anxiety disorder:** This condition manifests as relatively mild but chronic anxiety, tension, and concern with no apparent cause.

- **Panic disorder:** This is an intense and sudden onset of anxiety that results in attacks of frightening symptoms that include a pounding heart, weakness or dizziness, nausea, chest pain, numbness and/or tingling of the hands and legs, a flushing, and feelings of uncontrollable fear and impending doom. Commonly known as a panic attack, it is fueled by the chemical fight-or-flight response that causes a sudden and exaggerated release of noradrenalin in the brain. While these attacks seem to come out of left field, they actually originate from current stressors in one's life.

- **Post-traumatic stress disorder:** PTSD differs from panic disorder in that the attacks originate from painful flashbacks of distressing events, like childhood abuse or combat trauma. When a traumatic episode is reactivated by some unconscious stimulus or association, the brain may have difficulty distinguishing the powerful memory from reality. When it is tricked into thinking that danger is imminent, adrenaline floods in, creating tremendous anxiety.

- **Social anxiety disorder:** This social phobia develops from the rush of adrenalin produced from the fear of social interaction. This form of anxiety can develop from seemingly harmless and common social situations like eating or dancing in front of others. At other times, it can be as broad as a fear of open or public spaces (agoraphobia).

While there exists no real cure for anxiety disorders, they can be safely and comfortably managed with antidepressants, antianxiety medications, beta-blockers, and behavioral therapies like exercise and dietary changes. These treatments usually work best when they are administered in tandem with talk therapies and more event-focused treatments called cognitive behavioral therapies (CBTs).

CAUSE	→	PRIMARY DISEASE	→	SECONDARY DISEASE
EXCESS NORADRENALIN	→	GENERALIZED ANXIETY DISORDER; PANIC DISORDER; PTSD; SOCIAL ANXIETY DISORDER	→	ABUSE OF BENZOS (VALIUM, XANAX, ATIVAN, ETC.)

APPENDIX 2

REFERENCES

Origins in Brain Chemistry

Kranzler, H. R., H. Tennen, and Armeli, et al. 2009. "Targeted Naltrexone Reduces Alcohol Use among Male Problem Drinkers." *Brown University Psychopharmacology Update* 20 (11): 1, 6–7.
Long-term use of Naltrexone has been shown to decrease drinking by 19 percent in males with mild-moderate dependence levels. It may also benefit in short-term psychotherapeutic intervention. This does not apply to women.

Conner, B. T., and G. S. Hellemann, et al. 2010. "Genetic, Personality, and Environmental Predictors of Drug Use in Adolescents." *Journal of Substance Abuse Treatment* 38 (2): 178–190.
This study outlines the genetic, neurochemical, environmental, neurocognitive, and psychological factors that contribute to early drug use. Dopaminergic and GABAergic genes were the main focus. The research collected determined that it may be "possible to identify children at risk for problematic drug use prior to the onset of drug dependence."

Bukstein, O. 2008. "Substance Abuse in Patients with Attention-Deficit/Hyperactivity Disorder." *Medscape Journal of Medicine* 10 (1).
This article outlines the common co-morbidity of ADHD and substance use. More important, it supports the treatment of the primary disorder (ADHD) as a solution for the secondary (addiction). Early treatment of ADHD may also prevent substance use in the future.

Gass, J. T., and M. F. Olive. 2008. "Glutamatergic Substrates of Drug Addiction." *Biochemical Pharmacology* 75 (1): 218–265.
The role of the amino acid glutamate in the addiction process and the value of potentiation of said acid to allay addictive behaviors.

Leshner, A. "Understanding Drug Addiction: Insights from the Research." In
 Graham, A. W., et al. (eds). *Principles of Addiction Medicine.* 3rd edition.
 Chevy Chase, MD: American Society of Addiction Medicine. 2003: 47–54.
 Addiction as a neurological disease, not a social disorder.

Treatment

Netherland, J., and M. Botsko, et al. 2009. "Factors Affecting Willingness to
 Provide Buprenorphine Treatment." *Journal of Substance Abuse Treatment*
 36 (3): 244–251.
 *In this article advocating for the use of buprenorphine in opiate-dependent
 patients, the benefits of this drug are outlined. Ability to make buprenorphine
 use more widespread (especially for the middle and lower class), emphatic
 support from major medical groups (SAMHSA, NYAM, BHIVES, etc.), and its
 status as the most effective new treatment available.*

Carroll, C., and P. Triplet, et al. 2009. "The Intensive Treatment Unit: A Brief
 Inpatient Detoxification Facility Demonstrating Good Postdetoxification
 Treatment Entry." *Journal of Substance Abuse Treatment* 37 (2): 111–119.
 *Inpatient detoxification treatment accounts for 20 percent of patients admitted
 to public addiction care centers and is quickly becoming an industry standard,
 but it seems to be only half the solution. Of those discharged from the Intensive
 Treatment Unit in Baltimore for treatment, 80 percent moved on to some kind
 of postdetoxification program.*

Laudet, A. B., and V. Stanick, et al. 2009. "What Could the Program Have Done
 Differently? A Qualitative Examination of Reasons for Leaving Outpatient Treatment." *Journal of Substance Abuse Treatment* 37 (2): 182–190.
 *Of the 250 outpatients in this study, 54 percent did not complete treatment.
 When asked why they did not continue, a majority of patients cited "program-
 level barriers" (issues with program, counselors, inflexible scheduling, and lack of
 social service) and "individual-level barriers" (use of drugs, lack of problem
 perspective) as contributing factors.*

Stein, M. D., and D. S. Herman, et al. 2009. "A Motivational Intervention
 Trial to Reduce Cocaine Use." *Journal of Substance Abuse Treatment* 36 (1):
 118–125.

Isolating frequent cocaine users, this study proposes that intervention improves patients' likelihood for reduction in substance use following the event.

Gonzales, R., and A. Ang, et al. 2009. "Health-Related Quality of Life Trajectories of Methamphetamine-Dependent Individuals as a Function of Treatment Completion and Continued Care Over a 1-Year Period." *Journal of Substance Abuse Treatment* 37 (4): 353–61.
Methamphetamine users displayed great improvements in mental health quality of life after treatment.

Impact of Stress

Wu, P., C. S. Duarte, and D. J. Mandell, et al. 2009. "Study Uncovers Differences in Substance Use Following Mass Trauma." *Brown University Digest of Addiction Theory and Application* 28 (8): 1, 7.
Using studies measuring population substance abuse that had been completed shortly after a terrorist attack had hit the area, 77 percent of which were conducted after the events of September 11, 2001, in New York City. Ten percent of the studies tracked the substance use of survivors. The study concluded that the "probability of more than 15 percent of an exposed population reporting this type of drug use in a postterrorism environment was 55 percent."

Roozen, H. G., J. J. Boulogne, and M. W. Van Tulder, et al. 2009. "Treatment to Improve Social Network Can Aid Drinking Outcomes." *Brown University Digest of Addiction Theory and Application* 28 (8): 4–6.
Alcohol-dependent patients participating in a program designed to strengthen their personal support system, ridding themselves of enablers and fellow addicts, were far more successful in maintaining abstinence, "report[ing] an average of 80 percent abstinent days 2 years posttreatment, compared with just over 60 percent for the other two conditions." In fact, "40 percent of Network Support patients reported complete abstinence in the 90 days preceding their 2-year follow-up, compared with less than 30 percent for the other conditions."

Beets, M. W., et al. 2009. "School-Based Intervention Reduces Youth Problem Behaviors." *American Journal of Public Health* 99 (8): 1438–45.
By studying the efficacy of a 5-year trial of schoolchildren beginning in the first and second grades, researchers determined that by the fifth grade, students were

half as likely to use drugs of any kind. Interestingly, intervention students also had lower levels of sexual activity and (after 3 years in the program) "lower rates of all negative behaviors."

Genetics

DiMaio, S., and N. Grizenko, et al. 2003. "Dopamine Genes and Attention Deficit Hyperactivity Disorder: A Review." *Journal of Psychiatry and Neuroscience* 28 (1): 27–38.
A review of genetic studies that investigate dopamine-related genes in ADHD.

Johnson, B. A., and M. A. Javors, et al. 2008. "Can Serotonin Transporter Genotype Predict Serotonergic Function, Chronicity, and Severity of Drinking?" *Progress in Neuro-Psychopharmacology Biological Psychiatry* 32 (1): 209–216.
The place of modified genetics in reduction of alcohol abuse.

Montoya, I. D., and F. Vocci. 2008. "Novel Medications to Treat Addictive Disorders." *Current Psychiatry Reports* 10 (5): 392–398.
An examination of the few approved drugs to treat addiction and facilitate recovery.

Karp, P. D. 2008. "Genes and (Common) Pathways Underlying Drug Addiction." *PloS Computational Biology* 4 (1): e2.
This article is "a meta-analysis of 396 genes that were supported by two or more pieces of evidence to identify 18 molecular pathways that were statistically significant to both upstream signaling events and downstream effects."

Edwards, A.C., and D. S. Svikis, et al. 2009. "Genetic Influences on Addiction." *Primary Psychiatry* 16 (8): 40–45.
An examination of the genetic connections to addictive behaviors toward abused substances.

APPENDIX 3

ADDICTIONARY

Clarity is essential to understanding. With that in mind, this Addictionary defines words used throughout the book specifically in the context of the new paradigm of addiction medicine.

abstinence The conscious and total avoidance of abused substances and/or destructive behaviors.

abuse The deliberate or unconscious use of a dangerous substance or a damaging behavior.

addiction An assortment of behaviors that express a biochemical imbalance in the brain, frequently causing a destructive end point. These behaviors often continue despite known negative consequences.

antipsychotic A medication (like Seroquel) prescribed to restore a patient's sense of reality and functionality by reducing or eliminating agitation, hallucinations, and delusions.

anxiolytic A substance (like Valium) or behavior (like exercise) that reduces anxiety.

behavior A physical or emotional reaction to a change in homeostasis. Addictive (or destructive) behavior is a physical expression caused by the body's loss of homeostasis and the patient's instinctive efforts to restore it. Because behavior is often a reflection of an underlying medical problem, doctors consider behavior one of their best diagnostic tools.

blackout Unconscious behavior after reaching a toxic threshold from a drug or substance. A blackout is typically a red flag signaling the need for help.

brain chemistry The individual chemical soup that creates feelings and behaviors.

chemical dependency Compulsive use of substances even in spite of negative or problematic consequences.

circadian rhythm The body's natural cycle of sleep and wakefulness.

codependency A symbiotic and neurotic relationship with an addict. The
codependent feels worth and self-esteem only through the achievements or failures of the addict. The codependent is a "giver" rather than
a taker and is often self-deprecating. The opposite of narcissism, codependency is sometimes labeled "enabling toward narcissism" or
"enabling the narcissist." Codependency is almost always coupled with
addictive behavior. Like addicts', codependents' behavior is hardwired
by genetics and background . . . and they need just as much help with
their affliction.

cold turkey The sudden and chemically unaided withdrawal from addictive
substances, causing severe physical and emotional pain and sometimes
leading to death.

constant A condition or process that does not change.

craving An unconscious drive toward an addictive substance. As the craving
intensifies, it can become an irresistible biochemical wanting. It is most
likely associated with the neurotransmitter dopamine and travels through
the brain on the reward pathways.

cross-addiction A dependency upon two or more abusive substances or
behaviors at the same time, such as a dependency on both heroin and alcohol or cocaine abuse paired with a gambling disorder.

denial The refusal or inability to acknowledge a problem, such as an addiction.
Denial is a part of every behavioral or substance addiction and must be
addressed as part of any effective treatment.

dependence A reliance on an addictive substance or behavior, usually unconscious and driven by the need to avoid bad and/or uncomfortable feelings.

depressants Substances that negatively impact mood.

detoxification (detox) The process of safely withdrawing someone from an
abused substance. In the past, detox was often done cold turkey in traditional facilities. Today, the new medical treatment detoxes safely and effectively on an inpatient or outpatient basis or even at home with proper
medical supervision.

diagnosis The determination or opinion reached concerning the nature and
cause of a disease or injury derived from the evaluation of all available
information (including family history, examination, and lab data).

disease A condition (such as diabetes, cancer, and addiction) caused by the
body's impaired physiology, resulting in imbalanced homeostasis. A disease
is primarily a medical issue; the associated behaviors are typically symptoms of the disease.

disinhibition An artificial and temporary removal of personal, social, and moral restraints or boundaries due to a substance's negative impact on the inferior frontal cortex of the brain. The opposite of *inhibition*.

dopamine The pleasure and reward chemical that plays a major role in addiction.

DTs (delirium tremors) A physical reaction to the abrupt withdrawal of alcohol related to the neurotransmitter glutamate, which causes agitation. DTs can include uncontrollable tremors and seizures, nausea, vomiting, sweating, dizziness, hyperventilation, and heart palpitations and can cause permanent memory and cognitive dysfunction, leading to dementia syndromes.

dual diagnosis The assessment of an individual's biochemical neurotransmitter imbalance with the attendant manifestation of addictive predilections and/or behaviors. The neurotransmitter imbalance is the primary disease that underlies the secondary disease—e.g., addiction.

Importantly, the secondary disease—typically, an effort to restore homeostasis and to feel better—cannot be "cured" without first successfully treating the primary illness. Addiction is most often a *symptom* of an underlying emotional problem that reflects a neurotransmitter imbalance.

Depression, for instance, is directly linked to a serotonin deficiency that often leads to alcohol, heroin, and chronic marijuana abuse. To treat the alcoholism or addictions, which are merely reflections (or *symptoms*) of the root cause, you first have to address the depression by treating the serotonin deficiency.

Likewise, agitated and/or bipolar individuals suffer from an abundance of the neurotransmitters dopamine and glutamate and often find temporary relief in cocaine or meth. To cure these addictions, the primary emotional maladies and their causal points (the neurotransmitters) must be treated first.

Dx The term *Dx* simply means diagnosis . . . and a diagnosis is the answer to whatever is ailing you.

empowerment Taking control of one's own life. This begins with the individual's awareness and understanding of her own issues, good or bad. The empowered patient becomes a partner in treating her medical disease, whether it's cancer, diabetes, or addiction.

enabling/enabler A narcissistic or controlling relationship with an addict that encourages or condones unhealthy behaviors in an addict to advance the other person's neurotic agenda. It's like the manager of a rock star living off (or feeding off) his client's addiction and unconsciously (and sometimes consciously) aiding the star's addiction for his or her own purpose. Enablers are "takers," not givers. Since they suffer from low self-esteem, they transfer their egos into another ego system, taking credit for the other's success.

endorphins The body's own natural pain relievers (or analgesics) produced by the pituitary gland and the hypothalamus during rigorous exercise, pain, moments of great excitement, and orgasm. Like opiates, endorphins engender a feeling of euphoria.

fix To repair a state of unwellness. In the past, addicts feeling really bad while crashing or coming down would say they "needed to get well," so a fix was a hit or dose of their specific substance. Today, a fix restores wellness by first addressing the patient's primary disease (neurotransmitter imbalance) to "fix" the secondary addiction.

GABA (gamma-aminobutyric acid) A neurotransmitter that soothes an agitated brain.

GABAergic A substance or activity that raises GABA neurotransmitter levels, thereby reducing agitation and instilling calm. In the medical detox, nonaddictive GABAergic medications like Neurontin and Lyrica are given to patients to calm and comfort them.

genetics The science of genes (the components of DNA) and heredity. Specific genes targeting people for addictive behavior have been identified and linked to specific abused substances and neurotransmitter imbalances.

genome (combining the words *gene* and *chromosome*) is the biological "genetic map" (or "bar code") containing the entire hereditary information encoded in your DNA. Scientists and medical doctors have just recently started to read the genome, leading to remarkable new and successful medical therapies and preventions. Their reading not only confirms that a predilection toward addiction is embedded in the genes but also points the way to curing addiction before it occurs by identifying and treating both present and potential neurotransmitter imbalances.

Using the genetic map, doctors will soon be able to detect very early on whether or not a person is at risk of addiction. And they will be able to uncover the primary causes years before they might develop into the secondary disease of addiction.

genetic traits External (physical) and internal (chemical) features passed down through family lines.

glutamate A neurotransmitter that agitates the brain. It is present in every withdrawal.

habit A repetitive, often unconscious, behavior. In addiction, habits develop as a way to survive through self-medication as a way to deal with stress and maintain equilibrium, or homeostasis.

heredity The transfer of biological characteristics (including behavior and a predilection for certain diseases) from parents to children through their genes. Addiction is a hereditary problem, created by neurotransmitter imbalances passed down the family tree, with primary roots (like depression, anxiety, bipolar disorder, sleep disturbances) and the secondary malady (addiction) encoded in DNA (genes).

hit A dose of a substance, as in a hit of cocaine, taking a hit (or toke) off a joint, hammering home a hit of heroin, etc. Hits come in all sizes, depending on the extent of the addiction.

homeostasis The body's self-regulating (and self-protecting) process for continuously trying to maintain stability and comfort while adjusting or adapting to various biological and chemical changes. Homeostasis is the body's way of keeping its own internal environment in balance and harmony.

homeostatic compensations Involuntary reactions to external conditions.

honeymoon In traditional treatment, a short period of time (perhaps a week or two) in which the addict feels better—happier, less anxious, and regaining a normal sleep cycle. This most often happens just after detox, when toxic substances have vanished and the brain chemistry is rebalancing itself. It's a state of relative wellness, a transition from the constant ups and downs of addiction toward a more constant and natural balance.

After a week or two, the feeling of rejuvenation typically fades as the natural imbalance in brain chemistry—the primary disease that initially led to addiction—returns along with all the bad feelings and the biochemical wanting for the abused substance.

In the new paradigm, medically restoring and improving the brain chemistry actually fixes the root cause of addiction, leading not only to an extended honeymoon but to a lasting marriage with sobriety.

hypnotics A category of sleep-inducing psychoactive drugs prescribed for insomnia. Since sleep disorders always accompany addiction, hypnotics like Ambien and Lunesta are useful in promoting sleep during detox in order to restore the patient's natural circadian rhythm.

imprinting A natural and rapid learning process by which the very young (infants and toddlers) establish recognition, attraction, and behavior patterns.

inhibition Social restraint.

intervention An attempt by others to intervene (or stop) a behavior or process that is self-destructive. Successful interventions depend on meaningful consequences.

Jones A period of high anxiety between the time the effect of the last hit starts wearing off and the next hit arrives. Since the arrival of a Jones often marks the first noticeable step away from homeostasis (and the initial sign of withdrawal), it usually promotes a highly agitated state,. The neurotransmitters involved are dopamine (reward) and glutamate (agitation).

kicking Quitting substance abuse.

metabolism The regulation of all bodily functions. Insults to metabolism (like taking drugs or overeating) create bad feelings that perpetuate addiction.

modality A particular type or form of treatment; a methodology.

neurotransmitters Nerve cells that relay news of emotional occurrences and the primary component of addiction. The neurotransmitter systems involved with addiction are serotonin, noradrenalin, dopamine, GABA and glutamate, and opoids. It is the imbalance of these neurotransmitters that define the primary disease (for example, low serotonin creates depression) and lead to the secondary problem of addiction (in this case, alcoholism).

noradrenalin The readiness-response chemical that plays a role in addiction.

overdose A consequence of over-self-medicating, sometimes with a lethal outcome. When referring to prescription drugs, an overdose means taking more doses within a given time than recommended; when referring to illicit substances, an overdose is taking more than the normal amount, or taking a combination of drugs that do not go well together, or mixing prescription drugs with alcohol.

paradigm A new idea, founded in fact, that profoundly changes existing beliefs, models, and perceptions.

predisposition A genetic predetermination to a disease. Predisposition is not a certainty; proper preventive care can often keep the disease at bay.

primary disease In a dually diagnosed patient, the primary disease is the condition that provokes a secondary disorder.

rebound A sudden and dramatic shift in neurotransmitter balance that creates a biochemical adjustment leading to discomfort and often to a wanting. For instance, when alcohol is withdrawn, there is a sudden surge in glutamate, which was the transmitter the alcohol was suppressing.

receptor Protein molecules that attach to and then enable neurotransmitters. An example is the neurotransmitter serotonin attaching to its specific receptor, which allows the serotonin to create a change in mood. The GABA transmitter must attach to its specific receptor to create calm, and the noradrenalin receptor must connect to its specific receptor to create anxiety.

recidivism After a period of sobriety, a return to acting out destructive behaviors like drinking alcohol or abusing substances. This is usually the result of failing to treat the primary disease (the neurotransmitter imbalance), which inevitably leads to a recurrence of the secondary disease of addiction.

recovery Striving to stay healthy on a daily basis: simply trying to do the best every day.

recovery advocates Sober individuals dedicated to guiding the newly sober addict through the initial phases (detox and stabilization) of recovery. Recovery advocates facilitate 12-step meetings, set up professional appointments with the sobriety team, and are available for support in person and on the phone during the patient's vulnerable moments.

rehabilitation (rehab) Literally, "to invest again with dignity." The goal of modern rehab is not merely to take the addict off the abused drug (the secondary disease) but to treat the depression, pain, etc. (the primary disease) as well.

relapse A short- or long-term reversion to negative or addictive behavior. A relapse is an interruption or sliding back from wellness, not a complete stoppage; relapses are a natural part of any recovery program and should be dealt with compassionately, not punitively or with humiliation. The factors leading up to the relapse should be assessed and new tools introduced to the recovery plan.

reward center The clearinghouse for good feelings and sensations; located almost midpoint in the brain. The reward center is fed and controlled by dopamine, the neurotransmitter responsible for pleasurable feelings.

reward pathways Neural highways in the brain that carry chemical messages of "rewards" from the reward center to the memory, cognition, and behavior centers to reinforce (or repeat) the pleasurable experience.

Rx From the Latin for *recipe*, an Rx is a specific prescription, remedy, or solution for a disease, illness, bad feeling, disorder, or problem.

safety net The support system at hand when someone needs help. Most addicts have eroded that support by the time they seek help.

secondary disease The behavioral expression (like addiction) of a *primary disease*.

sedatives Medications used to calm the central nervous system. Sedatives are needed when dopamine and glutamate levels are elevated, as in withdrawing from substance abuse.

self-medication The act of treating one's bad or uncomfortable feelings without a doctor's advice or prescription. Self-medication springs from the body's need to maintain equilibrium and balance (homeostasis). When something goes wrong physically or emotionally, the body sends a message to the brain to fix it, with or without an available physician. Every addiction starts with the addict's attempt to self-medicate a primary problem.

serotonergics Medications used specifically to raise serotonin levels. Examples include Prozac, Paxil, Zoloft, Celexa, and Lexapro.

serotonin The mood-regulating neurotransmitter that, when imbalanced, creates depression and obsessive thoughts and behaviors.

slip A short-term, temporary relapse. For instance, for an alcoholic, a slip would be drinking one cold beer on a hot summer day.

SNRIs (serotonin and noradrenalin reuptake inhibitors) A class of antidepressant and anxiolytic medications that raise serotonin while diminishing the effects of noradrenalin. Examples are Effexor, Cymbalta, Savella, and Pristiq.

SSRIs (selective serotonin reuptake inhibitors) A class of antidepressant medications that treat opiate and alcohol abuse by increasing serotonin levels in brain chemistry. Examples are Prozac, Zoloft, Paxil, Celexa, and Lexapro.

stabilization The steps required to correct the homeostatic unrest and agitation that results when someone begins detoxification. There are four steps: 1) Reengage the patient's normal sleep patterns and circadian rhythms; 2) reduce anxiety; 3) safely detox the abused substance from the neurotransmitter; and 4) restore the natural equilibrium of the neurotransmitter system and create and maintain new and stronger neurotransmitter balances that will last a lifetime.

stimulants Substances that increase awareness while heightening alertness, endurance, productivity, and motivation. Stimulants temporarily elevate mood. Adrenaline and glutamate are natural stimulants produced within the body. Coffee and nicotine are mild stimulants; cocaine, meth, and Ecstasy are powerful stimulants.

stress Any marked change, good or bad, in homeostasis. Stress can create a shift in neurotransmitter balance that leads to bad feelings and a breakdown of coping mechanisms.

support system Anyone who is in the addict's corner.

surrender Fully acknowledging the need for help and entering treatment by choice.

toolbox A personal and metaphorical kit filled with the resources with which someone can successfully treat her addiction during the recovery process. Toolboxes can contain medications, various therapies, support groups, counseling, diet and exercise regimens, and anything else that steers the patient toward wellness.

trigger An event, a place, a memory, or almost any stimulation that elicits a certain psychological or behavioral response leading to substance abuse. A plastic straw, for instance, might trigger unpleasant memories of cocaine use. Likewise, driving past your old dealer's house can trigger feelings, good or bad, that may set off a destructive and/or addictive behavior. Triggers are often deeply implanted. They don't come from a bad place, but they can initiate bad behavior. Addicts in treatment must learn to identify the triggers that mark destructive behavior and control them.

wanting An irresistible urge or craving that arises from a neurochemical reflex, creating bad feelings that need a "fix." No matter the object of the wanting, the drive for this object comes from the dopamine neurotransmitter and its effect on the reward center of the brain.

willingness to change An openness to admit problems and seek solutions; the first step and basic foundation toward realizing *The Addiction Solution*.

APPENDIX 4

RESOURCE GUIDE

Suicide Hotline

The National Institute of Drug Abuse (NIDA) and the National Institute of Mental Health (NIMH) have suicide prevention sources and hotlines nationwide. If you or someone you know is considering suicide, don't hesitate to call: **1-800-273-TALK [1-800-273-7255]**

Crisis Planning

The Substance Abuse and Mental Health Services Administration (SAMHSA) offers an action plan both to aid recovery and prevent the intensifying of addictive tendencies. This includes warning signs, priorities during treatment and even homeopathic aids. **http://nmhicstore.samhsa.gov/ publications/allpubs/SMA-3720/crisis.asp**

General Sources

The American Society of Addiction Medicine (ASAM) is a certification program aiming to improve the quality of substance abuse treatment. **http://www.asam.org**

Under the expanding umbrella of ASAM, most states now have their own societies—CSAM is the California Society of Addiction Medicine (http://www.csam-asam.org). To find your state's society, visit ASAM's Web site or do an online search.

The Mental Health Parity Act (2010) widens the parameters of the 1996 legislation to include several uncovered categories, including substance abuse disorders. **https://www.cms.gov/ HealthInsReformforConsume/04_ TheMentalHealthParityAct.asp**

This online version of the Physicians' Desk Reference is a source that allows doctors around the country to quickly find information on any disease or disorder. **http://www.pdr.net**

As a source for the latest medical news, Health World offers a wide berth of clear, easily accessible data that address your health concerns. **http://www.healthy.net**

Other useful sites for general information include:

The National Institute of Health (NIH) **http://www.nih.gov**

The National Institute on Drug Abuse (NIDA) **http://www.nida.nih.gov**

The Centers for Disease Control and Prevention (CDC) **http://www.cdc.gov**

The Substance Abuse and Mental Health Services Administration (SAMHSA) **http://www.samhsa.gov**

Drug Testing

Government approved drug testing information and resources are available via the National Institute on Drug Abuse Web site. **http:// www.drugabuse.gov/drugpages/ testing.html**

Addiction Treatment Centers and Programs

The Substance Abuse and Mental Health Services Administration offers a database of substance abuse treatment facilities. **http://dasis3.samhsa.gov**

Alcoholics Anonymous has become a staple of the rehabilitation process for many addicts of varied substances. Although we cannot vouch for every individual program's value, we present the information in case it helps even one person ease their stress. **http://www .aa.org** (When checking out local AA meetings, make sure that dual diagnosis and medical treatment is accepted.)

Vocational Services

The Department of Human Services offers a resource for finding and understanding vocational rehabilitation. **http:// dhs.sd.gov/drs/vocrehab/vr.aspx**

The Office of Vocational and Adult Education offers avenues for getting a new career started. This can serve as part of a rehabilitation process. **http://www2.ed.gov/about/offices/list/ovae/index.html**

Veterans' Addiction Treatment

The Department of Veterans Affairs offers services to those who've served in the past and suffer from addiction. **http://www.va.gov**

Mental Health Services/Treatment

The Substance Abuse and Mental Health Services Administration offers a source for locating recommended treatment centers nationwide. **http://mentalhealth.samhsa.gov/databases**

The National Association of Cognitive-Behavioral Therapists offers a directory of certified therapists in your area. This up-and-coming type of therapy allows you to change the behaviors that create a cycle of addiction. **http://www.nacbt.org**

Substance Abuse Research

The Office of Applied Studies offers the latest data on drug treatment, abuse, and the substances themselves. **http://www.oas.samhsa.gov**

The National Institute on Alcohol Abuse and Alcoholism focuses on research and resources for alcohol abuse. **http://www.niaaa.nih.gov**

The National Institute on Drug Abuse is a source for news, research, and treatment of addiction in general. **http://www.nida.nih.gov**

Medical Journals

Journals allow all members of the medical community to keep track of breakthroughs and new research on a monthly basis. Reading them as a patient can feel daunting, but if you can get past the medicalese and doctor slang, you'll be (essentially) reading over your doctor's shoulder.

Journal of Addiction Medicine
http://journals.lww.com/journaladdictionmedicine

Journal of Addictive Diseases
http://www.researchgate.net/journal/1055-0887_Journal_of_Addictive_Diseases

Alcohol
http://www.alcoholjournal.org/home

Detoxification Resources*

The National Alliance of Advocates for Buprenorphine Treatment offers information about the new frontier of opioid addiction treatment. **http://www.naabt.org**

*We *do not* recommend rapid detox. Make sure to research any detoxification center (and speak with previous patients) before entering care.

Pain Management Centers

The American Society of Anesthesiologists serves as a source for pain management treatment, offering various sources and a large breadth of advice for those suffering from the chronic pain that can tempt a new or dormant addiction out of the shadows. **http://www.asahq.org/patientEducation/managepain.htm**

Sleep Centers

Approved by the American Academy of Sleep Medicine, this site is a source to locate sleep centers in your area. **http://www.sleepcenters.org**

Eating Disorders

A list of National Institute of Mental Health approved clinical trials being held all over the United States is available at **http://www.nimh.nih.gov/trials/eating-disorders.shtml**

Sources for Family and Friends

Al-Anon and Alateen (for youths) are groups to support those affected by the addictions of their loved ones. They offer counseling, group therapy, and follow their own version of a twelve-step program. **http://www.al-anon.alateen.org/english.html**

Prevention

The American Council for Drug Education is an agency that works to teach people of all ages about substance abuse using the most up to date scientific data available. **http://www.acde.org**

The Center on Addiction and the Family offers support to those with parents suffering from an alcohol addiction. **http://www.coaf.org**

The Center for Substance Abuse Prevention offers the latest resources for deterring the onset of addiction. **http://www.prevention.samhsa.gov**

More Resources

For more resources, or to ask questions regarding those already listed, visit our Web site at **http://www.addictionsolution.com**

INDEX

Boldface page references indicate illustrations. <u>Underscored</u> references indicate tables or boxed text.

R

Receptors
  defined, 22
  drugs mimicking neurotransmitters
    for, 37–39
  matched to neurotransmitters,
    23–24
  preferences of, 37–39, <u>38</u>
Recovery process, 59–60
Rehab and recovery
  addict's rights during, 60–61
  costs of, <u>61</u>
  in new treatment paradigm, 59–60
  recovery process, 59–60
  rehab period, 59
  traditional treatment method,
    58–59
Relaxation techniques for sleep
    disorders, 55
Repercussion, fear of, 71
Reward center, 25–26
Reward highway, 26, 30–31
Rights of addicts, 60–61
Ritalin, 53
"Rock bottom" myth, 79, 80

S

Savella, 43, 53, <u>54</u>
School, addiction risk and, <u>13</u>
Secondary disease, addiction as, 49,
    63
Sedatives for sleep disorders, avoiding,
    <u>56–57</u>
Self-esteem, low, 69
Self-medication
  with addiction, 18, <u>30</u>, 36, <u>45</u>
  brain chemistry imbalances and,
    34–36, <u>40</u>
  defined, 17, 34
  feeling better as aim of, 35–36
  for feelings and emotions, 18
  positive examples of, 17–18
  trial and error choices for, 35
Seroquel, 55
Serotonin
  Addiction Prediction test, <u>40–41</u>
  in addicts vs. nonaddicts, 39
  antidepressant agents for treating
    imbalance, 53

  behaviors associated with, <u>42</u>
  discovery in blood serum, 27
  effects of imbalance in, 32–33, <u>48</u>
  life enhancements from, 28
  mimics for, 37
  moods regulated by, 24, 27, 28
  noradrenaline excess due to deficit in,
    43
  in opiate-based painkiller addiction,
    146
  primary diseases from imbalance, 33,
    <u>42</u>, 43, 257–60
  receptor preferences of, 38, <u>38</u>
  receptors for, 23
  responsibility for addiction, 22
  role in addiction, 111, 146, 168, 200
  similarities to heroin, 44
  similarities to other
    neurotransmitters, 43, **43**, 44,
    44
  substances abused with imbalance,
    <u>42</u>
Sex addiction, gender and, <u>48</u>
Signs of addiction, 79, 81–82
Sleep apnea, 55
Sleep disorders, 32, 55, <u>56–57</u>
Smoking. *See* Nicotine
SNRIs (serotonin and noradrenaline
    reuptake inhibitors), 43, 53,
    <u>54</u>
Sobriety, definitions of, <u>74</u>
Social anxiety disorder, 261. *See also*
    Anxiety
Sonata, <u>57</u>
SSRIs (selective serotonin reuptake
    inhibitors), 53, <u>54</u>, <u>65</u>
Stabilizing medications
  for alcohol, <u>54</u>, 204, 215–16
  anticraving agents, 53
  antidepressant agents, 53
  for benzos, <u>54</u>, 186–87, 194
  for cocaine, <u>54</u>, 114, 121
  for heroin, 133, 139–40
  for meth, <u>54</u>, 170–71, 177
  for opiate-based painkillers, <u>54</u>,
    148–49, 155
  role in treatment, 52, 58, 63,
    241–42
  stimulant agents, 53